The
WANDERING IRISH
in Europe

D1027339

ALSO BY MATTHEW J. CULLIGAN

The Quest For The Galloping Hogan
Ronald Reagan and The Isle of Destiny
The Curtis-Culligan Story
Seventy Million Dollar Decimal

ALSO BY PETER CHERICI

Celtic Sexuality: Power, Paradigms and Passion

The
WANDERING IRISH
in Europe

Their Influence from the Dark Ages to Modern Times

Matthew J. Culligan

Peter Cherici

CLEARFIELD

Copyright © 1999 by Matthew J. Culliagn and Peter Cherici

All rights reserved. No part of this book may be reproduced or utilized in any form or by any means, electronic or mechanical, including photocopying, recording or by any information retrieval system, without prior permission in writing from the publisher.

Printed for
Clearfield Company, Inc. by
Genealogical Publishing Co., Inc.
Baltimore, Maryland
1999

Library of Congress Catalogue Card Number 98-75387
International Standard Book Number: 0-8063-4835-6

Made in the United States of America

CONTENTS

PREFACE

We wrote *The Wandering Irish In Europe* to fill in the picture of the significant Irish contribution to European civilization and history. The story of the invaluable labor of the Irish monks in preserving the foundations of Western culture by copying the texts of ancient and early Christian authors is well-known, as is the journey of many Irish monks to Europe where they also copied texts from previous eras and founded monasteries. But after this crucial and widely recognized task performed by the Irish monks, the story of Irish involvement in the growth of Europe trails off.

It is not that the Irish involvement in Europe in the centuries after the Dark Ages and early Middle Ages has not been recorded. It is, however, so widely scattered in numerous histories and biographies that it is unrecognizable to the average person and even to many historians and scholars. For instance, no sound history on certain subjects or eras of France can be written without at least mentioning the connection of the first universities with the monasteries founded by the Irish monks, the style of combat and victories in battle of the Irish Brigade, and Marshall Marie-Edmé-Patrice de MacMahon, a descendant of Irish emigres who helped to balance monarchist and republican political aims in a period of instability in 19th-century France. Likewise, there can be no history on certain subjects or eras of Austria without at least mention of the Irish military commanders who led campaigns which helped Austria maintain its independence. Yet, the roles of such Irish emigres and their descendants usually become obscured int he multitude of faces and points of such works or overshadowed by their overreaching theme.

While the role of the Irish in European culture and history has not been ignored, it has not been presented in a cogent, comprehensive, systematic way. As far as we know, *The Wandering Irish In Europe* is the first book to do this. From extensive research over many years in a number of countries, we gathered material on many Irish emigres and their descendants in nearly all of the countries of Europe. Our study was motivated by our own curiosity stemming from our Irish background. We originally didn't intend to write a book; nor did we even imagine that we would have written this book. But the more we got into our study, the more we saw the reality and import of the activities of many Irish men and some Irish women in most of the countries of Europe. Because of the loyalty of the Irish to the monarchs and the conception of the countries they emigrated to—which the Irish viewed as replacements of their clans—their activities are ordinarily seen as part of the particular historical activity and direction of the monarchs and the countries.

This view of the activity of the Irish in relation to various European monarchs and countries is not wrong, or even limited. It is the usual view because it was the view the Irish themselves had of their activities and roles. Looking at the monarchies and countries to which they attached themselves as their new clans, the Irish saw their activity as benefitting these; their focus was on the "clan," not on themselves. Beyond this usual perspective however, with our Irish roots and knowledge of Irish culture and history, we began to develop another, broader perspective on the Irish in Europe as we gathered more and more material on this topic. We began to see more and more clearly that while the significance of different Irish persons was related to historical events or circumstances in the different countries of Europe, underlying the activities and roles of the Irish in different centuries in most of the countries of Europe were traits and capabilities that were identifiably Irish. While the various Irish over many centuries and in widely separated countries of Europe had significant parts in the reigns of different monarchs and the growth of different nations, similarities in the traits and capabilities of the Irish led to a realization that there was a connection among the activities and ideas of the Irish. Considering the workings of history, such a connection among so many persons playing significant roles in such a number of different European countries over such a long period of time undeniably had an effect. We realized there was a demonstrable Irish influence on Europe, a perspective which we present in this book.

Although our perspective is based on the Irish heritage of the men and women treated in this book, more broadly, *The Wandering Irish in Europe* traces the growth of European culture as a whole. For we do not see the Irish as injecting any characteristics or determining any directions which were not inherent in European civilization as a whole. The Irish were teachers, leaders and innovators in different fields, counselors, compatriots and sometimes examples; they were not invaders, conquerors or rulers. Characteristics of the Irish, knowledge and skills they had, and activities they engaged in helped to define certain major or significant characteristics in European culture and to concentrate certain trends and directions. For instance, there were Irish military men who led the modernization of the tactics, armaments and organization of the armies of major European countries; and there were Irish diplomats, advisors and political leaders who played important roles in the movement in some European countries to become nations.

The Irish were able to uniquely have such a part throughout most of Europe because their skills and capabilities were often readily put to use by the rulers and upper classes of the countries they emigrated to. The obvious reason for this is that the rulers and upper classes could benefit from the skills and capabilities of the Irish with virtually no risk to themselves. As outsiders, the Irish had no power base in the different countries which might threaten the rulers or upper class. Besides, the Irish had earned a reputation for loyalty to the rulers they served; and the Irish welcomed the opportunity to put their skills and capabilities to use in their new circumstances in foreign lands. But underlying these logical reasons for the unique part of the Irish in European history is the question of why different generations of Irish could have such a part over so wide geographical area. The answer to this is that the Irish uniquely bore the heritage of the Celts, the race that dominated Europe from Spain to Austria to Ireland from 800 B.C. until Caesar conquered the Galls in roughly the area of France in the 1st century B.D. Although a warrior culture, the Celts were unable to resist the relentless legions of Rome, and in later centuries, the hordes of Germanic tribes sweeping down from the north to topple the Roman Empire in the 5th century A.D.

During these centuries, Celtic culture was overlaid by Roman civilization and the cultures of the barbarian tribes. Nonetheless, Celtic culture was too deeply rooted in the peoples of these large geographical areas to die out. Toward the end of the Dark Ages, when the Roman Empire had vanished long ago and the stagnation of the barbarian rule was becoming onerous, the reinvigoration of Christianity and the stirrings of the Carolingian Renaissance brought on the origins of Western culture. Monks from Ireland played central roles in both of these seminal occurrences. Earliest among these Irish monks was Columbanus who arrived in France in 591 A.D. and over the next two decades founded monasteries at Annegray, Luxeuil, Fontaine, Breganz and Bobbio. With respect to the Carolingian Renaissance, Charlemagne—King of the Franks and Holy Roman Emperor— invited Irish monks from throughout Europe to come to his court at Aix-la-Chapelle to teach and to pursue their scholarship; and he sent envoys to Ireland to invite monks from there to come to his court as well.

The repression of the Irish by the English in the late Middle Ages and another period of intensified repression in the 1600's after England became a Protestant nation drove numbers of Irish men and women to emigrate to different countries of Europe. Like the monks from Ireland at the close of the Dark Ages and early Middle Ages, these later Irish were Catholic. But unlike the monks, the later emigres possessed a much wider range of skills; and they did not emigrate with the aim of missionary work. The later emigres had much experience and well-developed skills in the fields of the military, business, medicine, agriculture and diplomacy, as well as the fields of religious work and education. With their variety of skills and the initiative they took to apply them to their situations in their new countries, many emigres entered the mainstream of a number of European societies and some of them became leaders in their respective fields.

The areas of Europe where the Irish had the most effect are the areas where Celtic culture was dominant. These areas are roughly the modern-day nations of France, Spain, Portugal and Austria. Although Irish emigres traveled to Italy, Russia and other nations in central and eastern Europe, their influence in these areas was limited. It should be no surprise that those areas of Europe shaped mostly by the Roman Republic and Empire, Vikings and Mongols, and the Germanic tribes were those areas where the Irish had the least influence. Since the effects of Roman imperialism and barbarian invasions barely touched Ireland, Celtic culture was able to remain free of outside influences and to evolve according to its inherent tendencies. Christianity was the first external influence of any significance on Celtic culture in Ireland. (Later in the Middle Ages, the Vikings were present in Ireland, but they had only a limited effect on the fundamentals of Celtic culture.) And Christianity was accepted by the Celts because its spirituality and lore struck a chord in the immemorial Celtic culture. Christianity was modified by the surviving Celtic culture in Ireland, so that it became known as Celtic Christianity to differentiate it from the Roman Christianity in the rest of Europe.

It was Celtic Christianity, especially the concept of the White Martyr who would leave his brethren and homeland to become a missionary, which the early Irish monks bought to Europe. The rulers and local populations were hospitable to this mixing of Christianity and Celtic culture. The monks appealed to the spiritual yearnings of the Europeans toward the close of the Dark Ages; and they had practical skills to offer which had been lost in the turmoil of the barbarian invasions or scorned by the warrior cultures of the barbarians. This acceptance of the early monks and the unique position they had with the rulers and local populations laid the ground for the acceptance of later generations of Irish emigres. The major difference of the Irish—namely their reflection of Celtic culture unaffected by the historical tides that flowed across Europe—was not a difference which set them apart from the peoples of the European continent, but rather, a quality which made the Irish more appealing to them. This quality of representing Celtic culture was enhanced by the Christianity of the Irish monks since the European mainland was ripe for the growth of Christianity at the time of their appearance. The practical skills that the monks and following groups of emigres had to offer to the rulers and the population of the countries they went to were another reason the emigres were readily accepted and had a noticeable influence. The benefits of the skills of the Irish in medicine, crafts and agriculture were immediate and self-evident.

The elements of Celtic culture preserved by the Irish and brought by the Irish emigres to major European countries and the ancestral memory,

desires and directions of these countries at different historical moments
and phases complemented each other in a unique—and even remarkable,
it can be said—way so that Irish emigres had an extraordinary influence
on the history of Europe and the development of Western culture. This
influence extended to matters both large and small—from roles in
victories in decisive battles to the shape of household articles. If you look
at history as a migration, you can see the reason for this extraordinary
influence of the Irish. A nomadic people who migrated to most parts of
Europe, the Celts possessed a core of cultural traits and abilities which
they adapted to the particular conditions of the different places they
migrated to. In such adaptations, the Celts did not change so that their
traits and abilities were dissipated. Rather, by the process of such
adaptation, the Celts came to dominate the areas they migrated to—so
that Celtic culture came to dominate most of Europe.

The place of the Irish emigres in the history and culture of Europe is
similar. In different historical times and to diverse places, Irish men and
women migrated, bringing with them the core elements of their culture
rooted in the ancient Celtic culture and adapting to the historical and
regional conditions they encountered. In the process of their adaptation,
certain characteristics of the Celts as transmitted by the Irish to Europe
came to be basic aspects of Western culture. In *The Wandering Irish In
Europe*, we give an overview of the place of the Irish by focusing on
particular influential Irish emigres. So the reader can understand what the
emigres brought to European culture, we treat to some extent Celtic and
Irish culture. And for readers to understand the reasons and causes behind
the Irish emigrations in different periods, we summarize certain periods
of Irish history.

We hope that our book adds to knowledge of the place of the Irish in
European history and culture and also to the knowledge of the formation
and course of Western culture.

As we mentioned earlier, when we first undertook a study of Irish
culture and emigration, we were not planning to write a book. At this
time, we were simply pursing our personal interests arising from our Irish
ancestries. We read many books on different subjects relating to Ireland;
but this reading was based more on our feelings or curiosities at different
times rather than a systematic study. When we traveled to Ireland or

France or other countries of Europe, we visited national or local libraries to search through relevant archives. Before meeting for the first time in 1991 while working on the re-publication of Matthew J. Culligan's book *The Quest For the Galloping Hogan*, both of us had spent many years pursuing our similar interest in Irish history.

At this time, after discussions which led to a growing sense of the inter-connection of the diverse material we had covered and the larger issues it suggested, we decided to turn our informally pursued interest into a systematic study. Peter Cherici had focused on ancient and medieval Celtic-Irish history while Matthew J. Culligan had gathered material on the Irish in Europe in the centuries after the Renaissance. It was then that we began to read and collect books on Irish histories, biographies of Irish people, Irish emigration, Irish and Celtic culture, and histories of countries many Irish emigres traveled to. These many books which were resources for *The Wandering Irish in Europe* are listed in the Bibliography.

Besides these books documented in the time of our formal study, there are also a number of historical documents from European countries which were sources of this book. Among these documents are edicts by King Joao V of Portugal concerning rewards given to different members of the emigre family named Hogan for outstanding activities of theirs; a French military document about a duel between two officers of the Irish Brigade; and a genealogy of Leopold O'Donnell, a notable descendant of Irish emigres in Spain. As these and a couple of other similar documents were collected at the early stage of the research which ultimately went into this book, we do not have precise references for where they can be located. We can name the European libraries where we found them, but cannot name the precise files. Librarians at these institutions may be able to direct anyone interested in seeing the originals of these documents to where they are kept. We do, however, have photographs or the originals or good copies of them from which we can make copies for anyone interested in these. Requests for such copies can be made through the publisher.

Interviews with descendants of Irish emigres and other persons who know about the activities of particular emigres or the influence of Irish emigres in different countries were another source for the book. Fernando

Terry in Spain provided a great deal of information about his ancestors, as did Philippe de MacMahon in France.

The perspective on the Irish influence on European history and Western culture presented in this book is derived from varied and numerous sources studied over fifteen years. In order to keep our book in the style for the general reader, which we wanted, we did not include footnotes. We hope that the reader finds that this makes the book more readable without detracting from the credibility of the material. Besides, our perspective comes from the accumulation of diverse, but inter-related, accounts of the roles of Irish emigres and understanding of fundamentals of Western culture, not scholarly analysis. We trust that the reader will come to the perspective we present the way that we did—not by filling in the pieces of a historical puzzle (as with the question "who first discovered America?"), but by the growing recognition of what in the end is the undeniable phenomenon of the Irish influence on the formation of Europe in light of the wealth of material in support of this subject in our book.

We were sustained over the years of our research not only by our interest in the study from our Irish backgrounds, but also by the interest and support of family members and friends. We would also like to thank Henry Berry for the editorial hand he brought to our book. A freelance editor, he helped on our book from conception to the final writing. As he often told us, he wanted have us do a book which awakened every reader to the story we had to tell as he saw it materialize from our voluminous research.

We hope we have succeeded in this.

Matthew J. Culligan
Peter Cherici
New York, September 1998

INTRODUCTION

Europe And The Wandering Irish

See, cut in woods, through flood of twin horned Rhine
passed the keel, and greased slips over seas -
Heave men! And let resounding echo sound our heave!

The wind raise blasts, wild rain-storms wreak their spite
but ready strength of men subdues it all -
Heave men! And let resounding echo sound our heave!

—The Boat Song of Columbanus, c. 610 A.D.

One of the first of a long line of Irish emigres to strongly influence affairs on the European continent was a monk named Columbanus. Accompanied by twelve of his followers, he voyaged to France in 591 A.D., forever abandoning his native Ireland. Columbanus was forty-seven years old, an advanced age for such a bold undertaking in an era when many people died young from disease and hardship. But his desire to perform missionary work seemed to meld with the penchant for wandering in his Celtic heritage to create in him an overwhelming urge to voyage abroad.

Columbanus chose to leave behind the security of his monastery and the companionship of his brother monks because traveling abroad was the only way he could become a "White Martyr." This was a uniquely Irish concept of how a man or woman could gain spiritual merit. Since monks like Columbanus enjoyed high status and prestige in the Christian communities of Ireland, they could escape the temptation of pride from their social prominence only by traveling to a distant land where they would live humbly among strangers who would not give them special status. These Irish monks were not like the traditional "Red Martyrs" of the Christian faith who were tortured and executed for their beliefs, securing eternal rewards after enduring a relatively brief period of torment. Instead, the "White Martyrs" suffered daily pangs of loss for the family and friends they would never see again, an anguish they would carry with them all of their lives. According to the Celtic version of Christianity, both Red and White Martyrs earned equal amounts of virtue.

The urge which inspired Columbanus and his fellow monks to forsake their monastic home and companions in Ireland for the unknown of continental Europe went deeper than their professed desire to become White Martyrs for their Christian faith. This urge to wander was a part of their Celtic cultural heritage. For more than a thousand years before them, the Celts had roamed extensively throughout Europe and parts of Asia, spreading out from their traditional homeland in the Danube River basin. When a new community of Celts grew so large that the surrounding forests were stripped bare and the streams polluted, some members of the community would leave to take the strain off the dwindling resources and to find a new place where they could settle. This cultural practice ingrained in the Celts a readiness to move to new locations as a way to overcome undesirable conditions and an ingenuity for adapting to new circumstances and recognizing their promise. As generation after generation fell into this pattern of migration, the idea of wandering became a part of the Celtic worldview. It was seen not only as a practical answer to troublesome conditions, but also as a challenge and adventure testing the character and the ingenuity of an individual. The idea of wandering took a central place in the lore of the Celts. It is reflected in the intricate spirals and repetitive motifs of Celtic art. This idea of wandering could take the form of an entire clan seeking a new place to live or an individual joining a foreign army as a mercenary or journeying alone to explore the wonders of the world. The religious concept of the White Martyr which prompted Columbanus and his followers to leave their homeland for France was yet another manifestation of the Celtic desire to wander.

In 591 A.D., what is now modern France was broken into three kingdoms—Neustria along the Atlantic coast, Austrasia in the north, and Burgundy in the central and eastern part. Each kingdom was ruled by a descendant of Clovis, a warlord who had temporarily united all of France in 480 A.D. Each king bitterly hated his cousins, and they endlessly fought petty wars that impoverished both peasants and nobles alike.

Columbanus came ashore in Neustria and continued to wander with his band of monks to the Kingdom of Burgundy, ruled by Childebert. Trudging across France, Columbanus passed peasants whose poverty made their lives an endless grind of toil and misery. His own native land of Ireland had been relatively prosperous with its fertile soil producing an abundance of food which easily supported farmers, scholars and nobility. The rolling hills and lush meadows of France were capable of producing similarly large harvests, yet privation plagued both Neustria and Burgundy. Despite constant attention by the peasants, the fields where they grew wheat and rye produced only small yields.

Eventually Columbanus's journey brought him to King Childebert's stronghold in the Saône Valley. Although he called himself a king, Childebert did not have much wealth. The general poverty of the region affected even the King. He could barely administer his realm. Childebert had only a small amount of gold, and he did not even have the benefit of adequate supplies of farm products or farm animals which could have made up for his deficiency of precious metals. The same primitive agricultural methods Columbanus had encountered in his journey across France were practiced in Burgundy—which left little surplus crops for the King. Childebert had to pay his troops and retainers with parcels of land, further diminishing his holdings and his revenues. Yet he needed the continued military support of many men-at-arms for wars of both aggression and defense with his neighbors. Donations to bishops and priests were also necessary so that they would support the king in his squabbles with rebellious nobles and rival monarchs.

Adding to King Childebert's difficulties in governing his realm was his domineering mother, the Queen Regent Brunhilde. Beautiful and ill-tempered, she controlled Childebert and many of the other nobles in

Burgundy with the strength her personality. Her sole concern was to insure her personal power. Historical accounts portray her as a vicious and vindictive woman who used poison, torture and the garrote to eliminate anyone who displeased her. She had been a princess from Visigoth Spain married off to Sigebert of Burgundy to form an alliance. When Sigebert mysteriously died from poison in 576 A.D., she became Queen Regent. Even after her son, Childebert, came of age and was made king, she remained a sinister power behind the throne, overseeing his every move.

When Columbanus explained to Childebert that he had come to Burgundy to perform missionary work, King Childebert was greatly impressed with the monk's spirituality, which sharply contrasted with the greed and the conniving of the local priests. Because Childebert could make no decision without Brunhilde's approval, he urged his mother to let these Irish wanderers stay in his land. He sensed in these foreigners a source of knowledge and education that could make his kingdom wealthy and strong. Brunhilde yielded to her son's wishes because she saw no threat to her power from the Irish monks. She permitted her son to grant Columbanus a remote plot of land where he could found a monastery.

In the Vosges hills of Alsace near modern Annegray, Columbanus settled with the twelve followers who had accompanied him from Ireland. He chose to build his monastery on the ruins of a Roman temple to Diana because the site was considered holy by the local pagans. Celtic Christians often incorporated pagan customs into their religious practice when these customs did not contradict the fundamental beliefs of Christianity. The nobles and warriors in the royal court gave this outpost little prospect for survival. Surrounded by a thick and tangled forest, the monks labored day and night to clear the land in order to grow enough food to feed themselves. The soil was barren, and the first summer's crop was meager. But in later harvests, the monks' patient husbandry produced fields of wheat and alfalfa. Each year they cleared more land until they were cultivating large tracts and raising fat herds of cows, sheep and chickens.

Agriculture was one of the skills that Columbanus and his twelve Irish followers had practiced in the monasteries of Ireland. Farming was essential to the survival of a monastery during a time when there was little trade between communities. In addition to learning Latin, Greek, mathematics and astronomy, the monks had to master the fundamentals of planting, harvesting and animal care to insure that they could produce enough food for their tables.

The Frankish tribe surrounding Columbanus' monastery and fields at Annegray were known as the Suevians. Despite being an outsider, Columbanus was accepted by them because he was quick to share his knowledge of agriculture, medicine, crafts and other useful, beneficial skills. Impoverished and barbaric even by the primitive standards of the Franks, the Suevians were impressed by the monks' peaceful way of life that reaped such evident material rewards as full harvests. Before long, many young men of the local tribe were asking Columbanus and his band of monks to be converted to Christianity, believing that there was a connection between the religion and the ability of the monks to provide regular, adequate meals. The Irish monks welcomed them into the Christian faith despite the suspect motives of the Suevians. Soon there were so many novice monks to feed and house that Columbanus had to found two new monasteries, one at Luxeuil and another at Fontaine. All three of Columbanus's French monasteries flourished throughout the Middle Ages, with Fontaine lasting until the French Revolution when it was destroyed by Republican extremists.

Despite his notable achievements in the areas of agriculture and education and the high regard he was held in by the Franks, Columbanus remained at heart a Christian monk devoted to a spiritual ideal. As he grew older, his missionary zeal became even stronger and he became a fire-and-brimstone preacher who foretold dire consequences for anyone who strayed from the Christian path of righteousness. His message offended many local bishops and priests of the Arian and Roman sects who had become very materialistic. The contemporary historian Gregory of Tours wrote that the Christian clergy was corrupt, openly engaging in murder, theft and sexual excess. Often they ignored the spiritual needs of the impoverished peasantry, concentrating on the wealthy aristocrats who could give them land and gold.

Even as he enjoyed the fruits of his success by establishing prosperous monasteries, Columbanus was planting the seeds of his undoing. He frequently denounced the Frankish bishops and priests in sermons that predicted divine retribution for their misdeeds. Angry clerics countered by denouncing him, and outraged bishops demanded that he appear before them for judgement. Ignoring their challenges and plots to discredit him, Columbanus was shunned by the clergy and their supporters among the aristocracy.

While this religious controversy was going on, King Childebert died, and his son, Theodoric, succeeded him as King of Burgundy. The new king openly enjoyed relationships with many women. At the same time, Theodobert, another son of Childebert, became King of Austrasia. Brunhilde continued to dominate her grandsons as she had her son, maintaining control over both realms.

When Columbanus learned of the loose sexual conduct of Theodoric, he began to denounce the king along with his regular denunciations of the materialistic local clergymen. Brunhilde could not tolerate the spectacle of a foreign monk preaching against the king. As far as she was concerned, the words of Columbanus were more seditious than spiritual. So she demanded that Theodoric test the loyalty of Columbanus by asking the monk to publicly bless the illegitimate sons of the royal household. When Columbanus refused to comply, as Brunhilde was sure he would, she banished him and all of the Irish Celtic monks from the kingdom.

Brunhilde was as shrewd as she was wicked. In one clever stroke, she rid her realm of an annoying troublemaker. But she allowed the monasteries that Columbanus had founded to continue operating, inhabited only by Frankish monks who had learned the Celtic Irish farming techniques. From Annegray, Luxeuil and Fontaine, the knowledge of the improved methods of agriculture continued to spread throughout Burgundy.

Columbanus was determined to remain in Europe after his banishment. He wandered down the Rhine, settled in Switzerland for a time, and founded a new monastery at a place called Bobbio in the part of northern Italy known as Lombardy. Wherever he settled, he was welcomed for his knowledge and learning, and he was careful not to openly criticize the behavior of any king or queen.

The tale of Columbanus marks the beginning of the relationship between Irish emigres and European countries which would continue for the following fourteen centuries. Columbanus's reasons for leaving Ireland, his contributions to the local European culture, and the tightrope he had to walk between fulfilling his aspirations and adapting to the local authorities and society represent typical aspects of the story of Irish emigration which endured throughout the medieval and early modern periods.

Like Columbanus, many other Irish monks were prompted to pursue their calling in the lands of continental Europe. These early missionaries left Ireland for spiritual reasons—to fulfill their vision of the White Martyr and to spread the Christian faith. For the most part, later generations of Irish emigres did not follow a spiritual calling, but rather were driven from their homeland by oppressive political, social, and economic conditions. In the centuries following the Middle Ages, changing historical conditions gave different waves and groups of Irish emigres different motives and reasons for leaving Ireland. But like the vision of the White Martyr, the varying specific motives and reasons were manifestations of the ancient Celtic desire to wander to different lands to seek better fortunes and to test oneself. The pattern of migration of the ancient Celts became a pattern of emigration for Irish society in later centuries. Because of its link to the migration of the Celtic tribes who were their forebearers, emigration was a natural, acceptable, and common practice in Irish society. With its roots in Celtic culture, medieval and modern Irish society saw emigration as an opportunity.

When the people of Ireland ventured into different parts of Europe, they usually found that their skills and viewpoints were highly valued. Sometimes they saw possibilities in commerce or diplomacy that no one had noticed before. Other times, they offered competence and loyalty, earning the respect of both nobles and peasants. Wherever they went, they instinctively recognized the needs of their adopted lands and took positive steps to fill these needs. Their well-balanced political sense and their holistic approach to spirituality helped the Irish to fit into the cultures in the lands where they settled, thus allowing the Irish emigres of both the medieval and early modern periods to become a distinctive and enduring influence in European society.

The basis for the success of the Irish emigres throughout Europe was their education. Learning in all fields—philosophy, mathematics, and language primary among these—was a central concern of Irish culture. Compared with the educational standards of the early modern era, the emigres had practically the same level of learning as the scholars of the universities in Europe. In most cases, however, the Irish differed from scholars and academics by having an eclectic educational background, rather than one focused on a specialized subject. The mix of intellectual disciplines and practical skills which were a part of the education of the early Druids and which were the model for the education of the Christian monks of Ireland remained the model for Irish education into later eras. This mix of intellectual training and practical skills enabled the Irish to be effective in a range of areas beyond the disciplines and formal education in universities. The eclectic basis of their schooling came into use in fields ranging from military service to agriculture to commerce. With their educational background, in military affairs, Irish emigres could take advantage of the local terrain to deploy an effective defensive position; the background would enable them to implement productive agricultural practices across large parts of a country. In the field of commerce, the emigres brought with them an international perspective, as well as contacts with Irish emigres in other countries, all of which broadened the economic activity of the countries where they settled. As artists, Irish emigres were able to represent by pictures or words feelings and experiences that were universal.

By filling needs of the various European societies, the Irish were accepted into them. It was usually the royalty or the aristocrats of the societies who recognized the value of the emigres and were best able to put to use what they had to offer. In many cases, emigres were given or reached positions of military or political leadership. In addition to their evident military or political abilities, the Irish emigres were untouched by palace intrigue and were not tied to any faction which might be maneuvering for power or impeding a monarch's wishes. Thus, besides being effective in whatever tasks they were assigned, the Irish gave their loyalty only to the monarch. As long as the monarchs and warlords of Europe saw the Irish as non-threatening, they were tolerated. But if Irish emigres in their service became involved with a bothersome faction or tried to change any of the society's basic cultural practices or beliefs, they would quickly lose their position and be ordered out of the society.

Although they had a high regard for education and gave educated persons such as monks and teachers a high status, the Irish were basically a practical people. Because of their Celtic heritage with its tradition of migrating and wandering, the emigres were able to assess the dangers and the opportunities presented by a new situation—and thus they were usually able to make the best of their circumstances. Also, the Celtic child-rearing practices of gossiprage and fosterage made the emigres accustomed to dealing with persons outside of the narrow context of the family; and loyalty to the clan enabled the Irish to give their devotion to the structures and inter-workings of larger entities such as a monarchy or state. That the Irish were not enmeshed in nostalgia was another advantage they had as emigres. They did not pine for the life they left behind; nor did they endeavor to recreate a facsimile of it in their new lands. The Celtic lore involving shape-shifting and the view of life as a journey, represented in the intricate spirals of the Celtic artists which had been carried into Irish culture, led the emigres to see their changed circumstances not as a loss or a change of the fundamentals of their lives, but simply as another appearance of them. As the spirals of the Celtic artists suggest, the past, present and future are interwoven. This view led the Irish to see each new situation as a step in the journey of life which presented new challenges and new opportunities.

The Irish contributions to European civilization were widespread—and they are immeasurable. Because the early Irish emigrated with a spiritual purpose and later emigres gave their loyalty and devoted their skills to the monarchs and governments of the different European countries, the Irish do not stand out the way individuals of other cultures do in the history of the countries where they settled. The breadth of contributions from many Irish were absorbed into the cultures of the various parts of Europe so that they have become a part of them rather than noted particularly as "Irish contributions". During the Middle Ages, Irish monks and scholars preserved a vast amount of learning which might otherwise have been lost forever. They were also the founders and administrators of many universities. Attracted or invited to the court of Charlemagne in France, Irish scholars, intellectuals and clerics had a significant role in the Carolingean Renaissance of the 9th century, which is often looked to as the origin of Western civilization. The hundreds of monasteries established by Irish monks all over the continent not only provided spiritual guidance, but served as centers of learning and culture.

Irish ideas about the independence of individuals and communal government were reflected in the artistic and political ideas which emerged in the European Renaissance that brought the Middle Ages to an end. These Irish ideas developed into the concepts of democratic government and society in the latter part of this era. During the early modern period of 1500 to 1800, large numbers of Irish soldiers and notable diplomats helped to shape the nations which were arising in Europe. Because of their numbers, the regularity of their emigration, and their practical skills and ability to fill the needs of the countries they traveled to, the Irish emigres had an effect on western European culture greater than any other group from outside of the indigenous populations. The Irish influence is often not recognized because it has been so thoroughly absorbed into European culture. Because Irish culture was in many ways the successor of Celtic culture, the Irish emigres can be viewed as bringing aspects of this Celtic culture back to the peoples of Europe whose roots in Celtic culture had been lost under the dominance of the Roman Empire or was displaced by invading German tribes.

To understand what it was particularly that Columbanus and the subsequent Irish emigres brought to Europe, and why they were usually readily accepted as valued members of the different societies in a way that no other emigrant groups were, we must go back three thousand years before Columbanus to the plains and valleys and mountains of prehistoric Europe.

During the Bronze Age—about 2000 B.C.—the Celts began to become a distinctive group within the Indo-European people who had migrated from the steppes of Russia to nearly all of Europe and parts of Asia Minor and India. By 1000 B.C., centers of this Celtic culture had grown around forts in Hallstatt, Austria and in La Tène, Switzerland. The concentration of Celtic tribes in these areas and the permanence of the settlements allowed Celtic culture to develop in ways which had not been possible in preceding eras. It was in the Hallstatt and La Tène regions where Celtic culture emerged by developing cultural traits which diverged from those of the older Indo-European culture and which distinguished the Celtic people from all of the other branches of the Indo-Europeans which had taken root in areas of Europe, Asia Minor, and India.

In these regions, the clans, the agricultural methods, the style of warfare, the independent spirit, the equality of women, and the pagan spirituality which have come to be recognized as the hallmarks of Celtic culture were first developed. It was this culture which would be preserved and further refined on the distant island of Ireland. At the time, Ireland was known as Inisfall or North Island—and to the Celts who had spread across continental Europe and whose culture was flourishing in the central European centers, it was little more than a remote, quasi-mythological land.

CHAPTER 1

The Civilization Of The Celts

To live, to err, to fail, to triumph,
To recreate life out of life

—James Joyce

THE ORIGINS OF THE CELTS

Because the Irish inherited many of the traits and outlooks of their Celtic ancestors and carried these into modern times, many aspects of the Celtic way of life had a remarkable historical continuity. These customs and beliefs that originated in the distant past endured the unpredictable currents of time and history to serve the Irish as cultural moorings in both the medieval and modern worlds. When Irish emigres found themselves in strange and exotic lands, Celtic traditions long embedded in their society helped them deal with their new circumstances.

The saga of the Celts began in the southern steppes of Russia more than 8000 years before Christ. At that time, theCelts were not a culturally distinct people. They had yet to emerge from the great tribe of nomads called Indo-Europeans whose language, behavior, and view of the world would become the foundation of the heritage of all Europeans. Between

5000 B.C. and 3000 B.C., the Indo-Europeans began to migrate westward in successive waves which broke into small groups as they traveled further from their homeland.

Indo-Europeans were patriarchal and warlike. Their principle gods were males who were usually portrayed as warriors. Indo-European society was organized into clans led by a chieftain. In this rigid social hierarchy, warriors enjoyed the highest status while women held the lowest. A man's wealth was measured by the number of cattle he owned. To increase the amount of grazing land available for their herds, clans sent bands of mounted war parties to conquer neighboring tribes. Because the Indo-European warriors were so successful in defeating the less warlike societies they encountered, they became the dominant society in Europe; and hence their beliefs and customs became the foundation for all later European civilizations. The acceptance of their symbols throughout Europe which continued into the modern world demonstrates the enduring impact of the Indo-European way of life. Black was the color of death; evil was represented by the serpent; the bull illustrated male virility; and the sun was the emblem of life.

During the millennia of their migrations, some of the Indo-Europeans went south into Turkey and settled; while later generations of the Turkish branch resumed roaming as far as India. Other groups traveled into Greece and Italy. By 3000 B.C., the Indo-Europeans had spread across all of Europe and much of western Asia.

After this period of migration, when they had been settled in an area for several generations, the people who had been Indo-Europeans began to develop varied cultural traits which would distinguish them from one another to some degree. As time passed, the far-flung groups originating from the Indo-Europeans of the steppes became more and more distinct from one another in overt ways. The groups developed their own languages, building styles, clothing, tools and weapons —and even customs and mythology after a time. The link of these varied people to their Indo-European origin could not be erased, but as time went on, it became more and more attenuated.

The group of Indo-Europeans which settled in Central Europe along the Danube River was the group that would become known as the Celts. The Celtic language, the fierce warrior ethic, and the clan structure which was more or less a large extended family were aspects of their Indo-

European heritage which they retained, although in a refined or modified form. Aspects of Celtic culture developed in this central European setting that varied from other Indo-Europeans were a relatively high status for women, a decentralized system of government and the tri-partite nature of their deities. This period of cultural development during which the distinguishing cultural elements of the Celts formed lasted for roughly a little more than a millennium.

When between 800 B.C. and 600 B.C., the resources of the Danube River region became strained by the growing population of the Celts, bands of Celts and larger groups, sometimes entire clans, moved out of this incubator of Celtic culture. From the area of Hallstatt, Austria, which by 800 B.C. had become the center of Celtic society, the Celts migrated to other parts of Europe. Toward the end of this time of Celtic expansion throughout Europe, about 500 B.C., the center of Celtic culture had shifted to the La Téne region of western Switzerland. The westward expansion of the Celts primarily from these two cultural centers brought them to the Atlantic islands of Britain and Ireland between 500 B.C. and 300 B.C. By this time, the distinctive culture of the Celts formed in the Danube Basin had spread over all parts of Europe. Wherever the Celts settled, they carried with them the same cultural practices and beliefs that had developed in the Danube Basin.

The Celts got their name from the Greeks. When the Greek geographer Herodotus of Halicarnassus (c. 490 - 425 B.C.) encountered a group of strangers from the north, he called them *Keltoi*, which meant strangers. The Romans named the Celts in the area from the Alps of northern Italy to the Atlantic Ocean, in what is roughly present-day France, the *Galli*, or Gauls, after the Roman name for the area. Because the Romans regarded the Celts from other areas as culturally similar to the Gauls with the same basic language, social structure, weapons and ornamentation, the Romans used names for these Celts containing the root "Gal". When the Romans encountered a group of Celts who had migrated into Turkey after being defeated by the Greeks in a battle near Delphi in 279 B.C., the Romans called these Celts the Galatians. For the Celts of Spain, the Romans used the name Gallicians. However, some Roman geographers and historians relied on Greek writers for their information and referred to the Celts of Spain as Celtiberians. The Celts described themselves simply as the *tuatha*, or people.

The waves of Celtic migration came to an end about 300 B.C. From the Alps to the North Sea, from the Danube River to the Atlantic Ocean and the islands of Britain and Ireland, and down to the Iberian peninsula, Celtic tribes had migrated, driven off or subjugated the inhabitants of the various regions, and established permanent settlements. By 300 B.C., most of Europe was under Celtic control and influenced mainly by Celtic culture. The notable exceptions to this Celtic dominance of Europe were the Italian peninsula, which was controlled by Rome, and the Greek city-states.

This vast territory was not an empire in the usual sense of this term. For the Celts had not set out from their Danube Basin settlements with political or imperialistic ambitions, but rather for the purpose of finding new land and resources for the growing population. Although there was a pattern to the migration, it was not systematic. The pattern was determined not by the desire for conquest, but always by the needs for new land and resources as populations of existing Celtic settlements grew beyond the capacity of local resources to support them; and a segment of these settlements would in turn migrate farther westward or northwestwards to a new location. Although in their aim of finding a suitable location to support a new settlement, the Celts readily drove off the inhabitants of a location they found desirable, the Celts did not take on the position of a "ruling class," but followed their customary tribal way of life.

Although Celtic tribes and clans dominated most of Europe, their tradition of independence and their communal form of government based on the clan precluded a political organization or network throughout this area. Nonetheless, because the far-flung Celtic people all had the same origin and followed the same way of life, there was a homogeneity and stability over this area. Wars between Celtic tribes were fought by small numbers of warriors; the vanquished peoples did not become strong enough to challenge Celtic dominance; and the Celts occupied all the land that was available for them, so their migrations came to an end.

Evidence of the Celtic migrations and settlements has come largely from Celtic grave sites, often marked by a heap of stones which archaeologists call a tumulus. Celtic chieftains and warriors were sometimes buried beneath vertical boulders capped with a large flat rock—a type of grave site called a dolmen. Most of these graves have been found in clusters along rivers and streams. The Celts often buried their dead by rivers or streams because they believed that flowing water weakened the barrier between this world and the Otherworld. Believing in reincarnation, the Celts thought that the dead could most easily return to this world near a place where water flowed. For the needs and solace of the dead during their time in the Otherworld waiting to be reborn, the Celts buried with them tools, clothing, weapons, jewelry, vases and other familiar articles.

The grave sites along with the articles in them provided a guide by which the migrations of the Celts could be traced, and helped considerably in reconstructing the way of life of the Celts. Many of the blanks in the picture of Celtic history and society began to be filled in when numbers of Celtic grave sites were discovered in Central Europe in the late 1800's. Assessment of iron plows along with other findings in the graves led archaeologists to the conclusion that the Celts had been cultivating crops from 1000 B.C. The durability of the iron plows compared to the bronze agricultural tools of other cultures of the region also led archaeologists to conclude that the Celts practiced advanced agricultural methods. The Celtic migrations were linked to these advanced agricultural methods, which would have yielded an increased food supply leading to an increasing population outgrowing the resources of an area, and thus prompting the initial migrations.

Findings in these grave sites and others discovered later also disclosed that Celtic society was advanced in other ways compared to the surrounding cultures. Blades of weapons were made of iron, when weapons of most other cultures were still being made of bronze. The intricately designed handles of weapons and the designs of jewelry showed a superior skill in metalworking.

Because of the steadiness of the Celtic migration and the advanced practical skills of the Celts, Celtic culture came to dominate most of western and central Europe. It continued to dominate until the Celts were conquered by the Romans, first in Spain by Scipio in 204 B.C. and later in Gaul by Caesar about 53 B.C. After Caesar's conquests, Celtic society was confined to parts of central Europe, around the original Celtic lands of the Danube Basin, and the islands of Britain and Ireland. After German tribes pushing down from the north overran the Danube basin lands and Rome conquered much of Britain, Ireland became the center of Celtic culture. From 800 B.C. when the Celts first spread out from their Danube basin settlements until about 50 B.C., Celtic culture exerted its influence on Europe mainly because it was mostly benign, its clan structure offered a balance of security and independence, its mythology and spirituality were relevant, and it had much to offer in the way of agricultural methods and practical skills. The tolerance, capabilities, practicality, skills, and power of example the Irish would bring with them when they emigrated to Europe centuries later were evident in the Celtic tribes and clans which had spread across Europe.

GREEK AND ROMAN DOCUMENTATION

Archeological evidence confirms that the Celts were a dominant force in Central and Northern Europe during the first millennium B.C. But the picture derived from this evidence is far from complete. Having no written language, the Celts left no documents relating to their way of life—only fragments of artifacts. Observations by Greek and Roman historians help to fill in the picture to some extent. But these observations have to be taken with due skepticism because these historians were biased against the Celts. Taking the prevailing perspective of their own cultures which regarded themselves as being self-evidently superior, the Greek and Roman historians saw the Celts as crude and primitive; although they did acknowledge their fierce warrior pride and joy in fighting. Roman historians especially played up this warrior image to explain the defeats that Roman legions periodically suffered at the hands of the Celts.

Greek and Roman historians did not rely exclusively on first-hand sources such as their own observations. They often based large portions of their work on the writings of earlier historians. Thus, when it comes to the ancient historians who wrote about the ancient Celts, it is difficult to sort truth from half-truth and fact from misconception. With some historians, the Celts appear as fierce savages lurking in untamed forests; while other historians saw them as noble, but unsophisticated, warriors.

In his *Historiai*, or Researches, the Greek historian Herodotus of Halicarnassus wrote that the Celts occupied a vast area north of Greece.

He commented on their "simplicity" and the absence of cities and money in their culture. Coming from the perspective of a complex urban society of the Mediterranean, he believed that the wandering lifestyle of the primitive Celts promoted honesty and innocence. In the *Eudemian Ethics*, Aristotle gives an ambivalent portrait of the Celts—admiring their courage, but in the same breath questioning their sanity. He remarked that "anybody would be mad or completely bereft of sensibility if he feared nothing: neither earthquake nor wave of the sea, as they say of the Celts." Aristotle was referring to the practice of some Celtic warriors of battling against the sea or the land with their swords. The warriors believed these features of nature were living beings. They would beat their swords against the seashore or slash at incoming waves; or they would beat their swords against the ground, particularly when the earth tremored.

The Roman historian Diodorus (c.60 - c.21 B.C.) was the first to describe the physical appearance of the Celts. In his *Bibliotheca Historica*, he wrote they were "tall of body with rippling muscles and white of skin, and their hair is blond. But not only naturally so...they also make it their practice by artificial means to increase the distinguishing color which nature has given it...they wash their hair in lime water. The clothing they wear is striking—shirts which they have dyed and embroidered in varied colors, and breeches... and they wear striped coats, fastened by a buckle at the shoulder."

Greek and Roman historians often portrayed the Celts as barbarians. Their criticisms were usually exaggerated and their praises were granted only grudgingly. Because Roman legions were frequently defeated in battle by hordes of Celtic warriors, classical historians portrayed the Celts as formidable warriors. A Roman historian of the 1st century B.C. named Poseidonius noted that the Celts were "belligerent in their customs. They often have single combat at dinner in which real injury is possible and even the death of the combatants. There is great rivalry for the champion's portion."

Besides the Roman and Greek historians, Mediterranean artists have also left an image of the Celts. In sculpture, the Celts were identified by a torc around their necks which was a sign of leadership. Statues and scenes on friezes often depict Celtic leaders releasing captured prisoners, portraying the Celts with a primitive fierceness balanced by courage and a personal code of honor. A Roman frieze from Civitas Alba in northern Italy shows Roman gods driving Celtic raiders out of a temple, but the Celts appear defiant despite the daunting supernatural power arrayed against them.

Greek and Roman descriptions of the Celts often vary from the archaeological evidence and the oral tradition of the Celts which survived long enough to be recorded by Celtic Christian monks during the medieval period. Nonetheless, writings of the Greeks and Romans record how other societies viewed the Celts. Weighed with the archaeological evidence, such writings help in giving a fuller understanding of the Celts and their culture.

WOMEN IN CELTIC CULTURE

Many other Romans, not only the historians and artists, were intrigued by the Celts who dwelled along the northern fringes of their Empire. They were fascinated by the Celtic way of life, by the practices and beliefs that seemed so strange, so different from the customs of Mediterranean society. Of particular interest was the behavior of Celtic women, which Roman observers often found scandalous.

While Celtic society was a patriarchy, women enjoyed higher status than in other cultures descended from the Indo-Europeans. They had the right to bear arms, form contracts, and engage in a profession such as physician or scholar. On the field of battle, women warriors often led troops. In the epic poem *Táin Bó Cualinge*, Queen Maev of the Irish province of Connaught instigated a war with neighboring Ulster and oversaw the battles of her troops. To try to drive the Roman invaders from Britain, Queen Boudicca led the Iceni tribe into battle.

When Christianity first came to Ireland, women were allowed into the priesthood and given a full spiritual role and full spiritual powers, such as administering the sacraments and consecrating the host. Since women could become Druids in the older Celtic society, the Celts expected that women could naturally become spiritual leaders in the new religion. Although this practice of letting women into the priesthood was objectionable to the Roman Christians, the turmoil following the collapse of the Roman Empire during the early part of the Dark Ages, when

Christianity was becoming widespread in Ireland, prevented them from interfering with Celtic customs. During the 5th century, the quasi-mythical Brigid was elevated to the position of bishop so that she might consecrate other female priests without having to allow any men into her enclave of celibate females living at her monastery in Kildare. For the next several centuries, the Abbesses of Kildare who succeeded her had the authority of a bishop. As late as 703 A.D., women were still present in the priesthood and some of them achieved high status in the clerical hierarchy. The Venerable Bede records in his *Opera Historica* that Beverly, who was Bishop of Hexham, ordained him a priest in that year. The last records of women serving as priests are from the 8th century, after which Roman Christianity began to exert a stronger influence on Celtic Christian practices.

Although women were denied the opportunity to become priests when the Roman version of Christianity gained ascendancy over the Celtic version, women continued to maintain their status in the traditional Celtic culture. One prime example of the role and influence of women in this culture was their ability to shame a warrior or other man who was behaving dishonorably by becoming partially, or sometimes fully, naked before him. In such an instance, a woman would stand before the man and bare her breasts or more of her body as if the man were forcing her to disrobe. In the *Táin Bó Cualinge*, the destructive rage of the warrior Cúchulain faded when he was confronted by women who had bared themselves in front of him. But when Celtic women assumed that this practice would produce shame in non-Celtic warriors, the results were disastrous. At the siege of Gergovia in Spain when the Romans were mistreating their Celtic prisoners, Celtic women descended from the walls of the city and bared their breasts to try to shame the Romans. But instead of feeling disgrace, the Romans ravaged the women, responding to their nakedness as a stimulation to rape.

Marriage did not constrict the rights of women. Virginity was not important as a criteria to determine the desirability of a woman as a wife. Dowries were passed to the husband before the bonding ceremony, but remained the property of the woman. If a woman found the marriage dissatisfying, she could easily divorce her husband, taking her dowry with her along with all other property she had acquired independently from her husband. The purpose of the Celtic marriage was children, and a woman could find grounds for divorce in a wide variety of circumstances which interfered with procreation. Male impotence, sterility, homosexuality and obesity were sufficient to dissolve a marriage. In addition, a Celtic woman could also form legally-sanctioned relationships for procreation with several men at the same time, a polyandrous custom that Romans and Greeks found shameful and outrageous.

While most of the descendants of the Indo-Europeans traced their ancestry through their fathers, the Celts traced their lineage through their mothers. A mythological Celtic king was known as Cónchobar mac Nessa, Cónchobar son of Nessa, his mother. Even Christ was referred to as mac Mhuire, the son of Mary. This custom reflected the fact that children could never truly know the identity of their fathers. Since women in Celtic society could choose the person who impregnated them, and often had multiple sexual partners to increase the chances of procreation, no man could be absolutely certain if any child was indeed his offspring.

In the patriarchal societies surrounding the Celts, the rough equality between the genders in Celtic society was scorned by Roman writers and historians as further evidence of their barbarism. This difference with respect to women between Celtic-Irish culture and the Romanized cultures of Europe continued through the medieval period and into modern times. When Irish women began emigrating from Ireland as the wives of soldiers and merchants who made up the large majority of the emigres in the 17th century, they were restricted to the roles of housekeepers, mothers, and wives in keeping with the view of women in the patriarchal societies of Europe. Only within the Irish communities were Irish women given their customary status and able to engage in activities open to them in Irish society. Women could act as physicians only in their own communities. There were also occasions when the wives of Irish soldiers took part in battles, temporarily taking on the role of the female combatants of ancient Celtic culture.

THE CELTIC FAMILY

The Celts had a strong family structure based on the extended family. It was not unusual for sons and daughters to reside with their parents even after they grew into adulthood and formed their own families. A Celtic extended family included everyone in a clan who could trace their descent from a common ancestor, even if the ancestor lived many generations in the past. This family and clan loyalty was reflected by Celtic law making each member of a clan responsible for the behavior of other clan members.

To teach the children to behave in accordance with the norms of Celtic society and not to bring disgrace upon the clan, the Celts followed a child-rearing custom called gossiprage. The adults constantly observed a child's conduct and reported to the parents both the good and the bad behavior. Within the local area of a Celtic settlement, every adult assumed a degree of responsibility for raising children by acting as a surrogate parent, even if the degree of kinship was remote.

Fosterage was another child-rearing practice of the Celts, whereby a child was formally placed in a household of another clan. Young Celtic men or women placed in fosterage lived as an adopted member of the clan until they were adult. Sometimes fosterage was used to form an alliance between clans. Other times it was used so children could learn a particular skill from their adopted parents. Both gossiprage and fosterage demonstrated a high degree of community involvement in family affairs which caused children to develop loyalty to the entire clan.

The Celtic practice of fosterage helped the Irish to adjust to life in European societies. With their familiarity with this age-old Celtic practice, new emigres saw Irish communities abroad as large families to whom they could easily attach themselves while getting their bearings in the foreign lands. When the emigres were ready to take a larger role in their new societies, this step was taken smoothly because the emigres readily gave their loyalty and services to a monarchy or nation, which they viewed as an enlarged clan. Because by custom the Irish were loyal to clans and received loyalty in return and were used to interacting with all types of persons beyond the unit of the family, Irish emigres readily adapted to their new circumstances and opportunities in the different societies of Europe.

But even after immigrating to Europe and becoming involved in the affairs of the different countries, the Irish did not abandon their ties with the extended family they belonged to. In many cases, their relationship with family or clan members in other European countries would both help them in their chosen field of activity and also benefit their new country. Because of their close kinship bonds, many Irish emigres were able to establish commercial, military and political networks with relations of theirs throughout Europe. Members of the same clan could usually be trusted to carry funds, messages, or sensitive information to other family or clan members in different countries of Europe.

The bonds of the Irish with their extended families enabled many Irish emigres to thrive in the countries they journeyed to. It gave the Irish a sense of familiarity and comfort in their new lands. In so doing, it served as a means for adapting to them and also as a foundation for taking an initiative in their various fields of endeavor.

CELTIC RULERS AND WARRIORS

The Celts developed a form of government suited for the small, independent communities of their agrarian society. The families in an area formed a clan cluster whose members would elect a chieftain. If he was not a capable leader, the clan replaced him by electing another chief. When threatened by an enemy, the clan chiefs would elect a warlord to lead them into battle. After the war ended, the warlord relinquished his authority.

In those regions of Ireland and Britain where Celtic culture survived the longest, it was nonetheless affected by the form of government of the cultures that dominated parts of Europe, including parts of the British Isles. This form of government was a hereditary monarchy. Following this form, clan chieftains who had been elected became petty kings whose position was filled by their oldest son upon their death. This development in Celtic culture rarely extended beyond the clan. No charismatic or powerful ruler rose to unite a number of the clans into a permanent kingdom or nation.

The closest the Irish came to a united system of government was when clan chiefs began electing a High King during the early Middle Ages, about the 5th century. Mythology tells of even earlier High Kings in Ireland who behaved more as local warlords than monarchs by engaging in frequent wars with rival clans. The authority of the High King was limited and his effectiveness as a ruler depended on his ability to persuade the clan chieftains to agree with his decisions. In matters affecting all of the clans, the High King had to call a convention of chieftains to decide the issues and could not act on his own initiative.

The failure of the Irish to form a unified, cohesive government is one of the main reasons for the surge in Irish emigration in the late Middle Ages. Acting independently from one another, the clans were unable to resist the Anglo-Norman invasion of the 12th century. Although the invaders were vastly outnumbered by the Celts, the Anglo-Normans permanently established themselves in many parts of Ireland. Once all of the clans were defeated, the Anglo-Norman overlords instituted a strict rule decreed by the English Crown. By this rule, the Irish had negligible political and civil rights. Farmers could arbitrarily have their land taken from them, and Irishmen could hold no political or judicial office. This led to ineffective rebellions by the Irish against England during the closing centuries of the medieval period. By the early modern era, the Irish came to realize that they were not going to free themselves from English oppression and they began to emigrate in large numbers to various countries of Europe.

Although they were ineffective in their wars with other societies, such as the Normans and before them, the Vikings and the Romans, the fierceness and bravery of the Celtic warriors in battle was often noted by those they fought against. In his work *Geography*, the Greek Strabo wrote that "the whole race is war-mad, and both high-spirited and quick for battle...For those that wish to defeat them by stratagem, they become easy to deal with. In fact, irritate them when, where, and by what pretext you please and you have them ready to risk their lives with nothing to help them but might and daring."

The Celts favored individual combat between opposing champions instead of the coordinated deployment of disciplined units. Julius Caesar was struck by the tactics of the Celtic charioteers. In writing about one of his encounters with the Celts in his conquest of Gaul, Caesar described these charioteers as driving "in all directions hurling spears. Generally they succeeded in throwing the ranks of their opponents into confusion just with the terror caused by their galloping horses and the din of the wheels. They make their way through their own cavalry, then jump down from their chariots and fight on foot...thus they have the mobility of cavalry and the staying power of infantry." As Hannibal in his invasion of the Italian peninsula and as Caesar himself recognized in his own use of Celtic warriors in his army, with appropriate leadership and used in certain ways in warfare, the Celts made formidable soldiers. But their loose, compulsive and sporadic style of warfare was no match for the organization and persistence of Roman legions and other well-disciplined enemies the Celts faced in their history.

While a loose political organization based on clans was suited for the Celtic way of life, it did not allow the Celts to muster an effective defense when attacked by the legions of Rome. This was particularly evident when Julius Caesar easily conquered Gaul in a war that began in 58 B.C. Some Celtic clans sided with the Romans while other clans watched with indifference as their neighbors were overrun by the invaders. By 53 B.C. Caesar believed that Gaul was pacified. But the clan chiefs had finally awakened to the danger posed by Rome. They elected Vercingetorix of the clan Arverni to be their warlord. Under his leadership, twenty-nine Celtic clans revolted against Rome in 52 B.C. Caesar's legions were soon surrounded in a fortified camp, defending themselves against constant Celtic attacks. But after suffering a large number of casualties without annihilating the Romans, the Celtic chieftains withdrew their support of Vercingetorix and returned to their homes. Vercingetorix was captured by Caesar and ritually executed in Rome as an example to dissuade other potential Celtic warlords from defying Rome.

Although Caesar admired the courage of the Celts in Gaul, he was disdainful of the way that they gathered military intelligence and made important tactical decisions. He wrote in his *Commentaries*, "in the town, a crowd [of Celts] gathers around traders and forces them to say what country they are from and what information they have gathered there. Influenced by these reports, even when they are hearsay, the Gauls frequently adopt plans about important matters which they are bound to regret almost immediately...They are slaves to unsubstantiated rumors and most of the people they question make up answers they think will please them." This tendency of the Celtic warriors to make decisions based on unreliable information enabled Caesar to deceive them as to the strength and deployment of his forces.

At times, Celtic warriors from different clans would join together to form a sodality. This was a band whose members followed a charismatic leader and closely supported each other in combat. But the warrior sodality was more than a tactical unit. It was also a way of life based on honor among the members of the sodality and loyalty to a military ideal that superseded allegiance to clan or kin. These warrior groups formed an integral part of Celtic society, distinct from the social classes of nobles, scholars and peasants. The concept was immortalized by the hero of one Irish myth named Finn MacCumhail. His young warriors called themselves the Fianna and were led by his son, Oisín. In times of peace, they practiced their military skills by hunting and fighting in lands far from their own clan territories. When Finn's land was threatened by enemies either mortal or supernatural, the individual champions of the Fianna vied with each other for the privilege of engaging in a death struggle to protect Finn's territory. Most of the warrior sodalities were exclusive male fraternities who disdained the company of women. But the Irish epic poem *Táin Bó Cualinge* mentioned a female warrior band led by a woman named Scáthach, who also trained the hero Cúchulain in the use of weapons. This mythical female warrior sodality demonstrated the level of equality between men and women in ancient Celtic society.

The warrior sodalities provided a socially acceptable outlet for young Celtic men with an excess of leisure time on their hands. They gave warriors military training while forging bonds with other young people from different clans. During times of war, the sodalities provided a highly-trained force that was prepared to engage an invader while other warriors gathered to meet the foe. In Ireland, warrior sodalities remained in existence until the late Middle Ages.

Because of the Celtic tradition of the warrior sodality, many Irish emigres were prompted to join the armies of different European countries. In some cases, so many emigres filled the ranks of an army that they were made into a special military unit. There were also instances of emigre soldiers presenting themselves as a unified unit, complete with Irish officers. The model for these all-Irish military units was the warrior sodality of traditional Celtic culture. Although these fighting forces wore the uniforms of a foreign land and were often led by foreign officers, the strong bonds of camaraderie among their members and the fighting spirit they found in the company of one another was the same as with the medieval warrior sodalities which bravely, and sometimes desperately, tried to keep Vikings and Anglo-Normans from occupying Irish soil. There were times in European history when such Irish military units turned the tide of battles, and in some cases played a major part in winning a war. At Cremona in 1701, the Irish Brigade of France transformed defeat into victory by driving the Austrians from the city; and the Ultonia Regiment of Spain blocked a critical supply line of Napoleon's army by withstanding a year-long French siege of Gerona.

By the early modern era, Irish soldiers had adapted to the methods of contemporary warfare. They no longer approached the field of battle as champions seeking fame and glory in individual combat against an enemy champion, but rather plunged into battle as a cohesive, coordinated fighting unit. Such a unit's movements and objectives were usually a part of an overall battle plan. But in recognition of the exceptional courage and enterprise of the Irish soldiers, in most cases their units were given wide latitude in their actions on the battlefield.

Because of the fierce loyalty of the Irish emigres to their adopted lands, the kings and queens of Europe were not concerned about enlisting the services of so many foreigners in their armies. The Irish were not mercenaries offering their swords to the highest bidder. Instead they generally fought for the benefit of their adopted lands and for the kings and queens they had sworn allegiance to. Even when they found themselves in combat with other Irish emigres, their sense of duty to their adopted countries, which they saw as their foster clans, prevented any compromise with their cousins and former neighbors.

The casual political system and the style of combat of the Irish were unable to stand up to the powerful Anglo-Norman forces which invaded Ireland in the 12th century. The Celtic virtues of individuality and clan ties became fatal weaknesses in the increasingly complex and highly-organized societies of the late Middle Ages and the early modern era. Although these Celtic virtues could not save Ireland, they did save a number of foreign monarchs and societies when the emigres put them to the service of their adopted lands. As with other virtues and skills, the military abilities of the Irish emigres enabled them to take leading roles in the armies of foreign lands.

THE DRUIDS AND EDUCATION

The Druids were the spiritual leaders in Celtic society, and were given a social status equivalent to the warriors. They were known as the men and women of "special gifts," the *áes-dana*. They were shamen and seers articulating the unique Celtic vision of the world and the role of people in it. Spiritual guidance was only one of their activities. They were also scholars who served their society as doctors, lawyers, priests and poets. For the Celts, these were not separate professions as they were in other parts of Europe. Any *áes-dana* had the knowledge and skills to compose entertaining verse, decide a complex question of property rights or set a broken bone.

Many years of study were required for a person to become a Druid. Although most Druids were men, women could become Druids too. The Celtic association of knowledge and spirituality comes from the recognition of the value of the Druids to Celtic society. Julius Caesar wrote that a person had to study for twenty years before he or she could be made a Druid. This study included both formal education and apprenticeship with a Druid. During this time of study, the Druid had to learn a large body of law, the intricacies of human anatomy, the Celtic oral literature and the rules and rhetoric of poetics, and also the Celtic spiritual system and its rituals. Druid formal learning ordinarily took place in a fixed location at schools which were called colleges by the Romans. To complement this formal study, students would also travel about the countryside practicing their skills and learning how to interact with the communities. Students, as well as Druids, would visit different clans performing rituals, reciting myths and poems, healing the sick, and rendering other services in exchange for temporary lodging.

Because of their authority in Celtic culture, the Druids were singled out by the Romans historians for particularly hostile criticism. Many Romans believed that the Druids wielded dangerous supernatural powers. Roman generals also recognized that the Druids were a rallying force in Celtic culture that stiffened resistance to Roman territorial ambitions. In their chronicles, the Romans often accused the Druids of bizarre practices, only some of which have been confirmed by archeological evidence. Diodorus claimed that Druids would attempt to predict the future with "a strange and incredible custom: they devoted [i.e. sacrificed] to death a human being and stab him with a dagger in the region above the diaphragm, and when he has fallen, they foretell the future from his fall, and from the convulsions of his limbs." Pliny the Elder during the 1st century A.D. suggested that the Druids engaged in a ritual animal slaughter to prepare a magical potion of blood mixed with mistletoe. While the Roman historians do mention the legal, medical and philosophical roles of Druids in Celtic society, they dwell far longer on the lurid and the sensational, as if they were the tabloid journalists of their age. It is from writings of Roman historians that many of the European folktales about Druids sprang to life. Because the early Celts had no form of literacy, accurate knowledge of Druid practices can come only from archeological evidence which allows modern scholars to reconstruct Druid rituals.

One such reconstruction was based on the perfectly preserved body of an ancient Celtic man retrieved from a peat bog near Lindow, England in 1984. He had died around 60 A.D. from the "triple death"—a ritual slaying involving garroting him into semi-consciousness, severing his jugular and drowning him before he bled to death. Archaeologists assumed that each separate act was an offering to a different god. Because the victim was not bound and because he enjoyed a sumptuous meal prior to his death, archaeologists also concluded that he was a volunteer victim for the fatal ceremony. The evidence of Lindow Man together with the Celtic bodies recovered from other parts of Europe confirmed the Roman assertion that the Druids engaged in ritual slayings as part of their rites.

By 58 A.D., the mystique of the Druid loomed large in the minds of the Roman occupiers of Britain. In that year, concern over the Druids dictated military decisions of the Romans in their measures to put down a Celtic rebellion. Boudicca of the Iceni clan led her warriors in rebellion against the legions of the Roman Emperor Claudius. The Roman military commander, Gaius Suetonius Paulinus, decided not to deploy his soldiers against the insurgents, but instead marched north to the Druid enclave located on the island of Anglesey. He knew that the Iceni warriors would easily be able to assault his undefended headquarters at Londinum (London), but he believed that the magic wielded by the Druids was a more serious threat to the Romans in Britain. The Druids at Anglesey were defended by only a few warriors, and the battle was brief. The Roman legions quickly cut them down, despite the supposed magical powers of the Druids. Paulinus then marched his legions back to Londinum and defeated the Iceni rebels.

With the characteristic determination and methodicalness that they exhibited in all of the territories they conquered, the Romans undertook the Romanization of the parts of Britain they controlled. Londinum soon became an important, thriving administrative, military, and commercial center. Roman legions were stationed far north of Londinum as a deterrent against incursions into Roman territory by the warlike, unpacified Picts. The natural bellicose inclinations of the Picts had been heightened even further by a wave of refugees of fellow Celts fleeing from the advance of the Roman army. Once the bulk of Britain had been pacified, a network of trade and information exchange was formed among the conquered territories and the outlying areas. Given the proximity of Ireland to Britain and the varied activity of this network, Celtic culture in Ireland was inevitably exposed to elements of Roman civilization. Nonetheless, Celtic culture maintained its distinctiveness not only due to the independent spirit of the Celts, but also because of Ireland's unique geographical position which kept it safe from any Roman territorial ambitions.

Writing was one of the elements of Roman civilization which found its way into Celtic culture. With their recognition of the value of knowledge, the Druids of Ireland, like the Druids of Britain, quickly grasped the importance of writing and realized its uses. About 200 A.D., the *áesdana* of Britain and Ireland developed a script known as *ogham*. This was a runic form of writing in which each letter was represented by parallel lines inscribed at different angles from a main vertical line or stem. It resembled the runic scripts used in Scandinavia and Germany at the time. Although modern scholars disagree on the origin and purpose of *ogham*, many of them believe that the keen interest in writing among the Druids was prompted by the success of Christian missionaries in spreading this religion by emphasizing reading and copying the Gospels.

Within Celtic society, the Druids were secretive about the use of *ogham* and discouraged the development of other forms of writing in order to guard the secrets of their herbal remedies and religious rituals.

It was used extensively on tombstone inscriptions, suggesting that it may have had a significance in religious rites for the dead. Contemporary Roman observers record that the Druids occasionally passed messages to each other written in *ogham* runes carved on wooden staves. To the Romans, this script seemed to be magical symbols, which they related to the supernatural powers attributed to the Druids. This Roman misunderstanding is the basis for the "magic wand" which frequently appears in the myths and folklore of the British Isles. The wizard Merlin of the Arthurian legends and his "magic wand" and other supernatural powers are based on the Druids of Celtic culture.

The Celts of the British Isles who embraced Christianity spread their religious message by using the Latin form of writing. When the Christians of Ireland saw how easily spiritual doctrine could be transmitted with just a few scratches on parchment, every monastic school began to teach the invaluable skill in order to attract converts to the new religion. During the early Middle Ages, the Celtic passion for education inspired monks and nuns to use their newly-acquired literacy to copy thousands of intricate manuscripts such as the famous *Book of Kells*, thus preserving a vast trove of Celtic and Christian wisdom for future generations. They also wrote down their own ideas and observations in chronicles and in the margins of manuscripts, putting their personal interpretation on historical events and social practices. At the same time, they preserved a substantial body of literature, philosophy and law.

To relieve the tedium of copying manuscripts, the monks played elaborate Latin word games with each other in which they invented words and altered grammatical rules. This eventually produced enough variations of standard Latin to create a language of their own which was called "Hisperic-Latin" by later historians. Because only the Celtic Christian clergy understood this language, they used it whenever they wished to pass secret messages to each other, much as the Druids used *ogham*. This practice was particularly useful when the medieval monks of Ireland communicated with other Irish monks who had settled in Europe. Because of the rivalry between the Celtic Christians and the other Christian sects in Europe, they wanted their messages to be understood only by the intended recipients.

As Celtic society evolved, Christian clergy gradually took the place of the Druids. Yet the high regard of Celtic society for intellectual pursuits based in the reputations and importance of the Druids was not lost. The Irish monks of the medieval period were noted for their intellectual achievements as well as their religious work. Only persons convinced of the crucial importance of the written word would have anonymously toiled the long hours many of the monks did in copying classical and Christian writings. Many Irish monks had leading roles in the Carolingean Renaissance of the 9th century. Many of the early monasteries in Ireland and later in Europe were founded to provide education for students and scholars from near and far as well as serve as religious centers. The outlawing of education for the Irish under the oppressive rule of the English during the early modern era could not stamp out the Irish desire for learning. This prompted numbers of Irishmen to emigrate to European countries where they could pursue the studies denied to them in their own land. It was mainly for this reason that the Irish Colleges at Paris, Salamanca and Rome were founded. The respect for education in Irish culture and the realization of its role in the well-being of society, the abilities and ingenuity of individuals, and in the practical arts such as medicine and agriculture can be traced back to the place of the Druids in Celtic culture.

CELTIC ART

The Celtic view of reality, which was also a manifestation of their spirituality, was embodied in their works of art. Like may other ancient cultures, the Celts had a holistic view, or sense, of reality. There was an interconnection among all things in the world of nature, and human beings were a part of this. Birth and death were experiences belonging to the natural processes which governed the life of a person. The essence of a person, or soul, was endlessly reincarnated in the world of nature. While their spirituality was similar to that of other ancient cultures, the objects and articles the Celts made to express their spirituality had a sophistication and permanence that set them apart from the artistic creations of other cultures.

The distinctive style and imagery of Celtic art were developed in the La Téne region about 500 B.C. The most primitive Celtic art was carved into stones. Stones with the loops and interlacings which are chief characteristic of Celtic art have been found throughout Europe. These loopings and interlacings represent the central matters of Celtic spirituality—the interconnection of all things, the patterns of nature, reincarnation. This imagery was also used for the metalwork and the jewelry made by Celtic artisans. It appears frequently on metal shields and the handles of swords. Brooches, rings, bracelets, clasps and other pieces of Celtic jewelry were often made in the form of such imagery, or else the imagery was carved into the jewelry.

Celtic jewelry appealed to people of the more developed, urban cultures of the Mediterranean for its exceptional workmanship and attractiveness of its patterns. However, people from these other cultures did not realize the symbolic value such jewelry had for the Celts. They saw it being worn by the Celts merely for personal adornment. As the Greek Strabo wrote, the Celts had a "fondness for ornaments...both chains around their necks and bracelets around their arms and wrists." Strabo remarked only on the Celts' fondness for jewelry, not its meaning for them.

One of the more impressive works of art of the Celts is the Gundestrup Cauldron. Dated at approximately 100 B.C., it was discovered in the bogs of Denmark at the beginning of the 20th century. The silver Cauldron symbolized life and death for the Celts. Carvings of myths and scenes relating to life and death ring the Cauldron. One of these depicts a goddess dipping slain warriors in to the Cauldron to restore them to life. Another scene shows figures—probably prisoners of war—with decapitated heads lying between their legs. This scene tends to confirm Roman assertions that the Celts decapitated their prisoners.

The art forms of the Celts were not confined to molded metal and carved stone. The Celts were also skilled poets, using imagery and metaphor to articulate their beliefs about the interrelationship between humans and the world around them. In the Irish *Book of Invasions*, a collection of Celtic myths from early Ireland, a poem attributed to Amhairghin showed the interconnection of all living things.

> *I am the wind which breathes upon the sea.*
> *I am the wave of the ocean.*
> *I am the murmur of the billows.*

I am a powerful ox.
I am a hawk on a cliff.
I am a beam of the sun.
I am a wild boar in valor.
I am a salmon in a pool.
I am a lake in a plain.
I am a word of science.
I am a lance point in battle.
I create in people the fire of thought.

Amhairghin was not merely like the things he named. In his mind and the minds of his audience, he became a hawk on a cliff and he became a lance point in battle. His words underscore his belief in shape-shifting, in the ability for his spirit to enter the bodies of animals, the inanimate objects around him, and even abstract concepts such as a word of science. Like the intricate knots etched into Celtic stone and metalwork, the poem of Amhairghin demonstrated that the Celts believed that all natural phenomena were interrelated.

The elements and subjects of Celtic art remained the major influence on Irish artists into the medieval and early modern period. The Irish artists continued to use recurring patterns when making stone engravings or working with metal, and often used recurring imagery in their poetry. Because of its connection to the Celtic art of ancient times, the art of the Irish emigres during these periods had a universal quality. For this, many Irish artists gained prominence in countries they emigrated to, just like emigres with military skills, intellectual abilities, business aptitude and other skills. In some instances, an emigre was made the poet laureate in his new country, to write verse to entertain the monarch and his royal court. In the 9th century, the Frankish Queen Ermingarde took a liking to the poetry of the Irishman Sedulius; and she rewarded him with special recognition and riches. Later in the Middle Ages, Irish poets had a strong influence on the metaphor and imagery used in Norse sagas. Many Celtic art forms endured into the modern period, with the Irish emigres becoming especially noted for their Celtic-style jewelry.

Celtic art forms were part of the cultural inheritance of the Irish emigres during modern times. The theme of the interconnection of all living things contained in Celtic art became an integral part of the Irish view of the world and helped emigres feel connected to their adopted European societies. The themes of Celtic-Irish art also reflected the emigre's belief that although they may appear outwardly Spanish, French, or Austrian, they remained Irish in spirit.

The close connection between ancient Celtic culture and the Irish emigres was brought about by a series of historical events which began approximately 300 B.C. and continued for more than a millennium. During this time, the Celtic way of life vanished from continental Europe, and the British Isles became the last place where Celtic culture survived.

CHAPTER 2

The Evolution of Celtic Culture in Ireland

They came from a land beyond the sea,
And now o'er the western main
Set sail in their good ships, gallantly,
From the sunny lands of Spain.
"Oh, where's the isle we've seen in dreams,
Our destined home or grave?"
Thus sang they, as by the morning beams,
They swept the Atlantic wave.

— The Coming of the Milesians *
  Thomas Moore (1779-1852)

GEOGRAPHY AND IRISH HISTORY

The geography of Ireland played a major role in the preservation of Celtic culture. On the northwestern fringe of the continent, Ireland was separated from Europe by a span of of sea wide enough to make invasion difficult, but narrow enough to allow commerce. Had it been closer to the European mainland, Roman soldiers could have launched an invasion

*
The first Celts in Ireland were named Milesians after their leader, Mil.

armada against the Irish Celts. Had it been further away, the Irish missionaries of the Middle Ages would not have been able to reach the European mainland in their primitive boats.

This position first played an important part in the preservation of Celtic culture between the 2nd century B.C. and the 1st century A.D. when a relentless tide of war and conquest inundated Celtic civilization on mainland Europe. During these centuries, the legions of Rome marched into Spain and Gaul; and land-hungry and battle-hardened warriors of Germanic tribes overran the Danube basin and central Europe. With their undisciplined style of warfare, the Celts were unable to keep the Romans or Germans from overrunning their lands. Many of those who did not perish swiftly by the sword lived under the dominance of Roman or Germanic overlords. Some Celtic survivors of the turmoil on mainland Europe fled to Britain and Ireland in the hope that the islands would offer them sanctuary from Rome.

These refugees were not the first Celts to reach Ireland. Celtic clans had migrated there as early as the late Iron Age, about 500 B.C., and established permanent, prosperous communities. Although far removed from the main centers of Celtic culture on continental Europe, the Irish Celts nonetheless continued to follow the same cultural practices. The round strongholds they constructed, called ring forts, were similar to forts built by Celtic tribes in northwestern Spain and on the Atlantic coast of France. Brooches and swords discovered by archaeologists in Celtic burial sites in Ireland are like ones found in Celtic burial sites throughout Europe. There is no agreement on how the first Celts got to Ireland. There is some archaeological evidence to suggest, however, that they came to Ireland from Spain, after migrating there from Celtic cultural centers in central Europe. The mythology of the Irish Celts supports this origin too. The *Lebor Gabála*—The Book of Invasions which is a medieval compilation of early Irish myths—names Mil as the chieftain of a group of Celts that came from Spain to settle in Ireland in order to escape a famine. After winning a battle against the Tuatha de Danaan who inhabited Ireland, Mil's people claimed Ireland as their new home.

The first Celts in Ireland—wherever they came from—maintained contacts with the Celts in mainland Europe by being a part of the trading network among the Celtic settlements. There is evidence that the Irish

Celts traded with cities as distant as Tyre in Phoenicia and Alexandria in Egypt. In turn, the mainland Celts uprooted by the Romans and Germans were aware of the Celtic communities in Ireland as well as in Britain; and numbers of them saw the distant island as a sanctuary from the warfare and uncertainty of the continent.

The influx of Celtic refugees arriving in the 1st and 2nd centuries B.C. helped to concentrate and advance the Celtic culture in Ireland. After Rome completed its conquest of most of western Europe and after the Celtic tribes already occupying central Europe were overrun by Germanic tribes, Ireland was left as the only place in all of Europe where the original Celtic culture existed and was free to endure and grow largely unaffected by the mixture of Greek, Roman, Mediterranean, Christian and barbarian influences which were determining the nature of mainland European society. Because of its location on the perimeter of Europe, historical developments elsewhere in Europe inevitably had some effect on Ireland. Yet because of its remoteness, these developments did not affect the essence of Celtic culture which had taken root in Ireland.

IRELAND AND THE ROMAN EMPIRE

Because Ireland was not isolated from events occurring on the European continent, the growing power of the distant city of Rome eventually influenced the development of Irish Celtic society. Yet no Roman soldier ever set foot in Ireland and no Roman governor ever made laws for the Irish to live by. Instead, the effects of Rome on Ireland were indirect, coming about from an exchange of goods and ideas between the Irish and the Celts living in the Roman occupied lands of Britain and Gaul.

Because the Celts almost conquered Rome before the city had grown powerful enough to build an Empire, the Romans came to regard the Celts as a threat to their survival. This experience motivated the Romans to ultimately destroy Celtic culture in western Europe and attempt to conquer all of Celtic Britain. The first conflict between Romans and Celts occurred in 390 B.C. when Rome sent delegates to the neighboring Etruscan city of Clusium to mediate a dispute between the Etruscans and a clan of Celts. Since about 650 B.C., Celtic raiders from the La Tène and Hallstatt regions had threatened the city-states of Italy. By the time of the confrontation at Clusium, the number of Celts who had migrated into Italy from Switzerland and Austria was large enough to concern both the Etruscans and the Romans. Because the people of Clusium refused to consider the Celts' demands for land to settle on, the negotiations mediated by the Romans quickly broke down and a skirmish followed between the Etruscans and the Celts. The Romans joined the brief battle on the side of the Etruscans, angering the Celts with their flagrant violation of neutrality. Under the leadership of the chieftain Brennius, the army of the Celts abandoned their attack on the Etruscan city of Clusium and marched south to the greater prize of Rome.

Unable to halt the Celtic advance, the Romans built barricades around the Capitoline Hill to protect the Senate and the Forum. The Celts entered the city, burning and looting and laying siege to the Capitoline Hill. For seven months they tried unsuccessfully to defeat the Romans. Then, after sacking the city, the Celts abruptly departed. Historians are at a loss to explain the Celts' sudden departure from Rome. The Roman chronicler Polybius wrote that the withdrawal was due to the their concern over the Venetii and Etruscans endangering the Celtic route back to their homeland to the north. The historian Livy thought the Celts departed because many of them became sick after encamping near the mosquito-infested marshes of the Tiber River. The devastation wrought upon Rome left the inhabitants of the city with a hatred for the Celts that would fester for centuries.

For the next 150 years, the enmity between Roman and Celt was intensified by ongoing conflicts between Roman soldiers and the warriors of wandering Celtic clans. During the Punic Wars of the 2nd century B.C., the Celts of Spain were allies of Carthage, a city on the coast of North Africa which was the rival of Rome for control of the western Mediterranean. When Hannibal made his famous passage across the Alps to invade Italy and threaten the city of Rome, his troops were mostly Spanish Celts. After a series of crushing defeats in battle, the Romans fell back to the city of Rome where they were soon besieged by Hannibal and his mostly-Celtic army. Unlike the previous siege in 390 B.C., this time the city was better defended—with a high stone wall encircling it. Nonetheless, this second siege inevitably recalled for the Romans their earlier humiliation when they had been reduced to cringing in their fabled city while bands of Celtic warriors surrounded them and were free to pillage the countryside. With Hannibal at their head, Celtic warriors had reopened an old wound.

This siege of Rome was lifted as mysteriously as the previous siege after the victories of the Roman general Scipio in Spain. Hannibal abandoned the siege of Rome and departed the Italian peninsula to return to Carthage. He left no reasons for this sudden departure, but most historians attribute it to the need to defend Carthage from Scipio's armies after the fall of Spain. With their defeat by Scipio, the Iberian Celts—called Celtiberians by the Romans—were now subjects of the Roman Republic who could be used as soldiers against Carthage.

Hannibal's withdrawal ended the immediate threat to Rome from the Celtic warriors. But it did not end Rome's problem with the Celts. Seeing the prosperous, peaceful Roman colonial provinces along the Mediterranean coast of Gaul (present-day France) as easy targets for raiding parties seeking precious metals, domestic supplies, and slaves, the Celts frequently assaulted the towns and cities. Occasionally, their raids extended to the cities and farms of northern Italy. The small Roman military garrisons in these areas were unable to control these raids by the Celts, who would appear suddenly, ravage rich, defenseless targets, and vanish just as suddenly into the wilderness of central Gaul.

The Celts had been making such raids before the threat to Rome from Hannibal, and they continued making them after the threat ended. Having twice been humbled by Celtic warriors and having been victorious over their Carthaginian rivals, the Romans anxious to end the destructive, unsettling raids by the Celts which diminished Roman treasure and terrified Roman subjects.

In 125 B.C., Rome sent legions into the Rhone Valley to subdue the Celtic tribes bordering Roman territory. This was just the first step in a long conflict between the Romans and the Celts that would not end until Julius Caesar finally pacified all of Gaul in 56 B.C. After Caesar's conquest of Gaul, independent Celtic culture in continental Europe was confined to the Danube basin; but the defeated Celts of Gaul could not flee toward the Danube because of the threat posed by Germanic tribes migrating westward into the lands between the North Sea and Switzerland.

The Celts of Ireland felt no impact from Roman expansion during the 3rd and 2nd centuries B.C. when Rome was conquering the Celts of western Europe. The first indirect effects came in the 1st century B.C. when a trickle of continental Celtic refugees began to arrive at the close of Caesar's campaigns in Gaul. Grave sites in Gaul excavated by archeologists indicated that many of the Celtic warriors died in battle. Survivors and their families faced the choice of submission to Rome or flight to the islands of Britain or Ireland, which was then known as either Hibernia and the North Island.

After vanquishing the Celts in Gaul and establishing garrisons throughout the territory, Caesar turned his sights to Britain. As the superior strategist he was, Caesar knew he had to subdue the recently-defeated Celtic warriors who had fled to Britain and were likely to return to the mainland to harass Roman forces or raid Roman cities and farms as Celts had done throughout Rome's history. Caesar desired to have Britain under Roman rule not only because this was a military imperative, but also so he could then be able to return to Rome in triumph to increase his chances of ruling the Eternal City and the far-flung lands he had newly brought into its imperial fold.

Caesar opened his planned invasion of Britain with a reconnaissance-in-force in 55 B.C. Having gauged the strength of Celtic resistance, the following year he led a Roman army large enough to defeat the Celts and establish a Roman stronghold which would be the basis for the eventual conquest of the entire island—the pattern which he had followed with success in his campaigns in Gaul. But Caesar's carefully-laid plans were dashed when a storm in the English Channel destroyed many of the ships carrying supplies to his forces which had landed in Britain and at the same time, a rebellion broke out in northern Gaul. Caesar withdrew his legions from Britain to deal with the uprising in Gaul. After putting down the revolt, Caesar never returned to finish the conquest of Britain. When a political crisis developed in Rome, Caesar set off on his famous "crossing of the Rubicon" and the fate that awaited him in the Imperial City.

Caesar might not have been concerned about attacks from the British Celts. Without the threat of Roman legions facing them, the British tribes and the Celts who had fled to the island from Gaul could not unite so as to pose any threat to Rome. The British Celts remained safe from Rome until 42 A.D., when the Emperor Claudius decided the time had come to add Britain to the Roman Empire. Under the leadership of the Roman general Aulus Plautius, an army of four legions landed near Dover in 43 A.D. They moved inland and met fierce resistance from a hastily formed alliance of several Celtic clans at a battle near Camolodunum (London), where Celtic champions charged at the Romans in chariots. But the efficient battle tactics of the Romans eventually prevailed over the undisciplined Celts. Camolodunum became the main encampment of the Romans from which they succeeded in conquering the southern half of the island.

Gradually, year by year, campaign by campaign, the Romans increased their British domain. After Roman legions had conquered almost half of Britain, a rebellion erupted in 61 A.D. led by when the Iceni clan who inhabited a territory northeast of London. They were soon subdued, but the Romans continued to have difficulty in subduing the Celts of Britain, a land far from the Imperial City. Between 61 A.D. and 84 A.D., the forces of Rome continued to press northwards, but never conquered the entire island. Rome was unwilling to commit the expensive military resources needed to subdue northern Britain, a land the Romans considered too rugged to produce much tribute in any event. In 119 A.D., the Emperor Hadrian ordered the building of a wall across the border with present-day Scotland, then the home of the warlike Picts.

The Roman conquests in Britain divided the Celts into two cultural groups. One group of Celts lived outside the boundaries of the Roman Empire and continued to follow their traditional customs and beliefs. These Celts lived in Scotland, beyond the northernmost Roman garrisons of Carlisle and Newcastle, and they passed on their enmity for Rome from generation to generation. The second group of Celts lived within the boundaries of the Empire in the southern part of the island. These Celts gradually became Romanized by adopting many aspects of Roman culture.

Because Ireland and Britain were near to each other, traders regularly exchanging goods and information introduced Roman ideas into Ireland. In addition, sea raiders from Ireland in search of plunder and slaves abducted Romanized Celts from Britain and brought them back to Ireland. These British-Celtic captives taught the Irish about Roman government, religion and methods of war. Despite these influences, Ireland remained essentially Celtic during the Roman occupation of Britain since the Irish could choose which Roman ideas to accept rather than having them imposed on their society by Roman legions. The Irish borrowed some Roman ideas, such as writing, and adapted them for use in their culture. But the influence of Roman civilization was not strong enough to disrupt the cultural continuity of the Celts in Ireland, who were the only Celts following a way of life that had vanished in continental Europe.

CHRISTIANITY COMES TO IRELAND

As the Roman world gradually embraced Christianity, the Celts inevitably came in contact with the new religion. Christianity was introduced to Ireland by British traders, adventurers and missionaries who crossed the Irish Sea, and by captives brought to Ireland by raiders. During the early medieval period, Christianity had a profound effect on the development of Celtic culture in Ireland.

The earliest Christian symbols in Britain have been dated from 315 A.D., about the time that the Emperor Constantine sanctioned the public practice of the religion throughout the Empire. The Venerable Bede, an eighth-century Saxon historian, claimed in his *Opera Historica* that Christians worshiped secretly in Britain from the 1st century A.D. Bede wrote that the faithful practiced their rituals in the "forests ...or secret dens." Despite the laws against Christianity, the religion took root in Britain and developed a widespread following.

Just how and when Christianity took root in Ireland is not known. The use of Latin-derived words for aspects of Christianity in the Irish language by the beginning of the 5th century indicates that Christianity was having an effect on Celtic culture by this time. The Irish word *caplait* for Holy Thursday was derived from *capitalavium*, the word that Latin-speaking Christians used for Holy Thursday. *Peccatum*, the Latin word for sin, became the Irish *peccath*, which also meant sin. Irish *ortha*, or prayer, was derived from Latin *oratio*. These words demonstrate the presence of Christianity in Ireland during the time when Rome occupied Britain.

In most European lands, the arrival of Christian missionaries sparked religious conflict when pagan spiritual leaders tried to maintain their dominance over societies against the growing influence of the new religion. But in Ireland, there was little conflict between Druids and Christians. Because of their tolerance for other points of view, the Druids did not use their influence to stifle Christian missionaries. Legend claims that the 6th century Welsh Druid Teliesin spoke for all Druids when he said, "In Asia Christ was a new thing. But there was not a time when the Druids held not his belief." Celtic Druids and Christian missionaries focused on the similarities of their beliefs, not the differences. During the 4th and 5th centuries, Christian and Druid beliefs gradually blended to form a distinctive version of the Christian religion which incorporated many aspects of Celtic culture into its practices and doctrines. Since most Irish saw no distinction between priest and Druid, the converts to the new religion viewed the Christian clergy as the philosophers, physicians and law-givers of their society, just as they had viewed the Druids. This hybrid religion, which came to be called Celtic Christianity by modern historians, continued to thrive in Ireland during most of the medieval period and was carried to mainland Europe by Irish monks.

ST. PATRICK

Folklore has enshrined a 5th century Christian bishop named Patrick as the person who converted the Irish to the new religion. But in reality, he was not as successful as legends which sprang up around him in the 7th century portray him to be. While he did convert many Irish Celts to Christianity, his influence was in fact limited because the Irish resisted as too rigid the doctrines and administrative structures of Roman Christianity which Patrick tried to impose on them along with the spirituality of Christianity.

Patrick was born in western Britain about 418 A.D., in a time when the power of Rome was waning. In 401 A.D., the Emperor Honorius ordered the bulk of the Roman military forces in Britain to Gaul to help defend it from hordes of Visigoths who had crossed the Rhine River. Only a few years later, in 405 A.D., the Emperor lost control of Britain when the Roman soldiers stationed there named several of their own officers as candidates to be the Emperor of Rome; although they lacked the means to enforce their claim. By 410 A.D. with the Empire crumbling, Honorius abandoned Britain by decreeing that he would no longer send troops to Britain for its defense if the Scottish or Irish Celts attacked Roman lands. To add to the uncertainty facing the Roman colonists and Romanized Celts of southern Britain at the time of Patrick's birth, Irish raids along the coastline had increased. Some Celtic chieftains had even gone so far as to establish permanent military outposts in Wales and Cornwall.

Patrick was captured by raiders of the Irish clan chieftain Milchu near modern Dumbarton on the Clyde River and brought to Ireland. For the next six years, he labored for Milchu's clan as a captive shepherd. Being already a devout Christian, Patrick prayed daily for deliverance from his pagan captors. According to legend, he escaped when a divine voice in the night directed him to a cove where a foreign ship was anchored. The ship brought him to Gaul, where he studied for the priesthood. In 461 A.D., he returned to Ireland as a missionary consecrated as a bishop by Bishop Amatorex of Gaul especially for his task of converting the Irish.

To move freely throughout Ireland and perform his missionary work, Patrick had to obtain permission from the High King of Ireland, named Laeghire. So the first thing Patrick did when he arrived in Ireland was to go to Laeghire's court at Tara to present himself and request the High King's permission to do his work. At this time, Christian values and practices had hardly any impact on Celtic culture. In keeping with the Roman Christian practice of humility, when Patrick went to present himself to King Laeghire, he wore plain and simple clothing. But this was the wrong thing to do to make a favorable impression on the King. The Irish Celts looked at clothing as a measure of a person's status. The King and the members of his court mocked Patrick when he appeared before them in his plain garments, and Patrick was unable to continue petitioning the King for permission to preach in Ireland. To obtain sufficient status for his appearance before the King which was necessary if Patrick was going to do his work in Ireland, Patrick made gifts of gold and silver to prominent people at the court; and he hired a band of warriors to accompany him for his next appearance to make a display of power which would impress Laeghire. This time, Laeghire gave Patrick permission to preach and try to make Christian converts in Ireland.

King Laeghire had heard of the Christian religion before Patrick's arrival, but he was not particularly interested in Patrick's religious ideas. It was in keeping with the Irish tradition of tolerance for the free exchange of ideas that he gave permission for Patrick to preach wherever he chose.

Patrick went north to the citadel of Emain Mhacha, the seat of power of Clan Uliad in Ulster, and established a church near the present-day town of Armagh. In this part of Ireland, Christianity was unknown; and he was able to convert some warriors and bondservants to form his first congregation. Patrick consecrated as bishops some of his more devout followers so that he could institute a Roman Christian administrative system of dioceses. The Celts at the time found this system excessively rigid for their pastoral communities. During the late medieval period, the Bishops of Armagh claimed ecclesiastical leadership over all Irish Christians based on succession from Patrick—a claim which other Irish Christians rejected.

While folklore praised Patrick and his deeds, it also portrayed him as a dogmatic man whose intolerant behavior went against the Irish Celtic tradition of eclectic scholarship. Although St. Patrick lived in the 5th century, it was not until the 8th century, when Roman Christianity began to gain acceptance in Ireland, that a large number of legends grew around his life. One of the best known of these is about Patrick's banishing the snakes from Ireland. The origin of this legend is believed to be the connection between the Viking word for toad—*paug*—and Patrick's Irish name—Pádraig (pronounced paw-rig). It was the Vikings who first assumed that Patrick had received his name because he had miraculously ridded Ireland of snakes as well as toads and other reptiles. But the folklore and legends concerning Patrick go much beyond this well-known tale. Many of these were based on the *Life of Pádraig*, a book written by Muirchú in the 7th century A.D. that portrayed Patrick more as a Druid than a Christian bishop. The book filled in the gaps in Patrick's own autobiography, the *Confesio*, with fantastic occurrences for the time after his escape to Gaul when Patrick claimed he was wandering in a "desert". Although this desert may have been intended as a metaphor by Patrick, Muirchú claimed it was a real place where strange beasts and miraculous events were commonplace. The book blended many aspects of Celtic mythology with Christian doctrine. One such tale tells how Patrick shape-shifted into the form of a deer to escape pursuit by bandits. The popularity of *The Life of Pádraig* helped to make Patrick preeminent over all the saints of Ireland.

Although Patrick did not convert large numbers of Irish to Christianity as he had hoped for, the lore which grew up around his life and his activities in Ireland had a strong impact on Irish Christians of later centuries. When the rivalry between Roman and Celtic Christians intensified during the Middle Ages, the Roman Christians adopted Patrick and made him the patron saint of Ireland to advance their version of Christianity among the Celts. This preeminent position of Patrick among the Irish continued into the modern era. In the 16th century, when Irish Catholics were prompted to find a symbol for the religious and political freedoms they sought under English domination, St. Patrick was the natural choice. This attachment of the Irish to St. Patrick was carried by the Irish emigres to the various countries of Europe. For the Irish emigres, St. Patrick's Day was not only a religious celebration, but also an affirmation of their Irish heritage and culture. While Patrick had only limited success toward his goal of converting all of Ireland in his lifetime, in later centuries, the memory of him embellished by legend exerted an incalculable effect on the religious, political and cultural development of Ireland. Even today, St. Patrick is virtually synonymous with Ireland.

MONASTICISM AND CELTIC CHRISTIANITY

Although Patrick is commonly given most of the credit for conversion of Ireland to Christianity, this was accomplished primarily by Irish monks after Patrick's death in the late 5th century. These monks were involved in the monastic movement originating in the Near East and introduced to Europe in France by Martin of Tours, a 4th century Roman soldier who became a monk after serving with the Roman legions on the Hungarian border. The strict religious ideal followed by the Near Eastern and European monks became known in Ireland through a manuscript named *The Life of Martin* which favorably described the regimen of the monks in their monasteries.

The first monastery in the British Isles where a community of monks could follow this ascetic way of life was built at Whithorn, a place in

Strathclyde in northwest Britain. The monastery was founded in the early 5th century by the monk Ninian after he met with Martin of Tours while stopping at Martin's monastery on his way back to Britain after visiting Rome. Legend has it that Martin lent Ninian stonemasons to build his monastery. Ninian's monastery helped to establish Christianity in the British Isles, and served as a model for the founding of similar monasteries in Ireland from which Christianity spread with surprising success. As greater numbers of Irish were converted, the number of Irish desiring to follow the monastic life also grew, so that within a hundred and fifty years there were scores of monasteries scattered throughout Ireland.

The idea of a man or woman who abandoned hearth and kin to battle with the desires of their bodies in a struggle for perfection appealed to the Irish notion of the heroic. In pre-Christian mythology, Celtic heros would often enter spiritual realms to struggle with supernatural forces in a quest for wisdom. The Christian monks believed that the internal spiritual conflict emphasized in the ascetic ideal was another form of the heroic quest found in Celtic mythology. The monks of Ireland drew inspiration from these legends and myths, viewing themselves as spiritual warriors who followed a path similar to the one once trod by traditional heros.

In the early 5th century, the monks modeled their regimen on the strict asceticism of the monasteries of Egypt and Gaul. They shut themselves away from the world to devote themselves to purely spiritual matters. On the windswept Atlantic islands of Skellig Michael and Inishboffin, ascetics fasted and prayed in a life of voluntary hardship which would merit them eternal salvation at the end of their lives. They sought perfection in a daily battle with the urges of their bodies. A Celtic monk named Faustus summarized this monastic ideal in an essay entitled *De Gratia* where he wrote:

> "It is not for quiet and security that we have formed a community in the monastery, but for a struggle and a conflict. We have met here for a contest. We have embarked on a war against our sins. . . The struggle upon which we are engaged is full of hardships, full of dangers, for it is a struggle of man against himself."

During the 5th century A.D., many of the Irish monks turned the focus of their concern from themselves to the spiritual and physical welfare of the communities beyond the walls of their cloisters. The traditions of the Irish Celts placed monks in the position formerly occupied by the *áes-dana*, the Druids who gave spiritual guidance to people. The Irish Christians who had not chosen the monastic life expected that the monks would interact with them on a regular basis, providing the leadership once provided by the Druids. This tradition stimulated the monks to abandon their solitary quest for perfection and leave the confines of their monasteries to act as teachers and healers for the entire Christian community. By this time, much of Irish Christian life and culture centered around the monks who instructed the young, healed the sick, and dispensed justice.

From the example of the Druids, the Irish monks realized that knowledge was the key factor to their influence and prestige in their society. The Christian communities also recognized that the education of the monks made them valuable members of society. This appreciation of the benefits of education inspired the monks to establish schools in the monasteries. By the close of the 6th century A.D., monks could learn the fundamentals of reading, writing and philosophy in their local monasteries; and they could study agriculture, mathematics and astronomy at the larger monasteries at Whithorn, Bangor and Moville.

Although all branches of Christianity accepted the Gospels, the practices and doctrines of the Celtic Christians emphasized aspects of the religion different from those emphasized by the Roman Christians who were becoming the dominant Christian sect in Europe during the early medieval period. In general, the Celts focused on Christian spirituality while the Roman Christians stressed sin and the redemptive aspect of the religion. In Ireland, the few Celts who followed the Roman version of the religion did not have sufficient power and authority to dictate doctrine and ritual to their neighbors.

When Celtic Christian monks traveled to continental Europe, however, they often became embroiled in disputes with Roman Christians over the fine points of doctrine. One of these disputes concerned the ideas of the Celtic theologian Pelagius who emigrated from either Ireland or Britain to Rome, where he lived between 380 A.D and 410 A.D. The foundation of Pelagius's theological and moral ideas was the belief that human beings were entirely responsible for the good or evil in their lives. This foundation led to Pelagius's belief that perfection was attainable by both individuals and society; and for him, the pursuit of perfection was a person's chief moral obligation.

The relationship of Pelagius's ideas about human nature and morality to the Celtic spirit of independence and also the rigorous, ascetic life of the early Irish monks is evident. But Pelagius's ideas which were embraced by the Irish variation of Christianity conflicted directly with those of Augustine of Hippo, who was the leading theologian of the time. It was Augustine's theological ideas which were approved by the authorities in Rome and taught by the followers of the Roman variation of Christianity across Europe. Fundamentals of Augustine's theological ideas were the concept of original sin and grace from God. For Augustine, human beings were naturally sinful because they were born with original sin; and they could overcome this flaw only with God's intervention in the form of grace.

When Pelagius recorded his ideas in a book called *On Faith*, he was denounced by the clergy in Rome who followed Augustine's doctrines. In 410 A.D., Pelagius fled to Africa and settled near the city of Hippo where Augustine was bishop. Angered by Pelagius's arrival in Africa, Augustine called the Council of Carthage to comdemn Pelagius as a heretic and ban his teachings. This decision prompted Pelagius to flee again, this time to Jerusalem where a specially convened synod reversed the decision of the Council of Carthage. After this synod in Jerusalem, no further record exists of Pelagius's activities. But the doctrinal controversy he inspired continued to rage among Roman Christians until 494 A.D. when Pope Gelasius I placed *On Faith* on the Index of Forbidden Books and condemned Pelagius's teachings as heresy. The Celtic Christians, however, continued to accept Pelagius's doctrines.

During the 5th and 6th centuries A.D., incorporating the teachings of Pelagius into their beliefs, the Celtic Christians accepted personal responsibility for improving their own spiritual condition as well as the spiritual condition of others. In addition, they also recognized that most people were not ascetics. Because the Celts believed that the Gospels, along with their own cultural traditions, should dictate the nature of

Christian doctrine, they rejected the ideas of Augustine that either supplemented scripture or did not conform to Celtic customs. However, Augustine's teachings about grace and original sin became a fundamental part of the Roman version of Christianity, sparking many disputes between Roman and Celtic Christian theologians during the Middle Ages. When logical arguments failed them, the Roman Christians often resorted to name-calling such as Jerome's description of Pelagius as "a great mountain-dog through whom the devil barks" who was "full of Irish porridge."

The Celtic Christians were far more tolerant of different religious doctrines and beliefs than the Roman Christians. This tolerance gave Celtic Christianity the capacity to graft traditional Celtic ideas such as Druid shape-shifting onto Christian teachings. Because the principle of shape-shifting was a part of the essence of pre-Christian Celtic spirituality, incorporating it into Christianity helped the new religion gain rapid acceptance. Long before Christianity arose in Ireland, Druid shamen had been performing a ceremony during which they would go into a trance-like state where they saw themselves as entering the bodies of animals or other persons. The Celts believed that this communion with other living beings of the universe brought about a greater wisdom for those who could engage in it. As the shamen adapted to Christianity, they taught that Christ was a divine shape-shifter—a god whose spirit had entered a human being. This understanding of Christ enabled Irish Celts to readily embrace Christianity by expressing profound and often perplexing mysteries of Christ's nature in terms of a spiritual principle the Celts had been long familiar with.

In the western mountains of Kerry and Donegal, large pockets of pagan belief endured throughout the Middle Ages. As late as the 13th century, the English geographer Gerald Cambrensis commented on the widespread non-Christian practices and rituals that he encountered in western Ireland. He was especially shocked when he observed a newly-elected clan chieftain publicly copulating with a white mare in a ceremony for making him leader of the clan. Pagan practices existing side-by-side with Christianity exemplified the Celtic tolerance of different types of spirituality and customs of different cultures. This tolerance kept differences over religious issues from leading to the civil and religious strife which occurred in many European countries. The tolerance also enabled the Irish monks to perform their missionary work effectively; and it was a trait that enabled Irish emigres down the generations to ease their way into their new societies.

The formation of Celtic Christianity to meet the spiritual needs of the Celts was not an accident resulting from historical or geographic isolation, but instead evolved from series of choices made by the Celts. The Celtic priests and monks of the 4th and 5th centuries were aware of other versions of Christianity from their regular travels to mainland Europe to attend councils and synods. At these assemblies, they argued heatedly with Roman and Arian Christian theologians about acceptable variations in practices and doctrines. Although the Romans and Arians often described the Celts as obstinate, the decision of the Celts to follow their own version of Christianity was a reflection of the tolerance and other unique characteristics of their society. The Celts believed that no outside authority had the right to dictate how they should structure their church and which beliefs should receive official approval. Like legal and political matters, religious matters were governed by clan consensus.

Because many monks became uncomfortable with their high status in Irish communities after leaving the walls of their monasteries, they developed the idea of the *peregrinatio pro Christo*, the journey for the sake of Christ. This lent religious purpose to the traditional Celtic urge to wander. The *peregrinatio* was a journey away from friends and family to preach the new religion to strangers in another part of Ireland. But once Ireland became largely Christian, the monks who made the *peregrinatio* were revered and welcomed in most parts of the land. Their very success in converting the Irish to Christianity made them holy wisemen whose opinion was sought on all matters. Early law tracts indicated that they had status equal to a king.

This recognition granted to the monks ran against the ascetic ideals they saw as their primary calling. Not wishing to be in surroundings where they might be tempted by the sin of pride, however remote this might be for them, the monks expanded the concept of the *peregrinatio* to include lands outside of Ireland. In the late 6th century, the concept of the *peregrinatio* evolved into the notion of White Martyrdom, a way to gain the spiritual rewards of martyrdom without being put to death. To become a White Martyr, monks had to leave Ireland with no intention of returning. In place of being put to death for their beliefs, they would suffer the pangs of loss for the friends and kin they would never see again. During the early medieval period, White Martyrdom became the motive for Irish emigration, a new stimulus for the traditional instinct of Celts to migrate.

Because of the equal status of men and women among Celtic Christians in Ireland, women were not barred by social custom from becoming White Martyrs. But they usually chose not to voyage abroad. Although Christian women in Ireland often lived in the same cloistered monasteries with monks and could become the spiritual leaders of them, they knew the difficulties that a wandering women ascetic would have in the patriarchies of mainland Europe. No matter how wise their words, women would be met with scorn and disdain. Swords and daggers were forbidden by their Christian principles, so they could not protect themselves if they were attacked by soldiers or brigands. For Celtic women in the early Middle Ages, a *peregrinatio pro Christo* in mainland Europe must have seemed more certain to result in a martyrdom that was red instead of white.

The Celtic concept of the White Martyr was not found in other versions of Christianity. In the lands around the Mediterranean, only Red Martyrs who died in pain for their beliefs could be assured of salvation. The White Martyr reflected the Celtic Christian belief that human beings could effectively strive towards perfection in this world. The Roman Christians rejected the idea that perfection was attainable, preferring to adopt the view of human nature found in Augustine of Hippo's doctrine of grace and original sin. When Irish monks arrived on the European continent, this difference in essential doctrine became a constant source of conflict between Celtic and Roman Christian theologians. But the attacks against the Irish Celts launched by Roman Christian bishops and scholars had little effect on the great majority of Europeans, who did not have the literacy or education to fully understand the fine points of Christian doctrine. The ordinary Europeans accepted the Celtic monks as wise and holy visitors with a great deal to offer to their adopted lands.

COLUMCILLE OF IONA

The foremost of the early White Martyrs was an abbot named Columcille. He was born a member of the royal family of Leinster, clan ó Donnell, in Donegal in 521 A.D. He founded his first monastery in Derry in 545 A.D. when he was only 24; and according to legend, he founded 300 more before he was 40 years old. Columcille's pathway into Irish legend as one of the first White Martyrs began with his taking liberties with a Vulgate Bible of Jerome that he borrowed from the Abbot of Moville, named Finian. In the middle of the night, Columcille copied this Bible unbeknownst to its owner, the Abbot. When Finian learned of this, he complained to Dermot, the High King of Ireland at the time. Dermot summoned Columcille to appear before him at Tara, the site of his throne. When Columcille did so, Dermot made the pronouncement, "to each cow her calf, to each book its copy," and ordered Columcille to give Finian the copy of the Bible he had made. Columcille rejected Dermot's ruling with the rejoinder "The wrong decision of a judge is a raven's call to battle."

Dermot could not allow such a brazen, direct rejection of his authority to go unchallenged. After dismissing Columcille, Dermot sent warriors to seize the copy of the Bible. But Columcille was intent on resisting Dermot's ruling further. He gathered warriors of his clan ó Donnell to prevent Dermot's warriors from taking his Bible. The two opposing forces met at Cúl Dreimne in a conflict which became known as The Battle of the Books. Columcille won the battle—but in subsequent events, he came out the loser in this disagreement with Dermot. Disturbed by Columcille's lawlessness leading to so much bloodshed between Irish Christians, the abbots of Ireland called the Synod of Teltown in 561 A.D. to decide upon an appropriate punishment for Columcille. The ultimate punishment of excommunication was being urged by many abbots when Columcille's friend, Brendan of Birr, appeared before the Synod to plead on Columcille's behalf for the lesser punishment of exile. The abbots relented, allowing Columcille to remain in the Church and thus eventually be recognized as a prominent and influential White Martyr.

Columcille left Ireland with twelve of his followers in 563 A.D. They set off from northeast Ireland in coracles, small boats made of bone and hide. Columcille had no particular destination in mind for himself and his followers. Once away from Ireland out in the Irish Sea, he left his course in the hands of God. The tides carried the coracles to Iona, a small island off the western coast of Scotland which had once been the site of a Druid school. Columcille decided to build a monastery there.

Iona was part of the kingdom of the Celtic clan named Dal Riada, Irish immigrants who had fled to the Argyll coast of Scotland after a famine in the early part of the 6th century A.D. The Irish clan chieftains of Munster claimed annual tribute from the Scottish colony, using the threat of invasion to extract payment. Although the Dal Riadans bridled at their political subservience, when Columcille arrived in Scotland, the Dal Riadan king Connell nevertheless grudgingly allowed the Irish monks to stay on the island of Iona because he assumed that a new monastery would benefit his realm. After Columcille established his monastery, he regularly intervened in the politics of the Dal Riadans. When Connell died, it was Columcille who crowned the new king, Aeden the Wily.

Involved as he became in the politics of the Dal Riadans, Columcille wished to see an end to the annual tribute the Dal Riadans paid to the Irish clan chieftains. The Convention of Drumceat convened by the High King in 575 A.D. gave him a chance to try to accomplish this. Conventions were meetings of many clan chieftains to decide on political and legal issues which had arisen since the previous Convention. In 575 at the Convention of Drumceat the chieftains were to consider the matter of Dal Riadan independence which would bring to an end the annual tribute. Columcille ignored the sentence of exile which had been imposed on him to attend this Convention as King Aeden's representative. He successfully argued for granting independence to the Dal Riadans and ending the tribute.

After later generations came to view Columcille as a model for all White Martyrs, his attendance at the Convention of Drumceat posed a problem.Since the gathering was held in Ireland, Columcille's attendance was a flagrant violation of his sentence of perpetual exile. To justify his return to Ireland with the ideal of the White Martyr, an ingenious folktale claimed that an angel named Axal granted Columcille dispensation from his vows in order to temporarily return to Ireland. Another tale recounted that he kept his face buried in his cowl so he looked at no former friends or kinfolk from his native land; and yet another, that he tied clods of Scottish turf to his sandals so he never actually set foot on Irish soil.

The adventures of Columcille became legendary in his own day. Every monk desired to imitate the great Abbot of Iona by embarking on a heroic foreign quest to gain salvation by spreading the Christian religious message. Glossing over the fact that Columcille was more or less forced into exile for his arrogant behavior, the monks and other Irish thought of him as a glorious White Martyr, a wanderer in foreign lands. As Ireland became predominately Christian at the close of the 6th century, the example of Columcille spawned a wave of Irish monks crossing the seas to mainland Europe.

CHAPTER 3

The Irish Monks In Europe

So, since your heart is set on those sweet fields
And you must leave me here,
Swift be your going, heed not my prayers,
Although the voice be dear...
Since, if but Christ would give me back the past,
And that first strength of days,
And this white head of mine were dark again,
I, too, might go your ways.

—Colman, a 9th-century monk

EARLY MEDIEVAL EUROPE

When the Irish monks following the footsteps of Columcille and Columbanus came to Europe in the 7th century, Europe was still feeling the effects of the Dark Ages which followed the collapse of the western Roman Empire in the middle of the 5th century. The date 476 A.D. is commonly given as the end of the Roman Empire. This is the year that Odovacar, chieftain of the Ostrogoths, ousted the last Roman Emperor, Romulus Augustulus. Prior to the Ostrogoth invasion, hordes of warlike and pagan Franks, Goths, Lombards, Vandals and Huns emerged from the lands adjacent to the northern and eastern borders of the Roman Empire and swept across all of continental Europe. The Roman Empire had been was so weakened from these earlier barbarian assaults as well as from political corruption and social indifference that the Ostrogoths met little resistance.

The barbarian invasions destroyed many of the institutions of the Roman Empire and disrupted the cultural practices—and these institutions and practices had been the main elements of the unity of the Empire. In place of the universal Roman government, barbarian chieftains established numerous petty kingdoms in France, Spain and Italy. There was continual strife among these kingdoms as various chieftains tried to enlarge their domains, increase their wealth, and rule over larger populations. But none of these covetous, bellicose chieftains succeeded in unifying a large territory and widespread population. During the Dark Ages, strife among the many barbarian tribes, and the related fear and defensiveness, was the norm throughout the area of the former Roman Empire.

With survival the primary social concern, there was hardly any communication among the multitude of petty kingdoms. Not only political development, but also basic skills and crafts were neglected and fell into a state of decline. The barbarians themselves did not have well-developed skills and crafts, and the artisans killed by barbarian attacks or conscripted into barbarian armies could not be replaced. Even the immemorial, necessary skill of agriculture fell into an impoverished state.

The barbarian invasions stimulated a resurgence of paganism within the lands once controlled by Rome. Although late in the 4th century, the Roman Emperor Gratian made Christianity the official religion of the Empire, much of the population continued to cling to their pagan ways in the countryside away from the urban areas. (The word pagan comes from the Latin *paganus*, meaning "rustic.") In one part of eastern Gaul, the religious leader Martin of Tours sent his monks into the countryside to stamp out any signs of paganism. Martin's monks followed his orders with excessive enthusiasm. They smashed pagan idols, wrecked shrines, and even assaulted worshipers taking part in pagan rituals. In 395, Gratian's successor, Emperor Theodosius, banned all religions other than Christianity. Yet despite the imperial decrees and virulent attacks by

Christian monks, paganism was not stamped out. Instead, just as the Christians had in the early days of their religion when they were persecuted, the pagans observed their spirituality secretly. They buried their idols so the Christians would not destroy them, and gathered in secret groves deep in the forests when they wanted to hold their rites. With the lifting of Roman rule and retreat of Christianity, the secretive pagan populations of the former Roman Empire once again brought their paganism out into the open. Besides, although they usually had different gods and myths, the barbarian invaders were themselves pagans and were not hostile to the ancient religions of the peoples of the former Empire.

Although Christianity had been decreed the official religion of the Roman Empire and had been aggressively enforced by government officials and Christian clerics, the religion practically disappeared in many parts of Europe controlled by the pagan invaders. The sphere of organized Christianity was reduced to the few square miles of the city of Rome, where the Bishops of Rome—who became known as the Popes—were recognized as the spiritual leaders. Once the worst of the anarchy and bloodshed of the barbarian invasions subsided and the many barbarian chieftains had carved up the former Roman Empire into their numerous petty kingdoms, there was a recrudescence of Christianity. Neither the pagans of the former Roman Empire nor the pagan invaders were opposed to Christianity once it was weakened so that it could no longer offer any resistance to either their political or religious practices.

During the Dark Ages, Christianity was but one kind of religion along with various types of paganism practiced throughout Europe. Because the pagans tolerated Christianity since it was not strong enough to oppose them, Christianity maintained its roots throughout the widespread lands of the former Roman Empire. In some limited ways, Christianity thrived. There was no central authority to bring unity to Christianity and guide it through the historical developments and various religious practices of the time. Although during the 5th and 6th centuries, the Bishops of Rome asserted that they had the authority to determine the doctrines and rituals binding for all Christians, in reality they had little influence on Christians beyond the city of Rome and neighboring communities.

The Arian Christians were one flourishing sect which opposed certain doctrinal positions of the Bishops of Rome. The Arians' most serious challenge to the Bishops of Rome involved a fundamental belief of Christianity—namely, the divinity of Christ. The Arians held that Christ was not divine and co-eternal with God the Father, but rather was created by God the Father. As Visigoths in Spain, many Frankish tribes in France, and Ostrogoths in Italy gradually converted to Christianity during the later Dark Ages, they embraced the Arian view of Christ. It was not until the 7th century that the Bishops of Rome and missionaries and ecclesiastic leaders sent out from the religious colleges of the Roman Christians succeeded in overcoming Arianism and bringing the large numbers of former barbarians to the belief in Christ's divinity.

Other Christian sects also attracted large numbers of followers. In parts of Spain and France, Manichean Christians taught that the world and the human body were creations of evil which God had allowed Satan to create to test an individual's spirit. There were also some Nestorian Christians in western Europe. They objected to calling Mary the "Mother of God" because they believed that Christ had a divine nature fully separate from his human nature. Besides the several diverse sects, Christianity was hampered from being a coherent, unified force affecting all of the societies of Europe because a considerable proportion of the clergy of the various sects failed to represent the Christian virtues of poverty and piety; they had become corrupted by power and wealth.

Conditions on the continent of Europe were very different from the conditions in Ireland to which the Irish monks who became White Martyrs were accustomed. The chaos and brutality of the Dark Ages throughout western Europe never extended to Ireland. Life in Ireland was rugged, and at times precarious. But Ireland was not involved in the upheavals and unpredictability brought to Europe by the barbarian invasions. Although skirmishes and sometimes extended warfare was common between clans in Ireland, by this time the Celts observed a code of honor which prevented wholesale massacres of defeated warriors and their families. Slaying an unarmed and unresisting person, whether it was a man or a woman, was a shameful act condemned in Celtic society. This code of conduct contrasted with   slaughtering defeated foes and massacring the   populations of villages frequently engaged in by barbarians. Even once the barbarians established their petty kingdoms and began to rule over the conquered peoples, the upper class of rulers and nobles believed that they had an absolute right to slay any person of lower status for any reason.

To survive and to be effective in their missionary work in the Dark Ages in continental Europe, the Irish monks had to tread carefully. In teaching Christian beliefs and practices opposed by the clergy of a local Christian sect or by just appearing to threaten the ruler of an all-powerful petty king, the monks could be banished from the community, and even sometimes killed.

In 7th century Europe, formal education was rare. Europe was just beginning to recover from the Dark Ages. The Irish monks were well-educated by continental standards, and were accustomed to tolerance of ideas and the careful examination of points of view followed by debate. The Europeans, on the other hand, saw theology as a form of science. Once a doctrine was accepted by a council or a synod, it became dogma, an incontrovertible fact that no one was permitted to challenge. Only the small group of European scholars had any learning at all, and the nobility and the clergy were not necessarily members of this scholar caste. The Irish monks carried the torch of learning with them, but it flickered dimly in the intellectual darkness of mainland Europe.

Because of the constant warfare during the early medieval period, and the harsh way of life that resulted from it, historians often call the 6th and 7th centuries the "Dark Ages". To survive and prosper in this hostile environment, the Irish monks who came to Europe during this time had to tread carefully. One misstep could lead to swift death from an angry warlord or bitter condemnation from rival clergymen.

EARLY IRISH MONASTERIES IN EUROPE

Despite the danger and difficulties facing the Irish monks of the 7th century, they were prompted to travel to Europe by the heroic example of Columbanus. The three monasteries he founded in France continued to thrive even after his banishment from Burgundy by Queen Brunhilde, and many Irish monks visited them as they wandered throughout Europe. When Columbanus's wanderings brought him to Switzerland and Italy, he founded still more monasteries which became influential centers of learning in early medieval Europe.

After Queen Brunhilde ordered Columbanus to leave her kingdom, she took no chances that the troublesome monk would return. She instructed armed soldiers to escort him and his Irish companions as far as Nantes and put them on a barque bound for Ireland. But once the barque was out at sea, a fierce storm arose. The boat's captain believed that the storm was a form of divine intervention to prevent him from taking Columbanus back to Ireland—and he turned back to shore, where he quickly released Columbanus and his band to wander where they wished.

Risking Brunhilde's wrath, Columbanus led his followers back into France, where they came upon the Rhine River. They obtained some boats from villagers and followed the River south. Eventually, they came to Breganz in Switzerland, a place which Columbanus thought was suitable to build a new monastery near a pass across the Alps. Breganz lay in the territory of Austrasia, whose king, Theodebert, granted Columbanus permission to build a monastery because the monk was the enemy of Theodebert's Burgundian rivals, Theodoric and his grandmother, Brunhilde. But war and politics soon thwarted Columbanus's plan. After the Theodebert was defeated by Theodoric at battle of Tolbiac   612, Burgundy annexed the territory of western Switzerland. Columbanus decided to move on rather than face the wrath of Brunhilde.

But one of Columbanus's followers named Gall was too ill to travel. Nonetheless, Columbanus insisted that Gall accompany him across the jagged, snow-capped Alps. When Gall refused, the two men quarreled bitterly. After hurling maledictions at his former comrade, Columbanus left and journeyed southward into Italy, to a place called Bobbio. Columbanus died there shortly after founding another monastery.

Gall eventually recovered and became a solitary hermit. The local mountain people began to come to him for religious and practical advice. Gall gained such renown that after the death of Theodoric and Brunhilde, the monks of the monastery at Luxeuil in Burgundy founded by Columbanus elected Gall as their abbot despite his solitary lifestyle far from their community. Gall declined this position, but could not prevent local followers from gathering around his hermit's cell. He died in 640. A century later, the Benedictine order of monks began construction of an elaborate monastery at the site of Gall's cell. Upon completion, it became a model for the design of monasteries throughout the Middle Ages.

Although St. Gall's was never exclusively an Irish monastery, it did act as a magnet for many Irish monks. They contributed many volumes to its library, which became the largest and best known in Europe throughout the Middle Ages. Day after day, year after year, dedicated scribes carefully copied manuscripts in libraries and scriptoriums at St. Gall's. It was these monks who produced the manuscript *Gospel* in the 8th century, a book of scripture with illuminations to rival the best-known manuscript illuminated by the Irish, the *Book of Kells*. In the 9th century, they wrote *Priscian*, a Latin grammar with lyric verse in Irish written in the margins.

The patient labor of both Irish and European monks gradually remedied the shortage of books for scholars. Even small monasteries had libraries open to anyone who could read. But the task of creating manuscripts was so painstaking and tedious that it caused one Irish monk to lament:

Ah my poor hand,
How much white parchment you have scored.
You will bring the parchment glory
And be the bare peak of a heap of bones.

Other monks inspired by the example of Columbanus founded monasteries at Faremoutiers in 627, Jouarre in 627 and Rebais in 636 in the Brie region of France. Rebais eventually became a popular way station where traveling Irish clergy and traders could enjoy Irish meals and converse with others in their native language. Between 663 and 675, the monastery at Angoulême in France became a favorite resting place for the Irish Christians traveling in Europe. During Roman times, it was a monastic center, but was destroyed by barbarian invaders. The monastery was rebuilt by Ansoald, the Bishop of Poitiers, who put an Irish monk by the name of Toimeme in charge. He was succeeded by Ronan and Aillil, both Irish. At Angoulême, the Council of Bordeaux met to coordinate the development of monasteries in France, which had previously depended solely on the initiative of local monks. The Council established a plan that provided for Church assistance for monks who wished to found monasteries. This resulted in the creation of even more monastic centers under Irish guidance.

The Irish felt a special affinity for the monastery founded by St. Martin at Marmoutier near Tours. They regarded Martin as an inspirational figure for Irish monasticism because of the popularity in Ireland of the biography, *The Life of Martin,* and the assistance that he provided to Ninian to build the first Celtic monastery in Britain. By the 7th century, Marmoutier was a large and thriving monastic center with many chapels and dormitories surrounding Martin's original humble cell. Irish writers and illuminators contributed to the production of such manuscripts as the *Sermons of St. Martin* and the *Gospels of Marmoutier and St. Gatien.*

Within a hundred years after the arrival of Columbanus in Europe, there were scores of Irish monasteries scattered across France, Italy, Germany and Switzerland. During the remainder of the Middle Ages, the success of these early monastic centers in western Europe stimulated the foundation of more monasteries as each new generation of Irish monks sought to match the achievements of their predecessors. During the 10th and 11th centuries, these early monasteries also acted as temporary stops for Irish monks who wanted to settle in central and eastern Europe, regions that were often too remote to travel to directly from Ireland.

CELTIC AND ROMAN CHRISTIAN RIVALRY

During the centuries of the early medieval period, the Roman Christians were winning the religious struggle in western Europe. Unlike the Celtic Christian monks, the Bishops of Rome often used their influence as religious leaders to arrange alliances which helped win wars for the Frankish and Lombard kings who were favorably disposed towards the Roman Christians. Eventually, the Bishops of Rome had enough political support to assume exclusive use of the title "Pope," a word derived from the Greek *papas*, meaning father, which had previously been used for the religious leader of any Christian community. The Bishops of Rome often banned as heresy competing interpretations of Christianity. Although the Irish Celts were not branded as religious heretics by the Roman Christians, the Irish often came dangerously close to official condemnation. The Celtic Christians found themselves under increasing pressure to accept Roman Christian dogma and ecclesiastical authority.

The suspicion towards the Celtic monks ran through the European ecclesiastical authorities from the Pope down to the local clergy. In 813, the Council of Tours censured the Irish wandering monks—"Hiberniae epicsopi vagantes"—for their extreme asceticism. The ostensible reason for this censure was that in following such a strict, forbidding ideal, the Irish ascetics presented a remote, harsh picture of Christianity which could interfere with the aim of converting the pagan populations of Europe to the religion. But the real reason the Irish were censured, so it seems, was that their asceticism sharply contrasted with the comforts and political influence enjoyed by Roman Christian clergy. At times, the Irish monks explicitly criticized the relative luxury and political involvement of the Roman Christian priests and bishops. When they did so, the European clergy would quickly condemn the critical Irish monks for some deviance from Roman Christian doctrine.

Since the Celts came from a culture which recognized the importance of the individual, they believed that people were responsible for their sins because they could choose to do good or evil by using their free will without divine assistance in the form of grace. The Celts also believed that abbots and bishops could not be appointed by either church or secular authority. But in keeping with the Celtic traditions, the people should elect their own religious leaders. The Celtic and the Roman Christians also contested other doctrinal issues, often arguing heatedly and rarely achieving full accord. Yet the controversy over the fine points of dogma did not hamper the Irish Celts from building monasteries and gaining converts for Christianity throughout Europe.

Quite often Roman Christian complaints about the Irish Celts focused on symbols rather than essential doctrinal issues. The Romans objected to the Celtic clerical tonsure made by shaving the entire front half of the skull. The Druids had shaved their head in this manner as a symbol of their authority in Celtic society. The Roman Christians objected to this because they claimed that it was the style of tonsure worn by the apostle Peter's arch-rival, Simon Magus, who Peter excommunicated from the early Christian Church for claiming that spiritual benefits could be purchased with money. The Roman Christians came to associate heretical doctrine with the tonsure of Simon Magus, who they believed to be a Druid who had embraced Christianity. This issue of the tonsure was important in the semi-literate world of medieval Europe because symbols often expressed complex concepts that could not be otherwise grasped. The Roman Christians used every opportunity to condemn the Celtic tonsure, and preached that it was a symbol associated with pagan practices. Their clergy instructed their flocks to revere only the men who wore the small circular tonsure at the back of the head which they claimed commemorated Christ's crown of thorns. At the Synod of Whitby in 664, King Oswy of Northumbria, who presided over the Synod, outlawed the Celtic tonsure in his realm; and the Roman Christians encouraged other monarchs to follow Oswy's example.

Another point of controversy between the Roman and Celtic Christians was the way each branch of the religion figured the date of Easter. The Celts celebrated the event on the fourteenth day after the first full moon after the vernal equinox. Using this calculation, Easter could fall on a weekday that sometimes coincided with the Jewish holy day of Passover. To avoid this scandalous coincidence, the Roman Christians followed a different method to calculate Easter. It was Pope Felix III who decreed in 527 that Easter would always be the first Sunday after the first full moon after the vernal equinox, thereby insuring that Easter always fell on a Sunday. The Roman Christians pointed to the reluctance of the Celts to adopt Pope Felix's computation as a sign of pagan influences in Celtic religious practices.

When they settled in Europe, the Irish Celts were clever enough to avoid open confrontation with Rome. When directly challenged by the Church, they usually agreed with the Roman Christians. After the Celtic Christians avoided conflict by apparent acquiescence, they continued to think and say whatever they pleased. Irish monks who were writers and poets became especially careful in expressing their thoughts and beliefs. In the European countries dominated by Roman Christianity, they had to be very guarded in their choice of words. They could be excommunicated for a phrase or simile that contradicted Roman Christian doctrine. So the Irish writers and poets resorted to a remarkable technique possible only in the Celtic language. They wrote down phrases that seemed to have one meaning in writing; but because of the peculiarities of the Celtic language, the same words spoken aloud could take on an entirely different meaning. A verse attributed to a bard named Moling (d. 696) demonstrates the technique. Moling wrote:

Ar is cach beo beires breth besa hea thoga
Everyone alive bears the judgement which will be his choice

But when spoken aloud, the Celtic syllables could run together in a completely different combination to give a completely different meaning:

Héris cach bé ob hérisbreth bésa hé a thucca
Every source of heretical judgment is heresy, it will bring grief!

When the spoken words of Irish poets were attacked by defenders of orthodox Roman Christian doctrine, the poets used the written words to prove themselves innocent of promoting deviant thought.

Although Roman Christianity dominated mainland Europe, the Celtic Christians developed refinements of doctrine and practices that the Roman Christians incorporated into their doctrine. In the 4th century, the theologian, Hilary of Poitiers, applied Celtic concepts of a triune god to greatly enhance the Christian notion of the Trinity. In the Middle Ages, the Celtic Christian practice of confession in private gradually became the standard practice. Prior to adopting the Celtic practice, Roman Christians confessed in public, usually in church before the entire congregation. Not surprisingly, many people were reluctant to confess their sins in these circumstances. The Irish practice of private confession made it a common act engaged in by all Christians and was formally recognized as the approved method of confession at the Fourth Lateran Council in 1215.

Another practice of the Irish monks taken up by the Roman Christians during the Middle Ages was the use of rules of behavior known as penitentials. Originally, these rules applied only to sworn celibates of the Irish cloister and were difficult to follow. Transgressions were punished severely. In the penitential attributed to Columbanus, the penalty for needlessly exposing the body to another person was a lengthy period of reduced rations. Eventually, the penitentials became more moderate so they could be applied to all Christians. They gave people a clear guide for the practical interpretation of Christian doctrine in day-to-day situations.

Although the Roman Christians implicitly acknowledged that Celtic Christianity did have some desirable religious views and practices to offer Christianity, they nonetheless generally attempted to see that the Celtic

Christians did not have any significant influence on the version of Christianity observed in Europe. In Germany of the early 8th century, a bishop named Boniface waged a particularly aggressive campaign against the Irish monks. Whenever he found places where Celtic Christianity was being practiced, he sent out groups of monks to put an end to it. With denunciations and the fists of his fanatic followers, he persecuted the Irish so vigorously that he earned the title "Hammer of the Celtic Church." He had a particular dislike for an Irish abbot named Fearghal, who was also known as Virgilius and was famous for his writings explaining his view of the cosmos. When the King of Bavaria offered Fearghal a bishop's miter, Boniface was outraged. He complained to the Pope that Fearghal's writings were unorthodox, and he urged the Pope to disqualify the Irish abbot from any ecclesiastical position. But after examining Fearghal's writings, the Pope could see no doctrinal threat in the work, and did not prevent Fearghal from becoming bishop.

Because Boniface was a Devonshire Saxon named Wynfrith before he changed his name at baptism, his dislike of the Irish Celts was rooted in the traditional enmity of the Saxons for the Celts, who the Saxons had warred against for generations in England. After the Saxons converted to the Roman version of Christianity, they viewed the German lands inhabited by their cousins as their exclusive territory for preaching. Boniface considered the Celts interlopers and resented the success of the Irish Celtic interlopers in Germany. In his native England, Boniface had been raised to view the Celts with loathing, a hatred which he carried with him to Germany.

During the Middle Ages, Celtic Christianity was gradually eclipsed because of the growing political power of the Roman Christian Church. The Roman Christians demanded that the Irish monks who settled in Europe conform to Roman Christian beliefs. The Irish avoided direct confrontation whenever possible by masking their religious views with ambiguous words. Although the Roman Christians could prove no outright heresy in the Celtic version of the faith, they remained suspicious of the religious doctrines of the Irish monks in Europe and always believed that all Irish Christians were strongly inclined toward pagan beliefs.

BRITISH CELTS IN EUROPE

The defeat of the Celtic Christians in Britain by the Saxon invaders sapped their missionary inclinations. By the close of the 6th century, a war in which each side tried to exterminate the other had been fought sporadically between Celt and Saxon for more than a century, a war that the Celts in Britain were losing. Continual battle and frequent defeat undermined their morale and their traditional way of life, making combat and survival their dominant concerns.

The strife engulfing the British Celts began in 449 when a High King named Vortigern sought the help of Saxon mercenaries in a conflict with neighboring clans. He hired a warrior band from Europe led by the legendary brothers Horsa and Hengeist to fight in the ranks of his army, offering them riches for their services. After their victory, the Saxon mercenaries mutinied and began to carve out a kingdom of their own in Britain. They sent for their friends and relatives on mainland Europe, and soon many Saxons arrived in Britain.

The Celts of Britain were unable to resist the Saxons on the field of battle. The Celts were not accustomed to an enemy who gloried in death and who indiscriminately skewered the vanquished and non-combatants with sword and pike. When the Celtic warriors were away from their homes, the Saxons slaughtered Celtic women and children. After being impoverished by Saxon bloodshed and pillage, Celtic warriors defeated in battle gathered together the surviving members of their clans and migrated westward into Wales and Ireland and northward into Scotland. In their anger and despair, the defeated Celts resorted to the worst punishment they could imagine for the destructive, victorious Saxons: after the warfare died down and the surviving Celts had settled in their new locations, they declined to try to convert the Saxons to Christianity, thereby denying their former foes the opportunity for everlasting life in Heaven.

Some of the British Celts fled to Europe, and a large group settled in Armorica, the early medieval name for the French peninsula of Brittany. The only chronicler to record the attitude of the British Celts who went to Brittany toward the Saxons was a monk named Gildas who wrote a book called *On the Ruin of Britain* in 560. Gildas was born in approximately 518, about the time of the Battle of Badon, the only Celtic victory in their long war against the Saxons, which temporarily halted the Saxon advance in Britain. After their defeat in this battle, it took the Saxons a generation to regain enough strength to renew their attacks against the Celts. During this time of relative peace, Gildas studied at monasteries in British territory still under Celtic control. When Saxon attacks resumed in the decade of the 540's, the Celts were unable to withstand the onslaught, and Gildas was forced to emigrate to Brittany to find safety along with members of other Celtic clans. In his book, Gildas cast angry blame not only on the Saxons, but also on the inadequate leadership of the Celtic clan chiefs who had been unable to form an effective alliance against the longstanding foe. Gildas's writings reflected the experiences which left the Celtic refugees in Brittany introverted and fearful that a brutal Saxon invader might come to their adopted land. In Brittany, they formed an insular community which had very little interaction with its neighbors.

Another group of British Celts migrated to northwest Spain and settled in the area which became known as Galicia, derived from the Roman word for Celt. These Celts felt that they had placed enough distance between themselves and the Saxon menace. Contrary to the British Celts in Brittany, the British Celts in Spain interacted with the local population. By the middle of the 7th century, they had established monasteries and schools which admitted native Spanish in accordance with the Celtic practice of universal access to education. The largest of these was the monastic center of Santa Maria de Bretona which flourished for most of the Middle Ages. However, the British Celtic monks in Spain had little impact outside the area where they settled because few of them chose to become wanderers. They felt as if they were already White Martyrs, living their lives far from their ancestral home.

During the Dark Ages, these pockets of British Celtic culture transplanted to mainland Europe had an influence on the Goths of Spain and the Franks of France. They provided an example of the Celtic way of life that was broader than the picture painted by monks. Complete with chieftains and farmers, grandparents and grandchildren, these groups were fully functioning societies demonstrating Celtic institutions and the Celtic way of life to their neighbors.

For the Irish Celts, the Saxons remained only a vague threat, a tale told around the hearth to frighten children. During the early Middle Ages, no outside force menaced their homeland. Thus, the Irish Celts had a great deal more confidence in their abilities to meet the challenges of medieval Europe than their British cousins who had grown dispirited by defeat. The Irish did not hesitate to travel to foreign lands and actively participate in local society.

PRACTICAL KNOWLEDGE OF THE MONKS

Although the Irish monks journeyed to parts of Europe primarily to engage in missionary work, they chose to live in self-sufficient monasteries somewhat away from local populations. In Ireland, the monks built the monasteries in order to create an environment where they could pursue their ascetic, often solitary, daily regimens and their intensively religious way of life. Such motivation also went into the building of the monasteries in Europe; but in fact in Europe, the monasteries were a necessity providing the monks' basic needs. Material trappings enabled the monks not only to continue to pursue their personal spiritual lives, but also to engage in their missionary work. For in the early Middle Ages, with Europe just beginning to recover from the disruptions of the Dark Ages, there was little trading between regions and usually the state of local crafts and skills was poor. In the monks' circumstances, carpentry, masonry, needlework, agricultural, and woodworking and metalworking skills which supported the monasteries in Ireland were essential to them. As things went for the monks in Europe, these skills not only enabled the monks to support themselves, but were also abilities which attracted the local populations to them, and in this way served as a means by which the monks introduced their Christian spiritual message. Suffering from the social impoverishment and stagnation of the Dark Ages, the western Europeans found the monks' skills in agriculture, metallurgy and medicine particularly welcome.

No field shows the improvements that Irish skills and knowledge brought to general European society more than the field of agriculture. The farm workers of Europe saw the ordinary agricultural practices of the monks as highly imaginative and new. The bounty of the fields of crops cultivated by the monks and the health and growth of their herds of farm animals were proof of the wisdom of those practices. Once the Europeans implemented the agricultural practices taught by the monks, they enjoyed similar results. The monks taught the farm workers to follow a pattern of mixed farming, which involved deep plowing in spring, rotating crops and planting a cover of winter grass in the fall. Another productive farming practice the Irish monks introduced to Europe was the use of large ox teams for plowing, yoking four to six animals together to pull the plow. Fertilizer was also essential to the monastic farm. Near the ocean, monks scattered seaweed and ground sea shells onto the fields. Further inland they depended on animal manure and lime. From time to time, they would move their animal pens so that they could plant crops in the heavily manured soil. The monks also taught the Europeans to balance herds of domestic animals with one pig and one sheep for each cow, so that if disease should strike any one type of animal, the others were likely to remain healthy. They were also careful to raise enough breeder animals to insure the replacement of aging or diseased meat animals in their herds.

On mainland Europe after the fall of Rome, there were vast regional differences in agricultural methods and technical knowledge. In Italy, where the estate system of the Romans endured the longest, farming was relatively advanced. In the late 6th century, the Roman Christian Church owned much of the land in central Italy. Farm production not only fed the clergy but was an important source of revenue for the Church. Before becoming Pope in 590, Gregory the Great was charged with reorganizing the estates of the Church to insure that the fields continued to remain productive. Because he performed this vitally important administrative task well, he became prominent among the Roman Christian ecclesiastical leaders and was soon after elected Pope.

But in many other parts of Western Europe, providing enough food for the local population was a major problem. The Franks, Saxons, Goths, and Lombards who had invaded the land in the previous century were nomads whose cultures were based on warfare and conquest. Living in one place generation after generation after they overran the Roman Empire was a new way of life for them. The aristocratic warrior class believed that farming was beneath them. Of course, they had to have enough food for their own tables and enough surplus to support their retainers, but they left the details of plowing, planting and harvesting crops, and raising herds of animals for meat and milk to the peasantry. The peasants were trapped between the demands of their overlords for sufficient agricultural production and their own lack of skills which had been lost when populations had been scattered or decimated by barbarian invasions. They learned agricultural skills by trial and error, and hoped that their fields would yield enough to feed themselves and their families as well as satisfy their lords.

Compared to the agricultural methods used by the Irish, the farming practices of Europe were primitive. The nobles and peasants of the regions surrounding the Irish monasteries could not help but notice the productivity of the monks. Just as Columbanus was besieged by Suevians seeking agricultural knowledge, so too were other Irish monasteries thronged by local people seeking to learn the farming methods of the monks. By example and formal instruction, the Irish monks were usually willing to teach their methods to anyone interested in them. Because there were monks in different parts of Europe, this resulted in standardizing agricultural techniques across most of Europe.

The monks' efforts played a major part in the emergence of the manorial system in western Europe during the 8th and 9th centuries. Like the monasteries, each manor was a self-sufficient unit providing all the food needed to sustain its inhabitants, from nobles to peasants. The agricultural techniques of the manors closely resembled the ones taught by the monks from Ireland, emphasizing manure for fertilization, larger plow teams and crop rotation

Metallurgy was another skill that some Irish monks were highly trained in during the early medieval period. All large monasteries required specialists in metals to make tools, hinges, and other metal devices so that they could be self-sufficient. Many of the monks who crossed the sea to Europe were master blacksmiths who forged iron, master white smiths who polished the forging until it gleamed, and braziers who produced lightweight bronze for sconces, candelabra and altar adornments. When the feudal lords of Europe and their warriors saw the quality of the tools and ornaments produced by the Irish monks, they gave the Irish metallurgists the task of making superior swords, pikes, and armor. It was during this period that warriors began to use plate armor, which was a solid piece of metal covering a part of the body. The Romans had used plate armor, but with the barbarian invasion of the Roman world, the processes required to make solid plates of armor molded to cover different parts of the body were lost. The Goths, Franks, and Saxons who had swept over the Roman Empire used less protective chain mail, which was a mesh made of metal rings easier to forge than plate armor. With the metalworking skills of the Irish craftsmen, however, plate armor resembling the former armor of the Roman soldiers came back into use.

In addition to monks with skills in agriculture and metallurgy, each monastery tried to have at least one monk who was trained in the advanced medical knowledge of the Druids. Hospitals were common in Ireland and among them were specialty hospitals that treated only one type of illness. Physicians usually prescribed herbal remedies, and surgeons had the skills to treat gaping wounds or amputate limbs. Irish healers were responsible for the outcome of their treatment programs and were subject to fines if the patient did not recover due to a healer's ignorance or incompetence.

The monks with medical skills became especially valued by the armies of the European lords since more soldiers died from disease than battle wounds. At times of battle, Irish monks would not only pray for victory, but also tended to the wounded. In the infirmaries set up at their monasteries, they would treat persons of all social ranks, from peasant to noble. From the healing powers of the Irish monks, which usually far surpassed those of local physicians, the reputation of the Irish medical schools spread throughout Europe. By the 9th century, the medical schools at the abbeys of Clonmacnoise, Cashel, Portumna, Clonard and Armagh in Ireland were teaching Irish medical skills to students from all parts of Europe.

The Irish monks settled in small groups in many parts of Europe separated by long distances. As with the native settlements and the petty kingdoms of the early Middle Ages, there was hardly any communication or any other inter-activity among the monasteries. However, coming from the isolated island of Ireland where Celtic culture had remained largely unaffected by the tides of the Dark Ages, the monks had similar skills and knowledge which had originated with the Celts and had made Celtic lands prosperous during the centuries of the Roman Empire. The monks introduced their skills and knowledge to most of western Europe even though the various monasteries were not in contact among themselves. With the permanent presence of the monks, as well as their instruction, the beneficial Celtic skills and techniques took root in European societies. As the Dark Ages receded into the past and commerce, education, and political consolidation once again became a part of European society, the uniform skills, techniques and practical knowledge brought by the Irish monks spread from the monasteries to become the foundation for crafts and arts throughout Europe. The skills and knowledge derived from the monks which came to be prevalent throughout Europe helped make possible the self-sufficient manors of the feudal age, and contributed to the increasing stability of European society at this time.

THE CAROLINGIAN RENAISSANCE

A formative, fundamental period in Western history which carried Europe out of the backwardness and insularity of the Dark Ages was the Carolingian Renaissance, initiated during the reign of Charlemagne in the early 9th century. Irish monks who were already established in European monasteries and also Irish monks acting on the invitation of Charlemagne to come to his court to participate in his revival of learning and spreading of knowledge had major positions in this Renaissance. The Irish monks were not the only scholars who played a substantive role in the Carolingian Renaissance. One of the main characteristics of this Renaissance, which helped carry Western culture out of the Dark Ages, was its breadth and openness, which reflected the generous nature and desire for learning of Charlemagne and his successors. Although the Renaissance affirmed and advanced arts, architecture, literature, religion, political forms, and other basic elements of Western culture which had been clouded and fragmented in the Dark Ages, it also helped to preserve classical Greek and Roman writings. The rediscovery of classical ideas helped fuse the perspectives of the barbarian invaders with Roman ideas of government, art and virtue; and included principles of logic, mathematics and science developed in Greece, Byzantium and the Near East. Even so, with their established presences throughout western

Europe, their role in the revival of the crafts and practical knowledge among artisans and peasants, and their educational skills and serious spirituality, the Irish monks had a role in this early medieval Renaissance beyond that of other scholars, clergy and teachers who took part in it. At a deeper level as well, with their connection to Celtic culture, the Irish monks represented the values, beliefs and way of life that the Carolingian Renaissance affirmed and advanced more than other people involved in it.

Charlemagne and the Carolingian monarchs of France were descended from Charles Martel. As "Mayor of the palace" for King Childeric of Austrasia from 719-741, Charles made all the decisions necessary for governing the kingdom because Childeric wanted to spend his time feasting and hunting. Because the Moslems who had invaded Spain were a threat to Christian France, Charles persuaded the Roman Christian Church to use its wealth to strengthen the army of Austrasia. With a greatly enhanced army at his disposal, Charles not only repelled a Moslem invasion of France, but also united Austrasia, Nuestria and Burgundy into one realm. It was his son, Pepin the Short, who gained the title "King" for himself by deposing Childeric in 751 A.D. To reduce the possibility that his bold act would spark a civil war, he stuck a bargain with Pope Zachary to gain the support of the Roman Christian Church. In return for Papal backing, Pepin promised to help Zachary regain Church lands seized by local Italian nobles. After he became king, Pepin kept his bargain. In various military campaigns, he captured the Church lands and turned them over to Zachary.

By 768 when Charlemagne came to share rule over France with his brother Carloman after the death of his father, Pepin the Short, the Irish monks were familiar figures in France. As Childebert of Burgundy had when he encountered Columbanus in the late 6th century, the monarchs preceding Charlemagne recognized the value of the Irish monks to their society, and respected their knowledge and spirituality.

The arrangement of shared royal power between Charlemagne and Carloman decreed by Pepin before his death proved unworkable. Civil war threatened; but in 771, before the supporters of Charlemagne and Carloman came to blows, Carloman died.

After Charlemagne became sole king of the Franks, the Pope asked for his aid in regaining Church lands seized in northern Italy by the King of the Lombards. The Pope also urged him to conquer and convert the German tribes who were pagan. In 773, Charlemagne began a series of wars with the petty kingdoms and feudal fiefdoms in Italy and Germany and he led his armies to victory after victory. In 800, Pope Leo II crowned Charlemagne Emperor of the Romans, a title that most historians believe has no direct connection to the later Holy Roman Empire which governed most of the German States.

Charlemagne ruled over a vast area stretching from Saxony to Spain and from Rome to Brittany. He established his Court from which he ruled over this territory at Aix-la-Chapelle (modern day Aachen), which became the center of the Carolingian Renaissance. Affirmed by the Pope as the ruler over both his inherited and conquered lands, Charlemagne's interests and energies turned to learning and culture. He desired to develop a Frankish culture to equal his exceptional military and political achievements. One of his first measures was to send emissaries to all parts of Europe and the Near East to invite scholars to his Court. Many Irish scholars answered his invitation. With scholars from other regions, they copied classical manuscripts, communicated with each other in Latin, and established a school using Roman architecture was the model for the new buildings. For copying manuscripts, the scholars devised a script that became known as Caroline minuscule, which eventually became the standard for documents and literature across Europe. The script was still in use in the 15th century, when it became the model for the moveable-type letters used in the new invention of the printing press.

In a listing of scholars living at Aix-la-Chapelle compiled by an Irish monk named Cappuyns, more than a quarter had names which were obviously Irish. In appreciation for the many Irish monks answering his invitation, Charlemagne donated a large sum of money to the monastery at Clonmacnoise on the banks of the Irish River Shannon. As word of the endowment spread throughout Ireland it prompted a new wave of Irish monks to go to the Court of the Frankish king. Even after Charlemagne's death in 814, his successors continued inviting Irish scholars to France. By 870, so many Irish scholars had arrived in France that Heiric, Bishop of Auxerre, lamented, "Almost all Ireland, despising the sea, is migrating to our shores with a herd of philosophers."

Clemens Scotus was a prominent Irish scholar who came to Aix-la-Chapelle in this new wave of monks in the 9th century. The name Scotus or Scot was a surname given to Celts by the mainland Europeans regardless of their actual place of origin. Clemens Scotus wrote a grammar book called *Ars Grammatica* he dedicated to the Emperor Lothar, Charlemagne's grandson who inherited the Carolingian Empire in 840. Lothar was so impressed with the book that he appointed Clemens as Master of the Palace School, the position vacated by Alcuin of York when he left the post. Other prestigious Irish scholars were Cruinnmael, who wrote a treatise on prose, and Dicuil, the first geographer of the Carolingian Empire. An Irish monk named Thomás gained popularity among scholars for his intellectually-challenging puzzles.

By the time of the Carolingian Renaissance, the motives for Irish emigration had changed. White Martyr fervor faded for the monks in Ireland as they sought personal comfort and enjoying the fame resulting from their scholarship. In addition, the ideal of the White Martyr became more difficult to achieve because of the success of the Irish monasteries in Europe. They had become flourishing centers of Irish Celtic society, each one filled with numbers of Irish-born monks revered by the local people. The monks of Ireland who visited the monasteries of St. Gall's in Switzerland or Bobbio in Italy were greeted not by strangers, but by former countrymen. Only in eastern Europe could a 9th-century Irish monk seeking White Martyrdom find the same sense of loneliness and heroic adventure experienced by his 7th-century predecessors.

When the Vikings began to maraud the Irish coastline, they posed a major threat to the monasteries and gave the monks a new reason to emigrate to Europe. Few parts of Ireland were distant enough from the sea to provide complete safety. For men who preferred to fight intellectual battles with quill and parchment instead of physical battles with sword and shield, the inland security of European monasteries was alluring. The monks were particularly drawn to the court at Aix-la-Chapelle where their intellectual talents were well rewarded.

Perhaps the most prominent member of the Irish "herd" of philosophers was John Scotus Eriugena, who was called Eriugena. In the early 840's, he arrived at the court of Charlemagne's grandson, Charles the Bald. At the time, Charles was not yet Emperor, but ruled over the Western Franks from Lyon. Charles granted Eriugena a post at the new palace school that Charles had created to continue the scholarly work started by his grandfather. Eriugena was a daring and original thinker for his time, and he was the only scholar at Charles' court able to read and write in Greek. No other scholar had learned Greek because the Roman Christian hierarchy had shunned it due to the ongoing quarrel with the Eastern Orthodox Christians centered in Byzantium. The Eastern Christians, who were considered heretical by the Roman Christians, used Greek for their rituals. The Greek language was such an anathema to the Roman Christians in the 7th century that, Gregory, the papal legate to Byzantium who later became Pope Gregory I, refused to learn it, despite spending six years engaged in diplomatic negotiations with the Byzantine Emperor.

Because Eriugena was the only scholar who understood Greek, Charles the Bald commissioned him to translate the writings of Dionysius the Aeropagite from Greek into Latin. Charles thought the work was important because he erroneously believed that Dionysius the Aeropagite was the same man as St. Denis, the patron saint of the Franks whose Latinized name was Dionysius. In translating Dionysius's works, Eriugena came to accept the Greek Christian perspective that human beings could gain some comprehension of divine mysteries only by comparing them to events and circumstances they were familiar with in the world around them. For instance, to gain an understanding of the mystery of Christ's ascension into Heaven, an individual had to picture Christ's body physically rising into the sky. Human beings could not directly comprehend the divine, mystical nature of such a happening. The Virgin Birth of Christ and the resurrection of Christ were other Christian beliefs Greek Christians believed could be explained only by analogy. In his book *De Divisione Naturae* written after he came to the Greek Christian way of thinking, Eriugena went so far as to state the position that human beings could directly understand nothing about God.

Greek Christianity and Roman Christianity came down on different sides of the issue of analogy as the way to know the nature of God. The Roman Christians had rejected the importance of analogy by the 6th century because they believed this approach would minimize Scripture by characterizing it as merely stories rather than literal. Nonetheless, the challenge to the Roman Christian view posed by Eriugena's book went unnoticed due to its complexity and subtlety. Medieval theologians read it, but they did not understand it to any depth.

On the basis of Eriugena's contributions to the Carolingian Renaissance, his erudite translation of Dionysius the Aeropagite, and his own learned theological writings and scholarship, medieval theologians held him in high regard. Because of this reputation, Pope Nicholas I praised him in a letter to Charles the Bald. Desiring to bring even greater renown to his court, Charles appointed Eriugena Master of the Palace School, a position in which Eriugena could influence the studies of numbers of scholars and theologians and have an effect on Charles' kingdom long into the future. For nearly 800 years, Eriugena was regarded as a leading, and even a representative, medieval theologian. Then in the late 1600's, when a reprinting of his *De Divisione Naturae* brought new scrutiny to this work, the basis of Eriugena's writings in Greek Christian beliefs came to light, and Catholic religious authorities hastily placed all of John Scotus Eriugena's writings on the list of forbidden books.

Eriugena's life was filled with more than study and philosophy. As a favorite of Charles the Bald, he was a constant companion to the king. The English chronicler, William of Malmesbury, claimed that once when the two men were sitting together and drinking, Charles asked Eriugena what separated an Irishman from a drunkard. Eriugena replied, "The width of this table."

It was not only the company and the wit of the Irish Celts that made them welcome in the noble households of Carolingian Europe, but also their play on words, their humorous tales, and their steadfast refusal to take themselves seriously. A manuscript preserved in the monastery of St. Paul in Carinthia, Austria, contains a brief poem written by an anonymous monk from Kildare. It sums up the light-hearted attitude that Irish monks often had towards their work:

> I and Pangur Ban my cat
> 'Tis a like task we are at;
> Hunting mice is his delight,
> Hunting words I sit all night
>
> So in peace our tasks we ply
> Pangur Ban, my cat, and I
> In our arts we find our bliss,
> I have mine and he has his.

During the Carolingian Renaissance, many Irish monks with poetic talent sought wealthy patrons to support them. One of the most famous of these, the poet Sedulius, attached himself to the Bishop of Liège, whose name was Hartgar. Sedulius's poems were read far and wide. By praising Hartgar in his poems, Sedulius helped to give the Bishop of Liège a reputation as an influential prelate who headed a cultured court. Hartgar rewarded Sedulius with a house and land. He also gave Sedulius a great deal of gold, which the famed poet used to start a poet's colony. The verse of Sedulius was so renowned that Ermingarde, wife of the Emperor Lothar, embroidered passages from his poems in silk tapestries.

Many Irish bards gathered in Liège to share in Hartgar's beneficence. The poets Fergus, Marcus, Blandus and Beuchell were permanent residents. Sedulius called them the "Four Charioteers of the Lord" for their religious poetry. Anomalously, their verse was usually light and even frivolous, a stark contrast to the solemn themes usually associated with religious poetry. Many Irish poets visited Liège for a time before settling elsewhere. Some of the poets wrote their signatures on manuscripts Sedulius had written, as if having their names associated with Sedulius enhanced their own prestige as poets.

Throughout the Carolingian Renaissance, Irish monks played a leading role in preserving the knowledge of the ancients and establishing the curriculum that became the model for education in Europe for centuries. In addition, the Irish monks took the initiative in teaching craftsmen, farmers, and other laborers practical skills which helped bring prosperity, self-sufficiency and stability to Europe after the tumult and ignorance of the Dark Ages. In various ways in religious, intellectual, and practical fields, Irish monks played a major role in laying down the groundwork for the development of European society. Since the Carolingian Renaissance of the 9th and 10th centuries is commonly regarded as the origin of Western civilization, the place of the humble, indefatigable and selfless labors of the successive waves of Irish monks in the formation of Western civilization is plain.

THE IRISH AND EUROPEAN FOLKLORE

Although they were outsiders, the Irish monks affected the societies where they constructed their monasteries and shared their knowledge and skills so that folklore and legends often grew up around them. Such folklore and legend might recount events in the lives of certain monks, acknowledge the origin of a valuable skill, or portray a monk's good works for the local population. Or a tale or legend might be like a parable teaching some moral lesson or illustrate the spirituality of the monks. The folk tales and legends involving the monks not only affected the place of the monks in the history of a society, but also helped to keep alive the virtues and spiritual message of the monks within the society.

The first Irish monk to make an impression in Europe, Columbanus, was among the first to find his way into folk literature. In the medieval tale of Columbanus's deeds, the storm which arose forcing the boat carrying him back to Ireland to return to France was attributed to Columbanus's own powers. As medieval storytellers and villagers saw this event, Columbanus summoned the storm so he could return to Europe to continue his missionary work. In another improbable, yet meaningful, medieval tale, the 8th-century Irish monk Renan of Brittany raised from the dead an infant girl who had been murdered by her mother to hide the child's birth. As with other characters of medieval literature, supernatural powers and miraculous deeds which delighted and instructed medieval audiences were attributed to various memorable Irish monks when they were brought into the tradition of folk literature.

The memory of the presence and the deeds of the monks did not always die out with the passing of the medieval era and the changing nature of literature in the opening of the modern age. The 7th-century monk born in Wexford who came to be known as San Cataldo was the spiritual guardian of Italy's armed forces during World War II. At first known by his Irish name, Cathal, this venerable monk was shipwrecked near the Italian town of Taranto on his way back to Ireland from a pilgrimage to the Holy Land in about 666. Interpreting Cathal's unexpected appearance as divine intervention to provide them with a spiritual leader, the local people appointed Cathal as their bishop. Because the Italians had difficulty pronouncing Cathal's Irish name, they called him Cataldo. Cathal remained in Taranto until his death. His body was entombed in the local cathedral. As legend tells it, when his sarcophagus was opened two centuries later, his body had not decayed—and lying across his chest was a crucifix with the inscription

Cataldus Rachau, which referred to Rathan, the site of an old monastery in Tipperary. Having survived a shipwreck, Cathal became recognized as a protector of anyone facing mortal danger, and because of his good works as Bishop of Taranto, was made a saint by the Catholic Church. In the 19th century, the newly-independent nation of Italy adopted the saint as the spiritual guardian of its armed forces.

Many Irish monks such as Columcille, Columbanus and Gall enjoyed local veneration and were elevated to sainthood after their death. Sometimes, the bones of long-dead monks were enshrined. In Pisano, remains purported to be those of the Irish Celt Fridian, who had been a hermit living on Monte Pisano, are still kept in a glass case beneath a church altar. Other times, the bones of dead Irish monks were disinterred and distributed to people for their reputed curative powers, a practice which helped spread the local folktales surrounding many sainted Irish monks as the bones were sold or given to sick people across medieval Europe.

The Irish monks also consciously created myths. The story of the Harrowing of Hell to encourage the pagans in Germany to adopt the Christian religion was attributed to an 8th-century Irish monk named Clemens. He learned that many pagans resisted baptism, believing that the ceremony would separate them in the afterlife from their ancestors who had died with no knowledge of Christ. Although it had no basis in scripture, Clemens created the legend that after the crucifixion, Christ descended into hell to liberate the souls of the righteous who had died before his coming. This would allow a joyous reunion in heaven between converts and their pagan ancestors. Because the tale was useful in gaining converts, orthodox scholars did not attempt to suppress it.

Besides the specific folktales the Irish monks devised in order to make Christianity acceptable to pagans in foreign lands, and the folktales and legends which grew around memorable monks in parts of Europe, the monks had an influence on European folk literature with the notion of shape-shifting that was central to Celtic spirituality. The frightening figure of the werewolf—a creature half beast and half human—found in the folktales of many European societies demonstrates the influence of shape-shifting on the popular imagination. Many other figures, both terrible and benevolent, of European folk literature reveal the effects of the shape-shifting concept found in Celtic spirituality.

The Irish monks left behind sturdy stone monasteries, intellectual standards, practical arts, and Christian spirituality as testament to their presence. But perhaps it is their works and teachings preserved in folk literature in all parts of Europe that best illustrate the lasting impression they made on the general populations. As well as imparting the wisdom and lessons of the Irish monks, folktales were a way of distilling the memory of them and transmitting it through the generations.

LATE MEDIEVAL ASCETICS AND THE CRUSADES

From the time of Columbanus in the early 7th century, there had been a steady stream of Irish monks coming to Europe. During these years, White Martyr fervor was a strong motivation, and there were plenty of opportunities to do spiritual and useful work in a Europe benighted by the Dark Ages. This flow of immigration inevitably slowed because of cultural changes in both Ireland and Europe, and by the late 10th century, it was no more than a trickle. Monasteries in both Ireland and Europe had lost much of the spiritual fervor that characterized them in the early medieval period. Abbots permitted many monks from wealthy families to bring luxurious furnishings and exotic foods into the monasteries. There were even occasions of monasteries warring with each other over disputed grazing land. Without the spiritual ideal of the White Martyr, there was little incentive for the Irish monks of the times to brave the hardships of travel and endure the separation from friends and family. During the late medieval period, most Irish monks were content to remain in the monasteries of Ireland. When they traveled at all, it was for a specific purpose such as a pilgrimage, study at a European scholastic center, or to attend a synod; and usually they returned home after a temporary visit to foreign lands.

This did not mean that no Irish Celts settled in Europe during the late medieval period. Some of the monks embraced a religious reform movement that sought to rekindle the ascetic spirit of the White Martyr. They called themselves the Cèli De, the vessels of God. But their practices were so rigorous that the movement attracted relatively few followers. Its most extreme form was the inclusi, monks who walled themselves into a cell for their remaining lifetime. The cell had a small opening for food and waste removal, but all other contact with the outside world as shunned. During the 11th and 12th centuries, monasteries in Mainz, Obermunster, Vienna and Kiev had Irish *inclusi* dwelling within their cloister walls. Because these ascetics did not interact with others, they had no impact on European society in general. Even within their monasteries, the *inclusi* had little effect on the other monks; few followed their example by embracing this exceptionally stark way of life.

During the 12th and 13th centuries, the Crusades to free the Holy Land from Moslem control indirectly stimulated immigration by providing a new spiritual motive for Irish monks to travel across Europe on their way to the Holy Land. Monks from Ireland again ventured abroad in large numbers, intent on making the arduous journey to Jerusalem, which the Pope ordained would result in forgiveness of their sins. Along the long and hazardous route, the continental monasteries established by their predecessors became way stations where a weary pilgrim could find a nourishing meal and a night's lodging. Sometimes sickness or advanced age forced Irish monks to remain in European monasteries far longer than they had originally intended. Other times, a monk on pilgrimage would become interested in the way of life or the work performed in a European monastery and settled there on the return trip from the Holy Land. During the late medieval period, these wandering monks who had come to Europe for reasons far different than the White Martyrs maintained a cultural link between Ireland and the monasteries on the mainland.

Due to the constant presence of the Irish monks and scholars in schools, monasteries, and royal courts, the French, Spanish, and Germans gradually became accustomed to them during the Middle Ages. The monks' knowledge and scholarship became as valuable to the kingdoms where they lived as supplies of food or weapons of war. Yet these Irish wanderers had a loyalty beyond their allegiance to the local king or political chieftain. They also adhered to their Celtic Christian view that all knowledge complemented spirituality.

The numbers of Irish monks who went to Europe concentrated on their own ascetic regimens, the missionary work of spreading Christianity, and practical instruction when this was sought by local populations. In these aims, the monks had considerable success, which caused them to have a much broader effect on European society. The monks embodied Celtic culture as it had been preserved in Ireland unaffected by the widespread and transforming historical developments of continental Europe in the centuries of the dominance of Rome and the barbarian invasions. In contrast to the Celtic culture of Ireland, the Celtic culture which had been the prevailing culture in Europe until Caesar conquered Gaul in 50 B.C. had become mixed with Roman forms of government and civic ideas; Greek forms of the arts which had been adopted by Roman civilization; a perspective on Christianity growing out of Near Eastern concepts of spirituality; and barbarian inclinations for destructive warfare. Nonetheless, Celtic culture was not abolished by these various influences. Rather, Celtic culture was the matrix by which these influences affected the societies of Europe; the matrix which allowed these influences to have genuine, enduring effects upon these societies.

Despite the strong influences on Celtic culture which changed it in significant and irreversible ways, there was a continuity to Celtic culture in Europe, and its essence remained coherent. With their frequent and extensive migrations and related adaptability to new situations, the Celts had long maintained the essence of their culture along with regularly assimilating new influences into it. Coming from the Celtic culture in Ireland, the monks struck a familiar chord in many of the peoples of Europe who were themselves rooted in Celtic culture. The monks aroused affinities between the Celtic culture preserved in Ireland and the Celtic culture of Europe which had been mixed with Roman, barbarian and some Near Eastern influences. The influence of the monks did not lead to a restoration of Celtic culture, nor was it even an affirmation of it. Celtic culture did not have this political edge to it—it never did. It did not have the self-consciousness of the imperialism of Rome or even the compulsions and lusts of the barbarians—characteristics which brought the Romans and barbarians to dominance in western Europe at different times. Rather, Celtic culture had its continuity in the respect for learning, the holistic outlook which bound spirituality and all fields of knowledge, the community spirit, exceptional craftsmanship, productive farming practices, a sense of independence, a code of honor for battle as well as domestic and clan life, and folk literature which kept heroes and supernatural figures close to ordinary persons—all characteristics represented by the Irish monks and revitalized by them in Europe. The monks did not implant or impose Celtic culture in early medieval Europe. What they did was stimulate its vestiges so that these vestiges acquired the potency to become fundamental elements in subsequent developments in Western civilization.

CHAPTER 4

The Emergence Of Irish Culture

*...to extend the bounds of the Church, to proclaim to a
rude and untaught people the truth...to root out
nurseries of vice...we are pleased and willing...that you
shall enter that island and do therein what tends to the
honor of God and the salvation of the people.*

—Pope Adrian IV from the Bull Laudibiliter, 1166 A.D.

THE VIKINGS AND EARLY IRISH HISTORY

In the beginning of the 9th century A.D., Viking raiders began to
plunder the coastal communities of Ireland. At first, they seemed to the
Irish like a scourge sent by a malevolent god, invincible marauders who
murdered anyone who stood between them and the gold they sought. As
time passed, however, the Vikings settled in Ireland and formed
communities of their own. Through marriage and commerce, they
eventually forged friendlier relationships with the Celtic Irish.

The first Viking landing was in 795 at a town on the east coast of Ireland called Howth, and was recorded in the *Annals of Inishfallen*. Like other Europeans, the Irish referred to the marauders as Vikings, a name derived from the Scandinavian word for bay, *vik*. Vikings originally meant "men of the bays." However, after suffering Viking depredations, the term Viking became synonymous with "pirate" for the Irish. During the next few decades, dragon-prowed long ships were a frequent sight in the coves and inlets of Ireland. The tall and fierce Vikings seemed invincible, a nightmare terror that feared no mortal force. Because their ships gave allowed them move rapidly along the coast, they could strike and retreat before any band of Celtic warriors could gather to challenge them. By 814, the Vikings had complete mastery of the coastline. They raided freely wherever they wished, and established coastal settlements with no opposition. To be able to continue their peaceful and solitary way of life, Irish monks from the island of Iona and monasteries near the sea enlarged the inland monastery at Kells. The monks of Iona were attracted to Kells not only because of its safer location, but also because, like Iona, the original abbey of Kells was founded by Columcille. The monks at Kells created the illuminated manuscript named *The Book of Kells*, and in the late Middle Ages, the monastery became a center of Irish scholarship.

According to the *Book of Armagh*, Viking raiders spent their first winter in Ireland in 840. They built fortifications around their encampments, which eventually grew into towns and cities. In 841, the Vikings made a camp which grew into the city of Dublin; and within a few years, other camps appeared at locations which would become the cities of Wexford, Waterford, Limerick and Cork. Because they now had permanent bases of operations, the numbers of Norsemen in Ireland swelled. They were able to mount inland raiding expeditions which posed a greater threat to the native Celts than the coastal attacks.

For more than a hundred years after the Vikings first arrived in Ireland, political quarreling prevented the Celtic clans from unifying to expel them. The Norse enemies of the Celts originated from different Scandinavian lands and were similarly disunited. Norse and Celt engaged in sporadic conflicts until 976 when a Celt named Brian Boru arose to become chieftain of the clan Dál Cais, won the High Kingship and unified all of Ireland under his banner. Brian was an ambitious and ruthless warlord who, he promised eventual Celtic victory over the Vikings if the chieftains submitted to his leadership; but any chieftain who refused to acknowledge Brian's authority was attacked by his forces. Within three years of becoming king of the Dál Cassian clan, Brian became the overlord of the clans of southern Ireland, and used his army to end the Viking menace in the territory that he controlled. Over the next few decades, he proved so adept on the battlefield against both Vikings and rival Celtic clans that he was able to force Maélsechlainn, the High King of Ireland, to relinquish his crown. Afterwards, the clan chieftains immediately elected Brian to be the new High King of Ireland.

Brian's success as a battle-leader and his ability to control the clan chieftains through a mixture of fear and charisma made him the most politically and militarily effective High King that Ireland had seen for centuries. Under his leadership, the Celts gradually overcame the Viking strongholds in the rest of Ireland. In 1004, Brian led his forces into the province of Ulster to crush Norse power in northern Ireland. The entries for that year in the *Book of Armagh* identified him as "Brian, Emperor of the Irish." In 1014, Brian marshaled an army large enough to challenge the Vikings in their main fortress in Dublin. The Celtic and Viking forces clashed at Clontarf, north of the city. The Celtic army won the battle, but Brian Boru was killed in the fighting. Although the Vikings and their descendants continued to live in Ireland, Norse political and military power was permanently broken by this battle.

Brian Boru's success in politics and battle stimulated new interest in the position of High King of Ireland. He was the only High King of Ireland during the Middle Ages to exact feudal fealty similar to the fealty commanded by monarchs in other parts of Europe. After Brian's death, however, no claimant to the crown of High King was powerful enough or charismatic enough to continue ruling all of the Celtic clans. Clan chieftains resumed struggling among themselves to become the monarchs of entire provinces, and every chieftain hoped to gain the throne of the High King.

It took almost two centuries of constant Viking menace to prompt the Celtic clans to overcome their tradition of factionalism and rivalry, uniting under Brian Boru's leadership. Once the Viking threat was eliminated, the clans returned to their customary feuds and skirmishes.

The Viking presence set in motion many changes in Celtic-Irish culture beyond the areas of politics and warfare. In the early 9th century, the threat of Viking raiders fueled the Carolingian Renaissance by causing a sudden upsurge in immigration to Europe by the monks who lived in the particularly vulnerable coastal monasteries. These monks were motivated not by White Martyr fervor, but by the urge to survive. The Viking raids, however, were not a temporary phenomenon like a brief and violent storm passing in the night. Skirmishes and pitched battles with Vikings became a continual aspect of Celtic Irish life for most of the 9th and 10th centuries. After a few decades, the Celtic monks reacted to the Viking menace not by fleeing from it, but by building fortress-like monasteries inland, hoping to find security behind stone walls. These monks also trained with sword and spear to defend themselves against the Viking marauders. This combination of the religious and military ways of life was a forerunner to the Knights Templar and the Knights of St. John who battled the Saracens during the Crusades.

Although the Viking depredations in Ireland terrified the Celts and kept them always on their guard, the Vikings were not bent solely on pillage and rapine and then returning to their homeland laden with captives and booty. They often settled in coastal areas building fortifications and following the Norse way of life. They also introduced minted coins as the primary medium of commercial exchange, and these coins gradually replaced the Celtic system of barter. Because the Vikings were a seafaring people, they maintained a continuous link between Ireland and other parts of Europe. When Celtic Irish monks or adventurers set sail for mainland Europe after the defeat of the Vikings by Brian Boru, it was usually in a Viking long ship.

The cities built by the Vikings gradually transformed Irish society by becoming trade centers for Irish and European goods. By the beginning of the 10th century, the Vikings permitted merchants from many nations, including Irish Celts from clans not at war with the Vikings, to live in the cities of Wexford, Galway, Cork and Dublin. These merchants reaped profits by using Viking ships to transport Irish linen, wool and butter to markets in continental Europe. They carried back to Ireland spices, perfumes and exotic foods that could grow only in warmer climates. During the later Middle Ages, the Irish came to depend heavily on the export of their products to Europe.

When Scandinavia was converted to Christianity by Roman Christian missionaries during the 10th and 11th centuries, Nordic Roman Christians settled in the Irish cities founded by the Vikings. These cities became centers of Roman Christian belief, although the large majority of the Irish population, who lived in the countryside, remained Celtic Christian. During the decades following their foundation, the cities were Roman Christian enclaves that lay outside of mainstream Celtic society. Prompted by the preaching of urban clergy who desired to establish conformity with Roman Christian doctrine in all of Ireland, more and more Irish people abandoned Celtic Christian practices. By the early 12th century, the "Romani", the minority of Celts who favored full acceptance of Roman dogma, had gained sufficient power to hold their own synods and to reform the Celtic marriage laws so that divorce was forbidden. Despite the Celtic tradition of religious tolerance, the Irish "Romani" were intolerant of Celtic Christianity. Prominent clergymen like St. Malachy preached that all Irish should follow Roman Christian practices and beliefs. The "Romani" regularly appealed to the Pope for financial and spiritual aid to bring all of the people living in Ireland into the Roman Christian fold. Nonetheless, Celtic Christianity remained the dominant branch of the religion until the 13th century.

After the Viking menace ended in the 11th century, fewer monks traveled to Europe than in the early medieval period. Some monks settled in established European monasteries, while a few wandered eastward to found new monasteries in Russia and Poland. Many Irish monks visited shrines and monasteries and attended ecclesiastical councils during brief journeys to Europe. These travelers maintained the link between Ireland and mainland Europe during the late Middle Ages, but were less influential in shaping the course of Western civilization than either their predecessors or their successors.

The Viking invasion and settlement of Ireland caused a cultural crisis for the Celtic Irish which lasted from the 9th to the 11th centuries. Celtic society found itself in turmoil and began a process of reorganization that prompted the Irish people to turn to their domestic problems. Celtic society was flexible enough to meet the challenge posed by the Vikings and endured with its fundamental beliefs relatively intact. But in 1169, the Anglo-Norman invasion initiated a second cultural crisis for the Celts, and set in motion a process of change that would transform the Celtic way of life.

THE ANGLO-NORMAN INVASION

When the Anglo-Norman nobles of England led an army of invasion into Ireland in 1169, they were a far more formidable foe for the Celts than the Vikings. The Anglo-Normans were well-organized and battle-hardened warriors with a mandate from their king to conquer the entire island. The origin of the invasion was in 1156 when an English king who was himself a descendant of the Norsemen desired to add Ireland to his domains. His name was Henry II, and he commanded some of the finest knights that the medieval world had seen. His warriors were Norman, descendants of the Norsemen from the French peninsula of Normandy who had conquered England in 1066. They combined all the physical hardiness of their Viking ancestors with a newly-developed discipline necessary for battlefield victories. Their tactics and their martial skills had been honed in desert battles against Moslem armies during the Crusades.

To help legitimize his territorial ambitions, Henry secured approval for an invasion of Ireland from Pope Adrian IV, who had been an Englishman with the name Nicholas Breakspeare before his election to the Papacy. In the Papal Bull *Laudibiliter*, Adrian gave Henry Church permission to invade to Ireland and use his secular power to curb the practices of the Irish Christians which did not conform to Roman Christian doctrine. In return, Henry was to pay Rome one penny for each Irish household, a tax which became known as "Peter's Pence" because the money went to St. Peter's successor, the Pope. Although the Vatican claims to have no copy of the Bull in its archives, the contents were confirmed in a letter by Adrian's successor, Pope Alexander III. In 1175, six years after the Anglo-Norman invasion, the letter was read publicly at the Synod of Waterford in Ireland. The Anglo-Norman chronicler Giraldus Cambrensis heard the reading of the letter and recorded it in his writings. The public disclosure of the Bull stirred anger and apprehension in most of the Irish. But for the "Romani", who strictly adhered to Roman Christian doctrine and ritual, whether they were ruled by Irish chieftains or English kings mattered little as long as everyone was brought into the Roman Christian fold.

Although with the Papal Bull, Henry II now had ostensible grounds for invading Ireland, he chose not to do so right away. Far from putting off his aim, he was instead craftily looking for the appropriate circumstances in Ireland which would make his intended conquest easier by lowering Irish resistance. Henry II's opportunity arose in 1166 when the loser in a quarrel between two Irish rulers came to England seeking his aid. The quarreling rulers were Dermot MacMurrough, the King of Leinster, and Tiernan ó Rourke, the Prince of Breífne. The basis for the conflict which broke out between them was Dermot's romance with Devorgilla, the wife of Tiernan. One night—so the story goes—Dermot carried Devorgilla off from Tiernan's castle. Although Devorgilla was a willing participant in this abduction, the two lovers spread the story that Dermot had taken Devorgilla by force in order to try to protect Devorgilla's reputation. Before long, Devorgilla tired of Dermot and returned to her husband, Tiernan. Tiernan never forgot this insult to his honor, and he never forgave Dermot. Fourteen years later Tiernan began a war with Dermot. Dermot was defeated and fled to England, where he approached Henry II for aid in returning to Ireland to defeat Tiernan and recover his lost lands and position as king. In exchange for Dermot's pledge of fealty to him, Henry II would allow Dermot to enlist the aid of any Anglo-Norman nobles who wanted to help his cause. With Dermot promising estates in Ireland for any noble who would offer him military aid, the English King knew that Dermot would have no trouble enlisting Anglo-Norman allies. Henry II would begin his long-intended conquest of Ireland by landing a large, well-equipped English army in Ireland in support of an Irish ruler trying to reclaim what he had lost.

Maurice Regan was a companion of Dermot's who went with him to England. In his poem, *Song of Dermot*, Regan depicts Dermot's appeal to Henry II for aid in regaining his land and power in Ireland:

> "May God who dwells on high
> Ward you and save you, King Henry
> And likewise give you
> Heart and courage and determination
> To avenge my shame and my misfortune
> That my own people brought upon me.

To you I come to make plaint, Good Sire,
In the presence of the Barons of your Empire
Your liegeman I shall become
On condition that you be my helper
So that I may not lose everything.
You I shall acknowledge as Sire and Lord
In the presence of your barons and earls."

While Dermot was preparing to return to Ireland with his Anglo-Norman allies, he learned about the new techniques of warfare developed by the Anglo-Normans in the Crusades. Unlike the Irish who favored wild and individual combat between champions of opposing sides, the Anglo-Normans fought in formations. The troops Dermot saw on maneuvers moved as one body under the direction of their general. After a victory, the Anglo-Normans remained in the territory they had seized by force of arms, quickly building fortified camps and stone castles. Using these fortresses as bases of operations, the Anglo-Normans would range out and defeat any remnants of the hostile forces. Then the Anglo-Norman nobles would seek a charter from the English king to posses the land that they had conquered on behalf of the king by pledging fealty and submission to the crown. The king would "own" the newly-conquered land and grant it back to the conqueror, who would become its protector in the name of the crown. If the noble subsequently offended the king, the charter could be revoked, often leading to bloody conflict between the king and a dispossessed noble.

To find Anglo-Norman nobles eager to acquire lands in Ireland, Dermot dispatched Maurice Regan to Wales with copies of Henry's "Letter of Patent," which pledged royal support for an invasion. Among the first to answer the call were Richard de Clare, called Strongbow, Robert Fitzstephen and Maurice Fitzgerald, all descendants of "the most beautiful woman in Wales," Princess Nesta. Many of the other nobles who accompanied these adventurers were the younger sons of noble families who had scant prospects of living a life of ease and luxury in England. Under the Anglo-Norman rule of primogeniture, the entire family estate would pass to the eldest male offspring of the lord, leaving the younger brothers without means of support. In Ireland, they hoped to create their own estates.

Strongbow was by far the most influential of the Anglo-Norman nobles who decided to cross the Irish Sea in aid of Dermot. His grandfather had fought beside William the Conqueror at Hastings in 1066 and the de Clare family had high standing among the Anglo-Norman nobility. Like his father before him, he was called Strongbow because of his skill in archery. He was a veteran of many battles and a skilled tactician. As an additional incentive to Strongbow to lend his support to the Irish expedition, Dermot promised him the hand of his daughter, Aiofe.

In 1169 a small group of Anglo-Normans under the command of Robert Fitzstephen landed unopposed at Bannow, on the southeastern coast of Ireland. According to *The Song of Dermot*, they were soon joined by Dermot, who mustered five hundred Irish warriors supporting his cause from the local countryside. The joint force marched on Wexford, quickly capturing the city, which was still inhabited mostly by Norse traders.

Fearing he would lose out on the conquests, Strongbow sent his own advance guard under the command of Raymond Fitzgerald, called Lo Gros. His orders were to secure a beachhead for the main landing. In early May of 1170, Fitzgerald came ashore at Baginbun Head, about five miles from Waterford. He hastily began construction of a stockade fort and captured cattle to feed his troops. Before his defenses were complete, Fitzgerald was attacked by a coalition of local Irish clans. According to *The Song of Dermot*:

> But many a wound was taken and dealt
> And many a life foredone
> And stark lay knight and gallowglass
> Archers and kerne in motly mass
> Before the post was won.

A less poetical account was written by the contemporary historian Giraldus Cambrensis, who paints a less grim picture of the battle:

> "Being besieged, by a general consent it was advised rather
> to rally and die manfully than to endure a lingering siege.

Raymond then commands the gates to be opened, the cattle was driven forth and followed with shouts and cryes, to offryght them, who braking on the Irish and put them into suche confusion as that the English obtained an easy victory."

The beachhead held until August 23 when Strongbow landed with two hundred knights and one thousand foot soldiers. The reinforcements enabled the Anglo-Normans to break out of their position and surround Waterford. Two attacks on the city were repulsed. Then Fitzgerald discovered a weak point in the defenses and breached the walls. The Anglo-Normans swarmed into the city, indiscriminately slaughtering the citizens.

Strongbow choose Dublin as the next target, and advanced north with his knights and foot soldiers. The High King of Ireland, Ruaidri Ua Conchobair mustered a large army and marched south to intercept the invaders. But the Anglo-Normans bypassed the Irish forces when Dermot—who had joined Strongbow in Ireland—led his allies through the Wicklow Mountains by a shepherd's track. When the Anglo-Normans approached the walls of Dublin, the Norse and Irish inhabitants sent Archbishop Laurence O'Toole to parley with the enemy. Since the clergyman was Dermot's brother-in-law, the Dubliners thought that he could arrange a peaceful settlement. As the two sides negotiated, Raymond Fitzgerald and Milo de Cogan assaulted the city without orders, breaching the defenses.

Asculf MacTorkil, king of the city, rallied his warriors to repel the intruders. But the wild battle tactics of the Norsemen and Celts were no match for the disciplined Anglo-Norman troops. After a brief skirmish, the Norsemen fled to their long ships and sailed for the Orkney Islands. Quite suddenly, Strongbow became master of the largest urban center in Ireland.

The Irish lacked the military and political unity of the Anglo-Normans. No leader like Brian Boru stepped forward to effectively guide them, no warlord roused the countryside against the invaders. The Irish who did not live close to the invasion points did not immediately view the Anglo-Normans as a threat to their way of life. Invaders like the Vikings had come to Ireland before and eventually had been defeated and assimilated.

Only after the Anglo-Normans established themselves by quickly expanding their territory and resisting all attempts to expel them did the Irish learn that they intended to reshape Irish society by destroying Celtic culture in the areas they conquered.

The Irish who fought against the invaders were usually defeated by the superior tactics and arms of the Anglo-Normans. The military disadvantage of the Celtic Irish was particularly apparent in combat against a formation of Anglo-Norman knights who wore steel armor from head to toe. The Celtic Irish wore only "soft" armor of leather, scant protection from a thrust from a broadsword or a blow from a mace. To reduce their casualties, the Celtic Irish resorted to the traditional Celtic tactic of ambush and maneuver by attacking small groups of Anglo-Norman knights who had strayed away from the main force. But this tactic was not effective in preventing the conquest of large parts of Ireland by the Anglo-Normans.

The Anglo-Norman invasion in 1169 signaled the beginning of the end of the purely Celtic culture in Ireland. During the next two centuries, the invaders introduced their laws, language and methods of warfare, which along with increasingly oppressive English rule, gradually transformed the Celtic way of life throughout Ireland. By the 16th century, the conqueror's policies towards the native Irish had grown so tyrannical that they stimulated new waves of Irish emigration to Europe.

ANGLO-NORMAN IRELAND

The first Anglo-Norman invaders conducted themselves as if they were members of a an elite warrior band under the leadership of Strongbow. Most of the leading knights were related by blood and were closely bound by personal loyalty to each other and to their leader. In battle, their armament and tactics made them invincible. After vanquishing Celtic armed opposition, they carved out fiefdoms for themselves. The advisors of Henry II noticed the cohesiveness of the Anglo-Norman knights, and warned the King that an independent Welsh-Norman kingdom in Ireland was a possibility.

King Henry was kept abreast of possible conspiracies by battlefield reports and spies who reported on the activities of the Anglo-Norman knights. His own political instincts, as well as the warnings from his advisors, led him to summon Strongbow to his court in 1171. Henry wanted to be sure that the conquered lands would indeed be subject to his rule. Strongbow delayed responding to the royal summons for almost a year. When he returned to England, however, he submitted fully to Henry by ceding his Irish territory to the crown without reservation. Satisfied with Strongbow's pledge of loyalty, Henry granted the lands back to him. Then Henry went to Ireland to affirm his sovereignty not only over the territory conquered by the Anglo-Normans, but over all of Ireland.

To insure the loyalty of Strongbow's men, Henry accepted their individual submissions and granted them fiefdoms in the territories they had conquered. At the same time, he sent Hugh de Lacy to persuade many of the Irish clan chieftains who lived outside of the territory controlled by the Anglo-Normans to pledge fealty to him. The Celts did not understand the feudal concept of surrendering land to the king, who could potentially grant the land to someone else. They believed that de Lacy was a peace envoy from a monarch similar to their own High King. De Lacy encouraged the Irish chieftains to performed a ritual of submission to Henry; which the Celts believed ended hostilities, but which Henry believed gave him absolute control over Celtic lands. The first conflict from this misunderstanding occurred when Henry rewarded de Lacy by granting him 800,000 acres of ó Rourke land after Tiernan ó Rourke submitted to the crown. Believing that his trust had been betrayed, Tiernan mustered his clan to battle the Anglo-Normans for possession of his lands, but de Lacy assassinated him while the two men parleyed under a flag of truce. The murder of Tiernan ó Rourke inspired many other clan chieftains to recant their submission to Henry.

Although Henry II and his successors, Richard I and John, continued to claim sovereignty over all of Ireland, they did not enforce their claim outside of the territory settled by the original Anglo-Norman invaders. The Anglo-Normans were most powerful in the areas where the first landings had taken place, in the eastern regions which became the counties of Meath, Louth, Dublin and Kildare. By the year 1200, they gained control of Galway on the west coast. This territory was connected to the eastern Anglo-Norman areas by a route secured by military patrols through the Celtic-dominated lands in the interior of Ireland.

The relationship between the Celtic Irish and the Anglo-Normans began to stabilize when the Anglo-Norman lords grew content with their current land holdings, and stopped using their military campaigns to acquire new territory. They turned their attention to developing prosperous manors to support their lavish way of life. In London, the Crusades and domestic problems occupied the attention of the English kings. They also stopped compelling the Anglo-Normans to force the Celtic chieftains to submit to the crown outside of the areas they presently dominated.

During the 13th century, the Anglo-Normans gradually introduced their way of life into Ireland. They administered their territory with a governmental system far more formal and structured than the loose political organization of the Celts. Many areas were divided into counties, which became the basis for many of the modern Irish county demarcations descend. Each county was administered by an earl with various barons appointed as lords over local estates within the county. The Anglo-Normans also used a governmental unit called the Liberty. This was a vast tract of land under the direct control of a single Anglo-Norman lord. Above the earls and lords of the Liberties was the king of England, who ostensibly controlled the land in a pyramidal chain of command. By the mid-13th century, this system proved inefficient when two lords of Liberties, de Lacy and Marshall, died without male issue. The Liberties were divided among the lords' brothers and sisters according to English custom. This created many smaller Liberties directly under the king, who had no deputy or viceroy in Ireland to act on the his behalf. Since London was far away and communications were slow, the lords of the Liberties could often act as if they were independent monarchs.

Because the earls, barons and lords of the Liberties initially had little trust in the Celtic Irish, they imported large numbers of Welsh and English peasants to work the land. These immigrants lived by foreign customs and spoke their native tongues of English and French. But the newcomers were not so alien that they did not share some cultural common ground with the Celtic Irish. Celts and Anglo-Normans gradually began trading their goods in marketplaces, their ideas in alehouses and their affections in bed chambers. The Celtic Irish grew accustomed to the foreigners living in their midst, no longer viewing them as an immediate threat to their society. At the same time, the newcomers adopted aspects of Celtic culture, forming the basis for a merger of Celtic and Anglo-Norman culture.

THE ECLIPSE OF CELTIC CHRISTIANITY

Before the coming of the Anglo-Normans, many Irish Christians practiced the Roman version of the religion. All Irish Christians recognized the authority of the Pope. Yet not all followed the Pope's decrees regarding ritual and doctrine. During the 11th and 12th centuries, the Roman Christians became increasingly intolerant of all other beliefs, whether pagan or alternative versions of Christianity. When the militarily powerful Anglo-Normans arrived ostensibly on a mission from the Pope, the "Romani"—who were Roman Christians—seized the opportunity to attack Celtic Christian practice and beliefs.

Because the Anglo-Normans had initially cloaked their territorial ambitions with religious justification, the Roman Christians of Ireland used the pretense that they had a clear mandate to act swiftly and vigorously to eliminate Celtic Christian practices in the territories under Anglo-Norman control. To accomplish this, the Irish Roman Christian clergy—whether Irish or Anglo-Norman—initially supported the Anglo-Norman government, recognizing that Roman ecclesiastical superiority was linked to English political domination. But during the 13th century, an ethnic rift occurred between the Irish and the Anglo-Norman Roman Christians. The Anglo-Normans viewed all Christian religious practices of the native Irish as potentially deviant, even the ritual and beliefs of those who claimed to be Roman Christian. In the eyes of the Anglo-Norman clergy, it mattered little which sect a priest or monk adhered to if the blood flowing through his veins was Celtic Irish. This attitude led the bishops of Anglo-Norman ancestry to oppose leadership positions for the native-born clergy even if the Irish clergy completely conformed to Roman Christian doctrine and practice. They went so far as to propose to the Fourth Lateran Council held in Rome in 1215 that anyone of Celtic Irish heritage be excluded from the office of bishop, a measure that was rejected by the assembly. The Council was attended by many European monks with links to the Celtic Irish, either because they had been born in

Ireland or through the history of their monasteries, who squelched official sanction for Anglo-Norman religious supremacy based on ethnic heritage.

Undaunted by their defeat at the Lateran Council, the Anglo-Norman clergy devised other methods to further their ambitions of total religious supremacy over Ireland. In the parts of Ireland under English control, the Anglo-Norman Roman Christians established a diocese system which placed all clergy and religious institutions in a region under the control of a bishop appointed by the Pope. The Celts had rejected this hierarchical system more than seven hundred years earlier when St. Patrick attempted to introduce it. The Anglo-Norman clergy also invited the mendicant orders of Dominicans and Franciscans to come to Ireland to replace the monks of the local Celtic monasteries. Both of these newly-formed orders were recently formed were directly under Papal authority. The Dominican monks and Franciscan friars gave their allegiance not to the Celtic way of life, but to the Roman Christian hierarchy.

Because in theory the Church was above politics, the Anglo-Norman clergy maintained that their claims of exclusive ecclesiastical leadership in Ireland were grounded in spiritual, not secular concerns. They insured that an English-born bishop was installed in the important urban centers. The first was John Comyn, who was appointed Archbishop of Dublin in 1181. His successor was Henry of London, who spent more time hunting red deer than tending to the duties of his office. Because Dublin was the most important city under Anglo-Norman rule, Henry claimed complete religious primacy over Ireland. Henry's claim rankled the Celtic Archbishops of Armagh. Because of St. Patrick's original work in Armagh in the 5th century, the Bishops of Armagh assumed that they were Patrick's successors and they alone could claim leadership in Irish religious matters.

The position of the Irish-born Roman Christians was undermined in 1213, when King John of England took the unprecedented step of making feudal submission to Pope Innocent III. On the surface, this meant that the Pope became the suzerain of England and King John was merely his vassal. In practice, it gave official Roman Christian sanction for the political aspirations of England. Deeds both base and noble could be justified as acts for the greater glory of the Church, and often Anglo-Norman priests openly supporting English domination were named Archbishops.

The Anglo-Norman clergy bound to Roman Christianity maintained its strong determination to eradicate Celtic Christianity, and they continued to press toward their goal by any means that they could The vulnerable, subjugated position of the Celtic Christians took an ominous turn for the worse in 1321 when the Anglo-Norman Bishop Richard de Ledrede of the Ossory Diocese located near Kildare obtained the authority to take the initiative in rooting out any heresy in his diocese. For de Ledrede, Celtic Christianity was a heresy. De Ledrede was granted such broad and exceptional authority by a synod which he convened in Ossory—specifically to grant him such authority. The means de Ledrede intended to use to reach his goal of rooting out Celtic Christianity once and for all were associated with the practices of the Inquisition. De Ledrede intended especially to use Pope John XXII's Bull which equated heresy with the diabolic art of witchcraft to reach his goal.

De Ledrede was an English-born Franciscan monk who had been appointed Bishop of Ossory by Pope John XXII. This same Pope issued his edict against heresy in 1315 because he was troubled by recurring dreams of seductive women that he believed were caused by spells cast by heretics. Equating heresy with witchcraft made sense in terms of medieval beliefs, which held that the world was inhabited not only by human beings, but also by invisible demons that tried to lure humans into evil. Since the Roman Christians maintained that any religious belief contrary to their doctrine was evil, it did not require much of a stretch of medieval logic to see opposing beliefs as a sign that the religion they were part of was inspired by demons.

Since de Ledrede's benefactor, Pope John XXII, had equated heresy with witchcraft and witch hysteria was sweeping across Europe at the time, de Ledrede was led to accuse Celtic Christians of being witches. Adopting the Inquisitorial tactics stemming from the Pope's edict was a way for de Ledrede to vigorously pursue his goal of eradicating Celtic Christianity as well as curry favor with the Pope, thereby strengthening his ecclesiastical and political position.

The first person de Ledrede targeted as a witch was Alice Kyteller, the daughter of a prominent Anglo-Norman knight. Alice was accused of being the leader of a group of heretics. The accusation against her rested partly on the fact that three men she had been married to had died, and her current husband, Richard Le Poer, believed that she was slowly poisoning him. Alice was also accused of consorting with a demon incubus named Robin mac Art, who was in fact probably her Celtic Irish lover by that name. Whatever the formal charges, Alice Kyteller was targeted mainly because of her open practice of Celtic customs and her Celtic beliefs.

Alice was not such an easy target, however. Besides being the daughter of a prominent Anglo-Norman knight, she was also related by marriage to the Viceroy of Ireland, appointed by King Edward II of England. Alice fled to Dublin, where she would be under the protection of the Viceroy. Frustrated, de Ledrede tried to prosecute Alice's son in her place. But this landed de Ledrede in jail for violating due process required by civil law. The matter petered out when de Ledrede was released from jail and Alice fled from Ireland. Not to be entirely deterred, de Ledrede prosecuted Alice's Celtic maid, Petronilla of Meath. The hapless maid was the first person burned at the stake for witchcraft in Ireland.

De Ledrede did not have much success in prosecuting alleged witches or initiating a campaign against reputed heretics throughout Ireland, however. The Anglo-Norman civil authorities were not willing to give up their own powers and prerogatives to the Anglo-Norman clergy, or even to share such powers and prerogatives equally with them. Moreover, with the tradition of tolerance for different religious beliefs and ideas among the native inhabitants of Ireland, the Irish accepting Roman Christianity were not willing to take part in de Ledrede's persecution. De Ledrede and the like-minded clergy met with resistance from all sides. Even so, there were occasional burnings of reputed heretics in Ireland during the 14th century. One other infamous instance besides Petronilla of Meath was Adam Dubh, a Dubliner who was sent to the stake in 1327 for denying the doctrine of the Trinity and the authority of the Pope.

Although de Ledrede's extreme plans were never put into effect systematically, the few instances of public burnings and the presence of some Anglo-Norman clergy allied with de Ledrede in different areas of Ireland did discourage the practice of Celtic Christianity. With both the large majority of Celtic Christians becoming guarded and even secretive about their practice, Celtic Christianity went virtually underground. For the most part, Celtic Christianity became a religion observed by individual families in private, and was passed on from generation to generation in an oral tradition. Despite the strong, continuing appeal of Celtic Christianity among the Irish—which lasted well into the modern era—the Roman Christianity favored by the Anglo-Norman rulers gradually, ineluctably, gained the ascendancy throughout Ireland. Civil and cannon laws favoring Roman Christianity and oppressing Celtic Christianity eventually accomplished what de Ledrede's Inquisitorial tactics stopped short of doing—virtually bring to an end the practice of Celtic Christianity throughout Ireland. Despite the adherence of many Irish to their Celtic Christian beliefs and practices in private, because of de Ledrede's terrorist tactics and the effects of the laws enforced by the Anglo-Norman rulers, in public the Irish came to conform to Roman Christianity by acknowledging the authority of the Pope, professing Roman Christian doctrine, and following its practices. Although Celtic Christianity never entirely died out and continues even today as an oral tradition passed down from generation to generation, Roman Christianity, i.e. Catholicism, became the official form of Christianity in Ireland and the religion widely accepted by the Irish..

ANGLO-CELTIC CULTURAL FUSION

As the Anglo-Norman newcomers settled into life in the Irish countryside during the 13th century, a process began that the nobles of England had not expected. Many of the Anglo-Normans began to adopt the customs of the Celts. Men whose grandfathers once attended the royal court in London grew their hair to shoulder length and shaved their faces except for long, drooping moustaches. Women whose grandmothers were bound by the feudal tradition that viewed women as property now rode horses bareback across Irish fields and through forests. In many households, the Celtic tongue could be heard on the lips of the Anglo-Normans as often as French or Middle English.

Intermarriage between Irish Celt and Anglo-Norman was common in all levels of society. Many of the leaders of the Anglo-Norman invasion immediately took Celtic wives after they staked out their fiefdoms, sometimes for love, sometimes to cement their claim to Irish lands. As he was promised before the Irish invasion, Strongbow wed Aiofe, the daughter of Dermot MacMurrough. Under English law, this gave him and his children a legitimate right to the kingdom of Leinster once ruled by Dermot. William de Burgh married the daughter of Donal Mór ó Brien; one of their descendants was Richard, Duke of York, whose claim to the English throne led to the War of the Roses in England during the 15th century. Hugh de Lacy married Rós O'Connor, daughter of the King of the province of Connaught. John de Courcey also took an Irish princess for his wife. Eventually, the Irish families of the Barrys, the Costellos, the Burkes (de Burghs), and the Fitzgeralds were formed from Irish-Norman unions.

The Anglo-Normans also embraced the Celtic child-rearing custom of fosterage. This form of adoption was an exchange of youngsters between Irish and Anglo-Norman families. It forged bonds of personal loyalty that transcended the gulf between cultures. Since the Anglo-Normans grew accustomed to treating all children equally, the issue of bastardy grew less important in Ireland than it was in England. Although paternity of the first-born male had to be certain to insure inheritance under the practice of primogeniture, it was not an important issue for the other children living in an Anglo-Norman household.

The Anglo-Normans even began to adopt the military tactics of their Celtic neighbors for warfare. On a battlefield, heavily-armored knights were the tanks of their day, relying on their impregnable mass to sweep the enemy from their path. When a line of knights charged, they were impervious to arrows and pikes. But when traveling alone or in small groups through the fens and forests of Ireland, they were highly vulnerable to ambush from the side or the rear. To defend themselves from Celtic insurgents, brigands, and rival Anglo-Norman nobles, knights began to use the Irish tactics of rapid maneuver, traveling without their armor so they could increase their speed and mobility.

For the Anglo-Normans, the Celtic way of life was alluring. By the early 14th century, they had adopted so many practices and customs of the Celts that they could no longer be called Anglo-Norman. They formed a new culture that was neither Celtic nor English, but a blend of both ways of life. At first they were called the Anglo-Irish, but the name was quickly shortened to simply the Irish from the Celtic name for Ireland, *Eire*.

Much of the attraction of the Celtic way of life for the descendants of the English conquerors lay in its less stringent rules of personal conduct. Feudal England was a maze of rules and regulations governing everything from which day of the week a knight could settle a private quarrel to how long a prostitute should stay with her client to receive payment. While Celtic society had laws and regulations to maintain social order, they were far less pervasive and intrusive than those in Anglo-Norman society. After a generation or two in Ireland, the descendants of the original invaders could see no sense in living by rules and customs that seemed rigid when compared to the Celtic way of life and relevant only to life in England. Despite their adoption of aspects of the Celtic way of life, however, most of the Anglo-Normans remained partially tied to English culture. They held to English customs and beliefs in major social and political matters.

Although Celtic culture did have a certain appeal for many Anglo-Normans and the large Irish majority of the population continued to follow the Celtic way of life, Anglo-Norman practices and perspectives dominated the fields of government, law and religion. These areas were controlled by the English Kings who often attempted to suppress the tendency of the Anglo-Normans to adopt Irish ways This made Ireland a divided society, with some Anglo-Normans adhering to English customs while other Anglo-Normans adopted the customs of the native Celts. The Anglo-Normans who remained most tied to the English Crown and way of life lived near Dublin, while Anglo-Normans open to aspects of the Celtic way of life lived in the rest of Ireland. The divisions and different cultural tendencies in Ireland were exacerbated by the succession of the indecisive Edward II to the English throne in 1307. The Anglo-Irish—the Celts and Anglo-Normans who had melded cultures—saw their opportunity to break free of English rule during Edward's weak reign.

In 1315, a group of Anglo-Irish nobles urged Edward the Bruce of Scotland to come to Ireland with a Scottish army to join with Irish rebel forces. When Edward landed in northern Ireland, his Scottish troops were joined by Anglo-Irish contingent to form a combined army with Edward as its leader. Edward was the brother of Robert the Bruce of Scotland, who had recently defeated an English army at Bannockburn in a war to achieve Scottish independence from England. Most of the Irish supported Edward the Bruce, while most of the Anglo-Normans opposed him. Edward led the combined Scottish-Irish forces to victory in eighteen battles against the Anglo-Normans. Within reach of his nineteenth successive victory in the Battle of Faughart near Dundalk, Edward was killed and his army defeated. His sudden battlefield death and defeat of his army brought an end the attempt of his Irish allies to throw off the English yoke. After Edward's death, most of his Scottish troops left Ireland and the Irish clan chieftains were unable to continue their rebellion because they quarreled among themselves.

Although the Irish did not succeed in gaining independence from English rule, their nearly-successful rebellion led by Edward the Bruce exposed the vulnerability of the English position in Ireland. Despite its power, resources and support for the Anglo-Normans in Ireland, the English Crown had not been able to ensure the security and the position of the Anglo-Normans throughout Ireland. Although they abandoned their armed rebellion, Irish nobles were quick to exploit the English weaknesses exposed by it to improve their position. The estates of many Anglo-Normans were seized by vengeful, opportunistic Irish chieftains. Revenge and retribution for excesses during the short war of Edward the Bruce became commonplace, forcing large numbers of Anglo-Normans to flee the country until Edward II made emigration illegal. The Irish clans of Kavanaughs, O'Hanlons and O'Tooles exacted tribute from the Anglo-Normans loyal to the English king in Louth, Dublin and Leinster. To preserve their wealth, dozens of Anglo-Norman families publicly renounced their allegiance to the crown of England. Some even changed their names, transforming families like the Manderville into the clan MacQuillan, the De Burghs into clan Burke and the De Angulos into clan MacCostello. This widespread repudiation of English authority was encouraged by the former supporters who continued to hope that the Irish would form a kingdom independent of England. The height of defiance was reached by the Earl of Desmond in 1341. He adamantly refused to attend a Parliament in Dublin called by King Edward III. Other Irish chieftains of both Celtic and Anglo-Norman heritage joined him in his act of defiance. The threat of insurrection forced the English king to accept the insult and agree to redress a list of Irish grievances.

In England, the nobility was enraged by the insolence of the Irish. They expected defiance from the Celts, all of whom the English considered barbarous, but they were particularly angered when the Celts were joined in their defiance by many descendants of the Anglo-Norman conquerors who they expected to be loyal to English customs and traditions. Edward III, who had succeeded the weak Edward II in 1327, instituted a policy of hostage-taking and bribery to keep Ireland at least marginally under control. For the first three decades of his reign, Edward III was more concerned with waging the Hundred Years War in France than he was with conditions in Ireland. But in 1361, he sent his son, Lionel of Clarence, to Dublin as Ireland's first Lord Lieutenant. On Lionel's initiative, the Statutes of Kilkenny were passed by an assembly of nobles loyal to the crown. These laws were designed to suppress the Irish way of life among English subjects by outlawing ordinary Irish behavior such as riding a horse without a saddle, speaking the Irish tongue, and wearing Celtic-style clothes. The Statutes' preamble claimed that the Irish were "forsaking the English language, manners, mode of riding, laws and usages, live and govern themselves according to the manner, fashion and languages of the Irish enemies aforesaid, whereby the said land and the liege people thereof, the English language, the allegiance to our Lord, the King and the English laws there are put in subjection and decayed, and the Irish enemies exalted and raised up contrary to reason." In areas where England had full political control, the Statutes were vigorously enforced by agents of the crown. They were also the first instance where the Irish were marked as "enemies of our lord, the King." The London government was sending an unmistakable message to its subjects residing in Ireland. Any Irish noble who wished to insure the patronage and largesse of the king had best remain connected to England not only politically, but culturally as well. Edward III attempted to stifle the desire to develop an independent Irish state and culture by making the reward for conformity with English values great and the punishment for defiance harsh.

In the hinterlands of Connaught and Ulster, the threat of arrest for riding a horse with no saddle and land confiscation based on a noble's hair length seemed more foolish than menacing. For the Celts and the Anglo-Normans who had adopted Celtic ways, words not backed by a sword were meaningless, and onerous laws could be ignored. They continued to live their lives as they chose, firmly establishing the new culture that was neither Celtic nor Anglo-Norman, but Irish.

More than a century later, in 1474, the English tried another stratagem to suppress the development of emerging Irish culture. They established a region around Dublin where English Common Law and the authority of the king were vigorously enforced. This area became known as "The Pale." Visitors from London or Bristol who set foot in Ireland were warned to beware of the curious customs existing "beyond the Pale"—customs which were a blend of the Celtic and Anglo-Norman ways of life,

IRISH CULTURE AT THE CLOSE OF THE MIDDLE AGES

The people of Ireland entered the 12th century as Celts and emerged from the 15th century as the Irish. This was the result of the gradual cultural merger of Celtic society with Anglo-Norman society. Initially, each group adopted customs and beliefs from the other. Irish culture came about after a majority of the people embraced the melded worldview during the 14th and 15th centuries, at which time it began to evolve as a distinct culture. Use of the Celtic tongue, respect for education, and loyalty to the extended family and clan remained important aspects of Irish society during the late medieval period and during the Renaissance. As writers and storytellers used ancient Celtic mythic themes in their works, Celtic myth enjoyed a resurgence of popularity in Ireland, thereby firmly implanting traditional Celtic views about the meaning of birth, death and the events in between into the new culture. Thus, many Celtic customs and beliefs that originated a millennia before the Christian era were carried into the modern age relatively unchanged over time.

The traditional Celtic urge to travel remained a part of the new Irish culture. When domestic strife engulfed Ireland in the later Middle Ages, emigration slowed as the Celts instinctively attempted to deal with the problems created by political and cultural change. Yet they could not completely stifle their urge to travel even during these troubled times. As the new Irish culture evolved after the arrival of the Anglo-Normans, the people of Ireland continued to voyage to Europe, visiting universities, trade centers, and shrines that housed the relics of saints. The difference between the Irish of the late Middle Ages and their Celtic predecessors of the early medieval period was that the former usually returned home after a sojourn abroad.

During the Renaissance, when England became a Protestant land and intensified its oppressive policies against Irish Catholics, the Irish regarded the Catholic countries of Europe as a haven from persecution. In the political and social changes of the continent as feudal kingdoms struggled to transform themselves into modern nations, the ancient customs and beliefs of the Celts the Irish emigres carried with them helped them maintain their identity and social and political perspective amid the unsettled conditions in their adopted lands. When encountering religious extremism, they were more tolerant of the beliefs of their neighbors; when asked to participate in political intrigue, they remained loyal to the monarch they looked upon as their chieftain; when Irish emigre women were told by European men that they could aspire to no ambition greater than tending a family, they nonetheless became teachers and physicians. During the early modern period, Irish emigres found influential roles in the fields of government, the military, and education; just as their predecessors the monks of the medieval times found influential roles in agriculture, metallurgy, education, and religion. The new waves of Irish emigres brought to European societies skills, knowledge and ingenuity which helped them adapt positively to the changes of the period.

CHAPTER 5

Religious Conflict And Irish Emigration

From where did I receive so great and so beneficent a gift
—to know and desire God,
relinquishing homeland and family for Him?

—St. Patrick's Declaration, 5th Century A.D.

THE PROTESTANT REFORMATION IN EUROPE AND IRELAND

Celtic culture gradually transformed into Irish culture during the two centuries after the Anglo-Norman invasion, religion remained a central element in the new society. Gradually, the Irish shifted away from the practices and doctrines that were uniquely Celtic, conforming outwardly the Roman Christian faith followed in most of Europe. Because "White Martyr" fervor faded as a motive for migration to Europe, the number of Irish monks emigrating to Europe decreased. As a result, some of the monasteries founded by the Irish to be abandoned while others were taken over by continental religious orders. By the 15th and early 16th centuries, Irish emigres rarely settled in Europe for religious reasons. Instead, they were seeking economic opportunities and safety from English tyranny after failed rebellions. But during the Protestant Reformation, a new conflict arose that would again make religion a pivotal factor in motivating emigration and shaping the Irish influence on Europe.

Christianity as defined by the Roman Catholic Church had been a stabilizing element for European civilization during the late medieval period. The name Catholic meant universal, and indeed the religion was found everywhere in western and central Europe. By the beginning of the 16th century, the Catholic clergy had grown widely corrupt as many priests, bishops and even some of the Popes sought wealth and personal power. For many people, the Catholic Church came to represent empty ritual that did not adequately address their spiritual needs.

In the last centuries of the medieval period, any individual suggesting reform was swiftly condemned as a heretic by the Catholic hierarchy. But in 1517, a German named Martin Luther openly challenged the Catholic Church, and garnered enough support from kings and princes to make himself immune from physical reprisal. His protest against Catholic religious abuses swelled into the movement called Protestantism that spread with astonishing speed. Jean Calvin in France and Ulrich Zwingli in Switzerland, following Luther's lead, defined new forms of Christian belief that not only condemned Catholic corruption but also challenged the validity of its dogma. Within the span of a few decades, the refusal of Catholics and Protestants to compromise on the issue of doctrine created a religious fissure that snaked across Christian Europe.

Because force had been usually used to quell religious dissension during the late medieval period, both Protestants and Catholics believed that oppression was the best solution for religious controversy. Civil unrest plagued kingdoms and embryonic nations because of religious differences. Public executions called "acts of faith"occurred in both Protestant and Catholic lands. By the end of the 16th century, the allegiance of each nation to the Protestant or Catholic religion became firmly established, despite continuing Catholic efforts to suppress rival doctrine and the efforts of the various Protestant denominations to spread the reformed creed. France, Spain, Portugal, Italy, Austria and the Flemish Lowlands remained Catholic while Germany, England, Scandinavia and the Netherlands became Protestant. These religious loyalties would guide the development of international alliances and conflicts over the next few centuries.

The religious strife that plagued Europe upset the traditional religious tolerance in Ireland by initiating a conflict between Protestant and Catholic that has endured until the present day. In 1534, Henry VIII of England broke away from the Pope to form his own religion and the London Parliament recognized him as "the only Supreme Head in earth of the Church of England." This also included his dominions in Ireland. His new religion came to be called Anglican, and Henry insured that it differed little from traditional Catholic doctrine and ritual. Initially, points of major variation were the rejection of the authority of the Pope and the affirmation of the right of the English king to appoint bishops. But Henry himself had not counted on the depth of desire for religious reformation among his people. The excesses of the Catholic clergy had predisposed the English for changes far more sweeping than Henry envisioned. During the course of the 16th century, there grew among the Anglicans a militant minority who sought to "purify" the new religion by forbidding statues, icons, vestments and any other external trappings associated with the Catholic Church. These Anglicans, who were fanatically anti-Catholic, eventually became known as Puritans and would play a major role in persecuting Irish Catholics and thereby stimulating Irish emigration to Europe.

In 1536, Henry VIII convened a Parliament in Dublin to help him reach his goal of being recognized as the head of Church and State in Ireland as well as England. At the time, Thomas Fitzgerald, Earl of Kildare, was leading a rebellion against England, which has come to be known as the Geraldine Revolt. This Revolt not only brought into question England's hold on Ireland, but it also strengthened anti-English sentiment among the Irish nobility. Henry wanted to be sure that this Parliament would readily grant him official recognition as head of Church and State.

So he was very selective about who was invited to attend. Irish nobles whose loyalty was in doubt were excluded, as were the clerical and monastic representatives who normally attended whenever a Dublin Parliament was convened. As Henry planned, the 1536 Parliament readily recognized him as the head of the new Church he had formed. The Parliament went on to declare that the Catholic religion was null and void, "corrupt for ever." After this action of the Parliament, the Lord Deputy of Ireland, a man named St. Leger who Henry had appointed to govern Ireland, demanded that all Irish lords immediately acknowledge Henry as being both head of Church and State. The "saint" in St. Leger was a family name and not a religious title. His demand extended to the Irish lords who were entitled to attend the Dublin Parliament and who had been excluded by Henry as well as to all the Irish lords who were in attendance at the Parliament. Any lord refusing to meet the demand would be accused of treason, and his title and his land would be taken from him. He even risked execution.

By the mid-16th century, the agents and allies of the English crown were vigorously enforcing the laws that the English government had enacted against the Catholic religion in Ireland. When the Anglicans began to destroy holy relics and shrines throughout Ireland, in isolated hamlets as well as cities, and assault and sometimes murder priests for saying Mass, the Catholics of Ireland began to resist. The laws passed to make the Anglican Church the only authorized religion stemming from Henry VIII's 1536 Parliament and the ensuing violence against Catholics were the beginning of the centuries of continual religious strife that plagued Ireland. At this time, the laws and persecution prompted a new wave of Irish emigrants to set out for European countries where they could practice their Catholic religion openly and escape the heightening of English oppression in their homeland.

IRISH RELIGIOUS REFUGEES

The first in this new wave of Irish emigres were members of the Catholic clergy. They left Ireland for the Catholic countries of Europe where they could continue to pursue their religious vocation openly. They went mostly to Spain, France and Italy. Monarchs and nobles in these countries readily granted them permission to settle in their lands to preach, conduct religious ceremonies and engage in other spiritual work. Some of the clergy went to Rome seeking spiritual support and financial aid to try to preserve Catholicism in Ireland. Since the Popes and Catholic hierarchy were mounting a "counter-reformation" to try to regain the preeminence and the influence the Catholic Church had lost in the Protestant Reformation, the Popes welcomed the spiritual fervor and the plans of the Irish clergy. The Popes elevated many of the Irish priests to the rank of bishop and funded their return to Ireland so that they could clandestinely help to keep the Catholic religion alive. While the Popes saw the Irish as valuable agents for their counter-reformation and for saving Catholicism in Ireland, at the same time, they saw the Irish as too unsophisticated to be given positions in the politically and diplomatically complex world of the European societies or in the Papal curia overseeing the activities of the counter-reformation.

A second group of religious immigrants from Ireland were the young men who wanted to study for the priesthood. With the closing of most of the monasteries and the schools associated with them by the Protestants of England, the opportunity to study Catholic theology and ritual in Ireland abruptly became limited. Many Irish students flocked to the seminaries attached to the universities in Madrid, Paris and Rome. When the number of Irish seminarians at a particular university grew large enough, they established their own colleges at the university which became known as "Irish Colleges" and could be found in more than two dozen major European cities. Some of the graduates returned to Ireland to perform Catholic mass and administer the sacraments in secret, but most of them remained in continental Europe shaping the direction of the Catholic counter-reformation at local levels.

Once they arrived in the Catholic lands of Europe, the Irish emigres enjoyed a relatively high status as religious refugees. By fleeing Ireland rather than submitting to English Protestant overlords, they had demonstrated their devotion to the Catholic faith. This higher social standing was granted even to those emigres who left Ireland to find fortune or adventure and who did not consider themselves religious refugees. The willingness of Catholic Europeans to accept the Irish into their society because of common religion enabled the emigres to quickly move into positions of power in government, education and the military.

A new missionary ethic began to grow among the emigre Irish priests, monks and seminarians, increasing their desire to influence the religious ideas of European society. They started to view themselves as the spearhead of a drive to eradicate Protestantism not only in Ireland but in all corners of the world. Many joined the newly-formed Catholic order of the Society of Jesus, popularly called the Jesuits. At the Council of Trent in 1551, Pope Julius III encouraged the expansion of the Jesuit order and gave it the task of stemming the tide of Protestantism through logical argument, and if necessary, political intrigue. The Jesuits saw themselves as soldiers willing to die for their cause and would often preach in Protestant lands despite the risk of imprisonment or execution. The Irish Jesuits often perceived themselves as heroic yet practical spiritual warriors in the tradition of the medieval Celtic monks.

Because the Society of Jesus dispatched its members to cities across Europe and to outposts in the New World, the opportunity of Irish Jesuits to exert an influence on secular affairs increased dramatically. Irish Jesuits, like all the other members of the Order, actively involved themselves in politics and civil government to insure that the Catholic cause would prosper. In their schools and universities, their objective was to mold the opinions of each new generation of scholars and leaders. Irish Jesuits became rectors of universities and confidants of royalty not only because of their personal talents, but also because they were members of the politically-powerful Society of Jesus.

The same missionary zeal also affected the Irish clergy who remained in continental Europe as parish priests. They were a constant grass-roots force resisting the spread of Protestant doctrine. Yet very few of them advanced to the position of bishop or cardinal.

As religious oppression continued in Ireland during the 17th and 18th centuries, it tyrannized not only the clergy, but all Catholics. The rebellion of the Confederation of Kilkenny in the 1640's and the Williamite War in the 1690's are instances of the various conflicts, ranging from sporadic spontaneous rebellions to full-scale wars, arising from religious differences in Ireland in the centuries after the 1536 Dublin

Parliament. The laws passed by subsequent Parliaments were the most onerous and unjust that Ireland had seen. For example, a series of laws made ownership of land at first difficult for Catholics and later outlawed land ownership completely. Following the clergy and nuns who were the first group to be affected by the anti-Catholic laws were Irish merchants, scholars and farmers seeking opportunities denied to them in Ireland. The laws had the effect not only of preventing the practice of Catholicism in general, but also of interfering with and often preventing Catholics from pursuing many enterprises, interests and trades in Irish society.

Another sizeable group of Irish emigres during these centuries was Irish soldiers. After the inevitable failure of the recurring rebellion and wars of this period when faced with superior English forces, many of the defeated Irish soldiers would flee to different countries of Europe rather than accept English rule. In some cases, such as the Irish defenders of Limerick during the Williamite War, large numbers of Irish soldiers who had surrendered were given the choice of exile or an oath of allegiance to the English Crown. Most of the soldiers, sometimes en masse in their entire surviving military unit, chose exile. In most cases, the soldiers went to a European country such as France or Spain which was a traditional enemy of England; or they made their way to such a country from a Protestant nation in Europe to which they had been exiled by England. The exiled Irish soldiers would then join the army of the enemy of England to continue their resistance against the oppressive English rule of Ireland from foreign soil.

By the 17th and 18th centuries, the majority of Irish emigres were no longer members of the Catholic clergy or religious orders of monks or nuns. The emigres belonged to various fields common to European society in the early modern era. They left Ireland not only because they could not freely pursue these activities due to oppressive English rule, but also because they could not freely practice their Catholic faith, which they regarded as an integral part of their Irish culture. Irish resistance to English rule arose from social, cultural, and religious grievances which were intermixed and could not easily be separated from one another. Although these later emigres became involved in areas that were different from those of the medieval monks desiring to be White Martyrs, and different from the priests, monks and nuns fleeing English oppression in the 1600's, they nonetheless left Ireland partly for religious reasons. This religious motive which was a factor of varying proportions for all Irish emigres well into the modern age—whether monks or merchants or soldiers or scholars—in a way bound the emigres over several centuries to one another. It was the religious factor which more than any other determined which countries in Europe the large majority would go to; the relationships they would make with monarchs, nobles and others in these countries; and the ties they would keep among themselves.

IRISH STEREOTYPES

The increased commercial, diplomatic and educational opportunities of the Renaissance led to an increase in travel to foreign countries. In many cases, learned travelers to foreign countries would publish books about their experiences and observations for their countrymen after their returns to their homelands. These books often revealed more about the biases of the authors than the countries they had visited. Even such a learned individual as Erasmus of the Netherlands was not free from this penchant. After his travels to different European countries, he wrote that Germans were crude, French were violent and Italians were vain and devious. These travel books of the Renaissance led to unflattering stereotypes of different nationalities.

The stereotype which clung to the Irish was that they were devoutly religious, but unsophisticated. They were often regarded as simplistic and somewhat superstitious in their understanding of the doctrines and beliefs of Catholicism. Because the Irish came from an agricultural society, the populations of Madrid, Paris and other Renaissance cities which were becoming increasingly complex did not feel that the Irish had the sense of refinement regarding religion—or other aspects of culture—as they had. This view of the Irish was especially strong in Rome. But this somewhat denigrating opinion of the Irish did not prevent them from becoming influential, and often leaders, in politics, military affairs, commerce, education and other fields.

By the time of the Renaissance, when the ethnic and national stereotypes were forming, Irish emigres were familiar figures to most Europeans from the folklore which had grown up around the monks of the

Middle Ages. This folklore tended to counter the denigrating stereotype of the Irish. In the folk literature of many parts of western and central Europe, the monks were depicted as larger than life, and sometimes as miraculous figures who had gained the affection of local societies and made important contributions to them. The later emigres did have a resemblance to the medieval monks in major respects. Like the medieval monks, the Irish emigres during the Renaissance were fervently religious, well-educated, and willing to impart their knowledge and teach their skills to the people around them. They lived by a code of ethics which allowed no compromise with honor, whether related to their religious beliefs or their service to an adopted country or monarch.

CHAPTER 6

Irish Influence in Spain

"The Irish established in these dominions shall keep and maintain the privileges which they have, by which they are made equal to native Spaniards; and that the formalities of the oath, to which all other nations have been forced to submit, shall not be exacted from the Irish, seeing that by the mere fact of their settling in Spain the Irish are accounted Spaniards and enjoy the same rights."

—Resolution adopted by the Spanish Council of State on February 3, 1792 at the request of Eduardo Murphy, Enrique Dowell and Juan Walsh to reaffirm the rights granted to the Irish by King Philip III in 1608.

SPANISH CONNECTION WITH IRELAND

King Philip's generous grant of full Spanish citizenship to Irish emigres stemmed from the close ties that had developed between Spain and Ireland during the 16th century. The Spanish regarded the Irish as fellow Catholics who were persecuted by Protestant England for the sake of their religion. After the 1560's, as Spain found itself pitted against

England for control of commerce in both Europe and the New World, the Spanish kings regarded the rebellious Irish as potential military allies. The Spanish also felt an historical affinity towards the Irish based on ancient and medieval Celtic influences in their land. In antiquity, the Celts had ruled Spain from the Pyrenees to Gibraltar. Local legends had also enshrined the deeds of the Irish medieval monks who had come to Spain to teach and found monasteries as they had in the other lands of Europe. From the perspective of the early modern Spanish, the colony of British Celts that had struggled fiercely against the Moorish invasions of their province of Gallicia during the 9th century were ethnically indistinguishable from the Irish.

This Spanish affinity towards the Irish continued to grow during the Renaissance era. In 1588 when the Spanish Armada was buffeted by fierce gales after its defeat by the English navy, many ships ran aground on the rocky shores of Ireland. A large number of the soldiers and sailors surviving the shipwrecks were massacred by English soldiers on the beaches as they swam ashore. But some managed to escape, hiding among the Irish clans that held no love for Queen Elizabeth and her often brutal deputies and generals. When they returned to Spain, the surviving sailors widely praised the chieftains Brian O'Rourke and Maglana MacClancey who had given them refuge despite the risk of English reprisals. As a result, the bonds between Spanish and Irish were further strengthened.

During the frequent rebellions of the Irish against the English overlords of the 16th century, Spain often provided military assistance to the Irish. In 1597, the King of Spain, Philip II, sent shipments of arms to Hugh O'Neill, the Earl of Tyrone, when he led an uprising which became known as the Nine Years War. Many of the Irish chieftains even considered asking Philip to be King of Ireland. In 1601, Philip III, who inherited the Spanish throne in 1598, agreed to send an invasion force to aid O'Neill's rebellion. When Spanish troops landed at the southern Irish port of Kinsale, O'Neill marched his army south to join up wit his new Spanish allies. But the two forces were prevented from joining by the English General, Lord Mountjoy, who defeated both the Irish and the Spanish armies in separate battles.

Spanish military assistance to the Irish gradually ended as Spain's wealth and political prominence began to erode during the 17th century.

But the conviction that Spain was a land friendly to Irish interests was firmly implanted in the minds of many Irish men and women. So when Irish men and women left Ireland the 16th and 17th centuries, the Iberian Peninsula seemed like a logical destination, a haven where they would be welcomed.

THOMAS WHITE AND THE IRISH COLLEGE AT SALAMANCA

One of the first Irish emigres to settle in Spain during the 16th century was a young Tipperary-born man named Thomas White. He would make an enduring contribution not only to the Spanish educational system, but also to universities in many parts of Europe. He went to Spain to study for the Catholic priesthood, a calling that was becoming extremely difficult to pursue in his homeland. The English Anglicans were closing more and more of the Catholic seminaries throughout Ireland. This land of Spain, where the one of the titles for the King was "His Most Catholic Majesty," seemed like the best alternative for becoming a priest.

As a lad, Thomas heard the legend of how the first Celtic inhabitants of Ireland had come from Spain many centuries before the birth of Christ. According to this legend, the Celts, led by a chieftain named Mil, sailed northwards across the Bay of Biscay to escape a famine. During their voyage, they were guided by the visions of a dying Druid who spoke of the rich and bountiful island named Innisfail, which was Ireland. But when the Celts finally made landfall, they were met by the people known as the Tuatha de Danaan who already claimed Innisfail for their own. With chants of magic and blades of sharp steel, Mil and his people dispossessed the Tuatha de Danaan, who retreated forever to the Otherworld. When Thomas White was a child in Tipperary, any mystical land beyond the sea was referred to as "Spain" in Irish legends and folklore.

Thomas White arrived in the Spanish port city of Bilbao, a northern city on the Bay of Biscay where his legendary forebearers may have set sail from. From there he traveled inland to the city of Salamanca, to a well-known university which had attracted a number of Irish seminarians. White enrolled in the course of studies for becoming a Catholic priest. As with the other Irish seminarians, White was in a situation which made his training for the priesthood even more difficult than it was ordinarily. The complex issues in his philosophy and theology courses were taught and debated in Spanish, giving White and his fellow Irish seminarians an academic disadvantage when compared to Spanish seminarians. In addition to this language problem, White, like most of the other Irish students, could barely afford lodging and food. At the time, there was monetary inflation and a rising standard of living in Spain created by riches from the New World passing into the country, as well as the traditionally high standard of living in the prosperous university town of Salamanca. The Irish students found it difficult to meet the basic necessities of life with funds available to them from Ireland—with its much different economic situation. With the little money he received from relatives in Ireland, White could afford only crude lodgings and simple meals; and he was never sure that he would be able to afford even these throughout his course of studies.

When the difficulties of student life seemed overwhelming, Thomas White sought the companionship and sometimes the solace of his countrymen who were also studying for the priesthood in Spain. After Protestant oppression had swept across Ireland during the 16th century, so many young Irish men wanted to study at Spanish seminaries they often had to wait several months for admission. The administrators of the Spanish universities welcomed them, viewing them as soldiers in the Catholic counter-reformation movement trying to combat the spread of Protestant doctrines.

This Spanish concept of the clergy as spiritual warriors had strong cultural echoes for many of the Irish seminary students, including Thomas White. Like the medieval monks of Ireland, the modern Irish seminary students believed that they were engaged in a struggle for the salvation of their souls. But the spiritual enemies of their era were different. The foe was no longer solely the needs and desires of their own bodies. Now the enemy was also Protestantism, a religion which varied from land to land, was inimical to Catholicism and was often backed by military and political force. The Irish seminarians of 16th-century Spain saw themselves as the vanguard of a spiritual army that would one day reclaim not only Ireland, but all the Protestant parts of Europe for the Catholic faith.

When he finished his studies, Thomas White entered the Society of Jesus along with many of his classmates. The order was relatively new, but had already gained a reputation for influencing areas as diverse as local education and international politics. The Society was structured as if it were a military unit, with a chain of command reporting ultimately to the Father General. All Jesuits thought of themselves as soldiers willing to die for the Catholic faith.

The Jesuit order sent many of its Irish priests educated in Spain back to Ireland to secretly preach and perform Catholic ritual. In 1592, Thomas White suggested that the Society keep him in Spain and assign him to an educational project which would benefit the Jesuits and Irish Catholics. He wanted to start a college exclusively for Irish students attending the University at Salamanca. Such a college was not a new idea. An Irish College had been established in 1590 at the University at Alcalá de Henares by a Portuguese noble whose mother was a MacDonnell from County Antrim. But this Irish College at Salamanca would be larger than its sister college and under the direct control of the Jesuit order.

Although the Father General gave his approval to Thomas White's plan, the Jesuits provided no resources for the college. To fund his project, Thomas White turned to Irish merchants and other Irish emigres who had settled in the commercial ports of Bayona and Bilbao along the Bay of Biscay. He received a grant of 200 reales from these merchants, a very modest sum to pay for the buildings and teachers necessary to operate a college. Eventually, this indefatigable Irish priest went to the royal palace of Escorial, near Madrid, and convinced King Philip II to endow the College as well as to give modest stipends to the students. Because the University of Salamanca waived tuition for the Irish by granting them pauper status, these stipends were enough to pay the living expenses of the students. As a result, many individuals of Irish heritage who might not otherwise have been able to afford it received an education. After several decades, the Irish College admitted Spanish students into its program.

In the Irish College at Salamanca, classes were held in the Irish, Spanish and Latin languages. The course work was quite eclectic by contemporary standards, educating students in Catholic theology, science, literature, and history. This not only reflected the Irish educational tradition which maintained that all knowledge enhanced human spirituality, but also reflected the Jesuit belief that Catholic orthodoxy could best be achieved by carefully examining events and ideas that seemed to contradict the faith and refuting them with clear logic based on extensive learning.

When the classes at the Irish College at Salamanca were opened to Spanish students, the school attracted Spaniards interested in the Irish and their methods of education. Eventually, the College grew so crowded that enrollment was limited only to candidates for the priesthood. From the example of the Irish College at Salamanca, the idea of Irish Colleges supported by both the state and the Irish community became extremely popular. Other Irish Colleges on the Salamanca model were founded in Santiago in 1605, Seville in 1612, Madrid in 1619 and Valencia in 1672. The success of the Irish College at Salamanca also influenced Irish emigres in other nations to establish their own versions of an Irish College modeled on the one begun by Thomas White. These Irish-inspired centers of learning provided an education for numbers of Spaniards and other Europeans.

By the mid-17th century, the Irish Colleges in Spain were controlled by the Jesuits. With a considerable proportion of graduates of each class joining the Society of Jesus, the Colleges were like recruiting grounds. They kept the Society's ranks filled with well-educated and highly-motivated young men, many of whom were Irish. As these Jesuits were sent to other European lands, they modeled the schools they established, whether to educate young children or university students, on the Irish Colleges of Spain. These schools and universities emphasized the study of Catholic theology, Greek, Latin and ancient history.

The Irish Colleges of Spain were not only the model for the administration and curriculum in many schools and universities established in several European countries, but they were also the model for the schools and universities of the educational systems established in the Spanish colonies of South and Central America. The Jesuits sent to these colonies believed that such schools and universities were essential for converting the native inhabitants to Catholicism, as well as keeping the Spanish colonists faithful to the religion in the New World. By the 18th century, most of the political, religious, and intellectual leaders born in South and Central America had been educated in these institutions established by the Jesuits.

Some of the schools and universities founded by the Jesuits in the 17th century are still operating. The University of Würzburg in Germany and the University of Córdoba in Argentina are among them. These institutions and many others which have not survived can be traced back to the Irish College established by Thomas White at Salamanca. In Europe, these schools and universities were a part of the Catholic counter-reformation. In the Spanish colonies of Central and South America, such schools and colleges played a central role in making Catholicism the prevailing religion. Thomas White's enterprise in establishing the Irish College at Salamanca hearkens back to the similar efforts of the medieval Irish monks. The College affirmed the importance education continued to have in Irish culture, and also displayed the Irish desire to make education available to others. Over the centuries of Irish emigration, founding schools, sharing knowledge, and teaching skills were important elements in the influence of the Irish in Europe.

THE IRISH REGIMENTS AND THE SPANISH ARMY

An institution like the Irish Colleges which attracted generations of Irish emigres influenced the development of Spanish society for centuries. Other such institutions were the Irish Regiments in the Spanish army which fought in battles across Europe and the New World.

These Irish Regiments in the Spanish army sprang from the policy of the English Lord Mountjoy who was attempting to forestall trouble in Ireland during the 1580's by recruiting many young Irish swordsmen to fight in the armies of England's Protestant allies in Europe. He believed if these potential rebels were fighting wars in Sweden, Denmark and the Netherlands, they could rebel in Ireland. One of the military units formed by this stratagem was called the Leicester Regiment under the command of a trustworthy Protestant, Sir William Stanley.

The Leicester Regiment was assigned to the English forces in the Netherlands to bolster it's strength in a war against Spain, whose forces occupied Flanders and claimed sovereignty over all of the Low Countries. The Irish troops fought in many engagements, but eventually they wearied of spilling their blood for a Protestant cause while their Catholic families and friends in their homeland were suffering religious persecution. The officers of the Regiment often debated theological issues with Colonel Stanley. In 1587, Stanley was convinced by their logic and became a Catholic. The Regiment then defected to the Spanish army in Flanders, surrendering the key city of Deventer to demonstrate their sincerity. The unit was immediately integrated into the Spanish forces.

During the Irish rebellion against England at the close of the 16th century that became known as The Nine Years War, the leader of the rebels, Hugh O'Neill, the Earl of Tyrone, asked Spain to lend him the services of the Leicester Regiment. While the Spanish king agreed, Archduke Albert who commanded the Spanish forces in Flanders had come to rely on the Irish soldiers in his army. So when he received O'Neill's request, forwarded to him from Madrid, he ignored it. Shortly afterwards, the Regiment took heavy casualties while guarding the withdrawal of Albert's army at an engagement in 1600 known as the Battle of the Dunes. The severity of their losses rendered the Regiment unfit for duty for more than a year while the Irish soldiers rebuilt the strength of their unit in the Netherlands by recruiting among the civilian Irish emigres in Spain. By the time the Regiment recovered, the Nine Years War in Ireland had ended.

When many Irish soldiers arrived in Spain seeking political asylum after the surrender of O'Neill and the end of his rebellion, they were sent to the Leicester Regiment in the Netherlands which was enlarged and renamed in 1605. It became known as the First Regiment of Tyrone and King Philip III placed it under the command of Henry O'Neill, a younger son of the O'Neill. When Henry died, his half brother John was placed in command. For the next hundred years, the regiment would have a direct descendant of Hugh O'Neill as its colonel. Because so many Irish men trained and experienced in warfare had come to Spain, the regiments of O'Donnell, Owen Roe O'Neill, and Preston were formed, all named for their colonels as was the custom of the times.

The numbers of Irish serving in the Spanish army were again inadvertently bolstered by the English in 1609. In that year, a convoy of transport ships laden with 6000 Irish fighting men who had been recruited by Lord Mountjoy was bound for the ports of Denmark and Sweden. But a storm forced the ships to find shelter in a Dutch harbor. Hugh O'Neill's nephew, Oghy O'Hanlon, seized the opportunity to lead a thousand men who had grown disgruntled with their lot over the sides of their ships.

They swam for shore, and eventually most of them made their way into the First Regiment of Tyrone stationed in Flanders.

During the 17th century, the First Regiment of Tyrone fought on many European battlefields. During the Thirty Years War, it was stationed in the Low Countries and fought at Amiens and Dourlen and in the siege of Louvain. Its valor became legendary, a model for other Spanish regiments to follow. Over two hundred officers and men were made Knights of Santiago by the Spanish monarchs in recognition of their exploits. Many of the commanding officers of the regiment were also admitted into the Orders of Alcántra and Culatrava, an honor which was usually reserved only for the highest of the Spanish nobility.

As the 17th century came to a close, Spain no longer needed a large army because it had lost most of its possessions in Italy and Flanders to France and the Netherlands. The grandeur and power Spain had enjoyed which had been largely supported by the riches from Spanish colonies in the Americas waned as imports from these colonies decreased, forcing Spain to reduce the size of its army. The First Regiment of Tyrone was disbanded in the 1680's. But the Spanish military leaders did not want to reduce the number of Irish soldiers since they were among the most highly trained and effective troops in the Spanish army. So what the military planners did was incorporate the Irish soldiers into other Spanish units.

All-Irish units were re-introduced into the Spanish military in 1703 when France lent the cavalry regiments of Daniel O'Mahoney—famous for his defense of Cremona in 1701—and Henry Crofton to Spain to bolster Spanish forces during the War of Spanish Succession. In 1709, Spain formed the Ultonia, Hibernia, Limerick, Waterford and Irlanda Regiments made up of infantry. In 1733, the Waterford Regiment was incorporated into the Irlanda Regiment; and in 1735, the Limerick Regiment was transferred to the army of the King of Naples. Throughout the 18th century, the officers from these Irish Regiments distinguished themselves in battle, were frequently promoted to general and were placed in command of Spanish troops, thereby exerting a widespread influence on the Spanish army.

The Irish soldiers in the armies of Spain felt an intense loyalty towards one another and to their units. The officers were usually Irish clan leaders who pledged their allegiance to the king of Spain. But many of the foot soldiers found the idea of a national monarch too remote from their day-to-day lives. Their loyalties lay with the regiment, with their comrades who shared their food and the dangers of combat. In essence, they transferred their clan allegiance to the military unit. It no longer mattered if the men they trusted with guarding the flank were members of the same clan. It was enough that they were Irish. This bonding based on common culture made the Irish Regiments extraordinarily effective fighting units. In accordance with the Spanish military practice of the time, individual Irish Regiments operated during wartime as a quasi-independent units that were assigned objectives that could be achieved without support from other units. Only when the Regiments were deployed as part of a larger force were they under the direct command of a Spanish general. Otherwise, a Regiment's officers were free to make decisions about when and where to engage the enemy. Hence, Irish Regiments were often free to harry or attack enemy forces with the ambush-and-maneuver tactics Irish warriors had developed in Ireland against the Anglo-Normans.

When cannons and hand-held firearms began to be used in warfare during the late 16th century, the value of the tactic of ambush-and-maneuver in many circumstances was reconfirmed for the Irish. Despite the devastating impact of cannon and firearms on a stationary body of troops, European armies continued to engage in battles where large bodies of troops would face each other in open fields. The opposing forces would take up fixed positions against each other and fire volley after volley into each other's stationary ranks of troops. Often, after many such volleys, the two sides would engage in deadly hand-to-hand combat with bayonets, pikes and sabers. Such a rigid style of warfare resulting in high, unnecessary casualties had no romantic or heroic allure and made no sense to the Irish. When they could, the Irish avoided pitched battles against large enemy formations in favor of attacking enemy forces when they were most vulnerable, such as when they were marching in a column or setting up camp.

Through the example of the Irish Regiments, ambush-and-maneuver became a tactic of the entire Spanish army. It was particularly effective during the Napoleonic Wars of the early 19th century when Spanish soldiers were faced with superior French forces invading their country. During this time, the Spanish soldiers became known as "guerrillas," Spanish for "small wars." This tactic has since become a standard part of military operations for all the armies of the world.

For the soldiers of the Irish Regiments in the 17th and 18th centuries, life was hard. Although the Regiments were headquartered in Spain, they was usually on operations in Flanders and Italy, and some contingents were even dispatched to Cuba and Mexico. Inefficient supply systems often deprived them of food and clothing. Pay was meager and frequently behind schedule. Yet despite the hardships, the Irish seemed to thrive on Spanish army life. Wives accompanied their soldier husbands as camp followers. The children of such couples grew to adulthood familiar with the tattoo of drums and the call of bugles. Although all written orders were issued in Spanish, the soldiers and their families continued to speak Irish among themselves. The Irish Regiments became outposts of Irish culture in Spain and its dominions in both Europe and the New World. For the soldiers and their families, the Regiments slowed the process of assimilation into Spanish culture and enabled them to provide an ongoing Irish influence on the Spanish military.

Besides their victories in battle and the tactic of ambush-and-maneuver they contributed to Spanish military operations, the Irish Regiments also made an important contribution in the field of medical treatment in the Spanish military. This contribution of the Irish emigres was similar to the role of the medieval Irish monks who attended to the illnesses and the battlefield wounds of the soldiers of the feudal lords and kings. As in feudal times, in the 16th and 17th century Spanish military, more soldiers died from disease and infected wounds than from direct combat with an enemy. Thus, the knowledgeable and skilled Irish regimental physicians were prized by the Spanish military. The physicians combined ancient Celtic herbal remedies with the surgical techniques and medicines being developed as a part of the increased interest in science at the time. With their knowledge and ingenuity, the Irish physicians were often able to cure illnesses and treat wounds that other physicians were helpless against. John Nynan was the first of the First Regiment of Tyrone's doctors in the early 17th century. He had been Red Hugh O'Donnell's personal physician and became a military doctor after Red Hugh's death. Nynan was succeeded as Regimental Physician by Owen O'Shiel, who eventually became chief of the medical faculty at the Spanish Royal Military Hospital at Mechlinburg. Both men emphasized the need for an effective system of military hospitals to care for sick and wounded soldiers.

The story of Lucy Fitzgerald, the wife of a captain of the Ultonia Regiment, shows a different aspect of the commitment of the Irish to the care of soldiers wounded in battle and illustrates the role women could take on among the Irish. In 1808, the Regiment was stationed in the northern Spanish city of Gerona to keep Napoleon's army from occupying it. The city had strategic importance because it was at the Spanish end of a pass through the Pyrenees. After the Spanish army had been defeated by the French and Napoleon had crowned his brother Joseph King of Spain, the Regiment remained in Gerona although they were no longer opposing the French.

The defeated Spanish army reluctantly pledged its loyalty to King Joseph. But the officers and men rankled under the leadership of the foreign King. The large majority of the population also continued to resent the French occupation of their country and the coronation of a Frenchman as their monarch.

In May of 1808, the people of Madrid rose up against the French. Other cities soon joined the rebellion. The first regular Spanish army unit to declare its support for the rebellion was the Ultonia Regiment, under the command of Antonio O'Kelly. Because they could not leave the strategically-important mountain pass in the hands of the Spanish, the French miliary leaders sent an army of six thousand men to capture the city from the Regiment. When the French attacked, murderous fire from the fortified walls of Gerona forced them to withdraw. After this defeat, the French commander sent an army of thirty-three thousand French veterans complete with artillery and siege guns. This force surrounded the city, attempting to starve the garrison into submission. But within the walls of Gerona, the heavily outnumbered Ultonia Regiment husbanded their supplies and would not surrender.

To bolster the combat strength of the soldiers manning the defenses, Lucy Fitzgerald organized the wives, mothers and daughters of the Ultonian soldiers into the Company of Santa Bárbara. Their mission was to support the soldiers by tending the wounded and passing the ammunition. Some of the women also took the place of soldiers on the ramparts who had been struck by an enemy musket ball or grape shot.

Forming the Company of Santa Bárbara and encouraging other Irish women to join it was an audacious step for Lucy Fitzgerald. She had been raised in the strict patriarchal culture of Spain which allowed women few choices in behavior, education or career. Women were under the "protection" of a man, either their father, husband or occasionally a grown son. Only in the strict regimen of Catholic religious orders could a women find an alternative way of life, but still the nuns remained under the "protection" of a bishop who could forbid any activity which displeased him.

As a member of an Irish emigre family, Lucy Fitzgerald had greater opportunity to take on roles not generally accepted for women in Spanish society. While Irish women were not as unfettered in their actions as their Celtic ancestors, they were active in affairs beyond the home and family. They expected access to education and the right to offer any skills they developed to the community. So when Lucy Fitzgerald married a captain of the Ultonia Regiment, she did not hesitate to participate as much as possible in the non-military aspects of regimental life. Since the Ultonian soldiers remained largely Irish in their customs and beliefs, they welcomed Lucy's active involvement in the defense of Gerona.

On August 10, 1809, the French wearied of the protracted siege and began an all-out assault. First they barraged a small outpost, called Fort Montjuich, beyond the town walls. In a short time, the fort was devastated, and every defender lay dead or wounded. Rather than abandon the defenders of Montjuich, Lucy Fitzgerald led her company of women volunteers through a rain of bombs and musket shot to the fort to evacuate the injured. Despite withering enemy fire, they carried the blood-soaked survivors back to the relative safety of the town. Inspired by her courage, the defenders of Gerona successfully resisted the French assault. The Regiment continued to hold the town for another five months until relieved by Spanish forces in December of 1809. Afterwards, the Company of Santa Bárbara became a model for other regiments of the Spanish army to form their own auxiliary nursing and convalescent organizations staffed principally by women.

It was unlikely that Lucy Fitzgerald's bold break from a traditional role for a woman would have been permitted in a fully-Spanish regiment. But because Irish heritage included active female intervention in the affairs that Spain considered the exclusive domain of men, the Ultonian Regiment encouraged and applauded her. The fact that the Company of Santa Bárbara became a permanent part of military life indicated the level of esteem that the other soldiers of Spain felt towards their Irish comrades.

For many Irish emigres, service in the Irish Regiments was often a stepping-stone to higher rank in the military. An Irish-born soldier who became commander-in-chief of the Spanish army in the late 18th century was from the Ultonia Regiment. Alejandro O'Reilly was born in Ireland, emigrated to Spain and became an officer in the Ultonia Regiment. Because he impressed his superiors in Madrid with his organizational ideas and abilities, he received rapid promotion. After becoming a general, he was detached from regular duty and sent to Prussia as an observer. There he studied the tactics and training methods of Frederick the Great which were bringing the Prussians victory after victory on the battlefield. Upon his return to Spain, he established the Spanish Military Academy at Avila which focused on engineering as well as infantry and cavalry tactics. After his promotion to field-marshal, he insisted that the entire Spanish army adopt the Prussian tactic of a three-deep line for combat on open terrain. This meant that companies would line up in three ranks, one behind the other. The first rank would fire their muskets while the other two ranks were reloading. Then the first rank would step behind their comrades, enabling another line to fire. This created a constant barrage of musket balls firing at the enemy. Other Spanish generals who began their military careers in the Ultonia Regiment were José O'Donnell and Pedro Sarsfield y Waters.

During the 17th, 18th and early 19th centuries, all of the Spanish people knew that their Irish countrymen would be at the forefront of the fighting whenever war broke out. It was not only the battlefield valor of the Irish that contributed to Spanish society and history. The Regiments also produced of innovators such as Alejandro O'Reilly who influenced training and tactics throughout the Spanish army, and Lucy Fitzgerald who improved the way that wounded Spanish soldiers received medical treatment. The loyalty, courage and dedication of the Irish emigres made their Regiments a respected institution in Spanish society.

THE SPANISH ADMIRALTY

Although they lived on an island, the Irish, as the Celts before them, were not drawn to the sea. Unlike the Vikings, the English, the

Portuguese and other island and coastal peoples, the Irish did not develop superior seafaring skills or build ships for trade, exploration or colonization. According to their legends, St. Brendan had set sail in the frail Irish boat made of hide and skin called a coracle and discovered a mystical land to the west. Since this mythic exploit in the 6th century, the people of Ireland confined themselves to coastal fishing and did not sail large vessels to Europe for commerce or into the Atlantic for exploration. During the 17th and 18th centuries, the English established the shipbuilding industry in Belfast, but these shipyards were far smaller than the yards in Rotterdam or Portsmouth. Yet despite their lack of a seagoing heritage, many of the Irish emigres entered the Spanish navy.

The Irish emigres were attracted to the Spanish navy because of the high social standing accorded to naval officers. In the 16th and 17th centuries naval officers were highly regarded because it was mainly the navy that protected Spain's rich, far-flung empire. Spain's large navy had a complex mission. Ships had to patrol the Atlantic, protecting convoys of galleons laden with the treasures and products of the New World. At the same time, ships had to guard the Spanish and South American shoreline from privateers and pirates who would raid coastal settlements. In times of war against naval powers like England, France and the Netherlands, the navy had to blockade enemy ports and engage enemy squadrons to deny them the use of the seas. To support its large navy, Spain needed many officers and sailors to crew the ships.

Because the Irish emigres were well-educated and many of them came from families that the Spanish recognized as noble, they were ideal candidates for naval officers. All naval officers required enough education to grasp spherical trigonometry and astronomy in order to navigate vessels on the high seas. Once naval officers advanced to the rank of captain and commanded a ship, they often operated independently with little communication with the Spanish Admiralty. Ship captains on an independent mission were at liberty to interpret and change their orders in accordance with the varying circumstances they encountered on distant seas. This self-reliance required of ship captains appealed to the vision of the lone Celtic warrior challenging his enemy in battle that was inherent in Irish heritage. The Spanish naval service provided one of the few opportunities in the contemporary world for an individual to exercise independent judgement in warfare.

Tómas Geraldino Fitzgerald was one notable Spanish naval officer with an Irish heritage. He was descended from the clan that initiated the rebellion known as the Geraldine Wars against Henry VIII in the 16th century. When Cromwell came to Ireland in 1642 to purge the island of Catholics once and for all, Fitzgeralds were among the leaders of the defense of the city of Drogheda when it came under siege by Cromwell's army. After the city finally fell and the English forces slaughtered all the Irish defenders had not fled into the countryside, the Fitzgeralds managed to escape by hiding in the countryside. A short time later, some of the clan fled to safety in Spain. A hundred years later, Tómas Geraldino Fitzgerald was born to successors of the Fitzgerald family in Spain.

Tómas joined the Spanish navy as a midshipman in the mid-18th century. By 1782, he had risen to the rank of captain and had led several expeditions to the Caribbean to keep the waters off Spanish colonies free from English privateers. Although England was not at war with Spain, the two nations were vying for supremacy in the New World and control of its wealth. English kings had granted authority to privately-owned warships to plunder Spanish ships in the Caribbean because England believed that if Spain were unable to protect the trade with its colonies, they would rebel against Spain and thus become markets for English goods. Tómas thwarted the activities of the privateers by keeping his ships at sea for long periods of time. During voyages back and forth across the Atlantic and across the oceans of the globe to discover unknown lands, ships had to frequently make landfall to replenish their supply of fresh water. But Tómas increased the length of time his ships could stay on patrol searching for English privateers by devising a filtering for sea water so that it would become fresh water. By the 1790's, Tómas's desalinization method was adopted for the entire Spanish fleet.

Ten years after serving in the Caribbean, Tómas again faced English ships, this time warships. Spain had been part of the First Coalition formed by England, Austria, Prussia and Holland to wage war against the recently-established Republic of France. In 1795, Spain not only left the Coalition, but made a military alliance with Republican France. Angered by this apparent betrayal, the English government declared war on Spain. Two years later in this war, attempting to drive off English ships blockading the port of Cadiz, Tómas was killed.

During the Napoleonic Wars a few years later, another captain of Irish ancestry in the Spanish navy clashed with British men o'war. At the Battle of Trafalgar fought off the coast of Spain, Rear Admiral MacDonald led a squadron against the English fleet commanded by Lord Nelson. He had started his career of service to the monarchs of Spain as a lieutenant in the army. Then MacDonald requested a transfer to the navy, and fought in naval engagements from Africa to the West Indies. For a time, he was detached from the Spanish Navy to counsel the Swedish King on tactics and strategy in Sweden's war against Russia. In 1814, MacDonald was promoted to the rank of Admiral of the Spanish Fleet.

One Irish family in particular stands out for its career in the Spanish navy. This family was the O'Doghertys. Although the family did not arrive in Spain until the late 18th century—quite a bit later than most other Irish emigres—the Napoleonic Wars of the early 19th century presented members of the O'Dogherty family with an opportunity to display daring and intelligence in a time of crisis for Spain.

The story of the O'Doghertys decision to emigrate to Spain began in the early 1600's, with the Irish rebellion against the English led by O'Neill. Seán óg ó Dochartaigh had remained neutral during O'Neill's rebellion, hoping that this would keep the English from seizing the family lands in Inish Eoghain between Lough Swilly and Lough Foyle which he had inherited. When he died in 1601, Seán was succeeded as Lord of Inish Eoghain by his son Cahir. After the unsuccessful rebellion and the Flight of the Earls in 1607, Cahir was the foreman of a grand jury convened by the English which produced an indictment known as a Bill of Treason against O'Neill. This Bill was necessary under English law for the crown to confiscate O'Neill lands. Despite the loyalty to the English of the ó Dochartaigh family, the Governor-General of Derry, Sir George Poulet, coveted Inish Eoghain. Attempting to acquire the territory by public insults and destruction of property aimed at driving Cahir off the land, Poulet provoked Cahir to a rebellion to try to save his family's land. Within a short time, Cahir, was killed in a skirmish with the English at the Rock of Doon in Donegal.

After Cahir's death, his brother Seán became Lord of Inish Eoghain and continued fighting the English. But Seán received no support from the other Irish clans, and his forces were soon defeated by the English. Poulet seized the ó Dochartaigh lands and Seán fled to Breífne in central Ireland where he lived in secret to preserve his own life. Seán and his descendants became farmers, eking out a meager living on land owned by an English lord near Clankee in County Cavan. By the mid-18th century, they were impoverished and bitter, the days of their former family prominence only a memory.

In the 1760's, a descendant of Seán's named Henry O'Dogherty emigrated to Spain to study for the priesthood. Once he saw how well the Irish emigres in Spain were living, once he saw that it was possible to be both Spanish and Irish, he wrote letters to his nephews in Ireland urging them to join him. In 1790, Seán, Henry and Clinton O'Dogherty arrived in Cadiz. Because they had become interested in the sea during their voyage from Ireland, the three brothers wanted to join the Spanish navy. To become officers, they had to present a genealogy which showed noble origins. While these documents were being compiled and certified, they were permitted to become cadets of the Ultonia Regiment, then stationed at Ceuta, a city under Spanish control on the African side of the Strait of Gibraltar. When the brothers eventually presented the Spanish Admiralty with their certified genealogy, the title of earl held by Seán óg ó Dochartaigh during the Elizabethan period was deemed sufficient to allow them to become midshipmen.

When the Napoleonic Wars broke out, both Clinton and Henry were dispatched to the Caribbean with the navy. A short time later, Seán achieved widespread fame for repelling a French invasion force attempting to land in the Atlantic port of Vigo near the Portuguese border. Spain had ended its alliance with France, and Napoleon sent his troops to invade Spain rather than risk having a potentially hostile nation on the southern border of France. At Vigo, Seán O'Dogherty had only two small gunboats to engage a much larger French force. He ordered his sailors to remove the cannon from the gunboats and place them in a castle overlooking the harbor approaches. From this fortified position, Seán was able to damage the French ships enough to force them to withdraw. O'Dogherty's victory became a part of Spanish naval tradition. The exploits of Seán O'Dogherty at Vigo were told and retold to each new generation of Spanish midshipmen, giving them an example of the courage and intelligence that Spain expected of its naval officers.

Many of the descendants of Seán O'Dogherty followed in their famous ancestor's footsteps by entering the Spanish navy. As was common in naval families, O'Dogherty's daughters and granddaughters married naval officers. One of his descendants was Pascual O'Dogherty, a 20th-century admiral who was an internationally-known authority on naval architecture.

Those emigres who had been nobles in Ireland saw the naval service as a way to obtain the prestige and position they had lost with the English occupation of their land. Besides, naval service uniquely offered the Irish an opportunity for adventure which appealed to their ancient Celtic traits. Even though a life at sea was unfamiliar to them, with their ability to adapt to new situations and their desire to play a productive role in their new countries, many emigres readily, and eagerly, joined the Spanish navy—where many of them served with distinction and a few became legendary.

MERCHANT ADVENTURERS

During the 15th century, a large number of merchant families in the Irish port cities of Galway, Cork and Waterford had become wealthy by trading with European countries. They mostly shipped Irish butter and beef to the continent on English merchant vessels, which then returned to Ireland with casks of wine.

During the reigns of Henry VIII and his daughter Elizabeth, the Lord Deputies in charge of Ireland placed many restrictions on Irish merchants. Merchants who did not convert to the new Anglican religion found themselves harassed by customs agents, and sometimes they had their premises sacked by soldiers. As O'Neill's rebellion spread across Ireland in the late 16th century, Irish merchants were heavily taxed by the English to pay for the defense of Irish cities against a rebel army that many of them sympathized with. In addition, the continual strife between the warring sides and the scorched-earth policy of the English army frequently cut the merchants off from their interior markets for their imported goods and also from the domestic goods they exported. Seeing their revenues plummet with little likelihood of recovery, many Irish merchants moved their headquarters to European port cities such as Cadiz and Bilbao in Spain with which they had been trading for many years while continuing to operate in Ireland as best they could.

The majority of merchants in Ireland and Spain were small businessmen, usually employing only family members. With their base of operations shifted to Spain and business prospects in Ireland uncertain, they changed their business activity to importing goods and materials from the New World and the Far East and distributing these goods to other European countries. In the ports of Cadiz, Bilbao and Barcelona, the Irish merchants imported coffee, cocoa, rum and other products and made arrangements to send them to other European countries. To insure that their affairs abroad would be handled effectively and reliably, the Irish merchants often sent their sons or nephews to cities in Europe, the New World, and the Far East to be their agents. In many parts of Europe, though, the Irish merchants did not need to dispatch an agent to handle their affairs because they could call on members of their clans who had emigrated to do this. This was often the case in France and Austria and even in faraway Russia. Having clan members they could rely on in foreign countries usually gave the Irish an advantage over their business rivals.

After the Flight of the Earls in 1607, members of clan O'Sullivan, MacCarthy and O'Driscol settled in the cities of Santender and Bilbao on the shores of the Bay of Biscay. Within a few generations, they became very prosperous merchants who traded with all parts of Europe. But not all of the Irish merchants remained in the north of Spain. Some, like Pedro Alonzo O'Crowley, settled in the southern port city of Cadiz. He devoted his time not only to his business interests, but also to writing and historical research. The king acknowledged his scholarship by ennobling O'Crowley, granting him the right to call himself *hidalgo*, the equivalent of an Irish baron. After his death, O'Crowley left behind documents identifying him as a member of clan O'Sullivan who had changed his name to escape English reprisals for his part in O'Neill's rebellion.

One of the most noted and successful Irish emigres who went into business in Spain was not originally a merchant, but an emigre soldier who had served in the French forces sent to Spain in support of its new King, Philip V, in the War of Spanish Succession in the early 1700's. General Terry, one of the Wild Geese arriving in France in 1693, played a major role in the growth of the export of sherry from Spain to all parts of Europe; and he was also responsible for the famed Lippezaner horses of Austria. But Terry's path to becoming a prominent emigre businessman was roundabout.

After arriving in France in 1693, like most of the other Wild Geese, Terry joined the French army, where he rose to the rank of general. He left the military when Philip V of Spain renounced his claim to the French throne, thus ending the crises to the European balance of power from the possibility that Philip could wear the crown of both Spain and France. Philip V, who had been named heir to the Spanish throne by his uncle, King Carlos II of Spain, was also in line to be King of France as a grandson of Louis XIV. Shortly before the death of Carlos and his will appointing Philip as his successor was known, France, England Austria and the Netherlands made an agreement to partition the Spanish territories in Europe after the death of Carlos II—who was childless. The agreement came apart when Louis XIV of France learned that his grandson, Philip, was to be King of Spain, and France might control all the Spanish territories in Europe as well as Spain itself. Alarmed by Louis XIV's reneging of the agreement and the possibility of an increase in French power and territorial possessions which would upset the balance of power, England, Austria and the Netherlands went to war against France and Spain—hoping to replace Philip V with the Archduke Charles of Austria. The Archduke felt that he had the stronger claim to the Spanish Throne because he and Carlos II belonged to the royal family of the Hapsburgs; and thus, with him as the Spanish King, the Hapsburg lineage as rulers of Spain would continue.

Philip V rewarded Terry for his service to Spain with a tracts of land. Terry was given an estate with vineyards near the southern city of Jerez, in the region of Andalusia. The area surrounding the city was famous for its sweet wine which was known as sherry from the garbled attempts of foreigners to pronounce Jerez. Terry decided to stay in Spain to oversee his estate. When he went to take over his estate, Terry found that the harvest of grapes produced by the tenant farmers on their plots of land varied widely. Some plots were adequately fertilized and produced satisfactory harvests; while with others the soil was so depleted that they yielded hardly anything. Having no farming background, Terry went to other Irish emigres who were farmers for advice on agricultural techniques which would improve the harvests of his estate. After following their advice to organize his vineyards into a single agricultural unit with uniform methods of cultivation and fertilization taught to him by the farmers, Terry's estate began to yield consistently good harvests. In fact, his estate became widely known for the abundance of its harvests, and Terry's neighboring landowners soon began following the Irish farming methods he had implemented.

It was about this time in the early 1700's that sherry became a "fortified" wine by adding brandy to it to give it a higher alcohol content.

No record exists which credits General Terry with this innovation, but what is known is that he began to produce fortified sherry around this time. He quickly established trade connections with other Irish merchants throughout Europe for the export of the fortified sherry wine from his vineyards. Sherry already had a large market in England. Folklore in Jerez claimed that the English had acquired a taste for the wine from supplies of it on captured Spanish galleons. With the addition of brandy to it, this soon became popular in many other countries as well. General Terry led the way in stimulating not only greater production, but also greater exports, laying the foundation for Andalusia to become the most important viable wine-growing area of Spain. Terry's descendants continued in the wine business and today Fernando Terry heads the Terry Corporation, the second largest exporter of Spanish sherry.

Besides wine production, General Terry became involved in raising horses after visiting the Cartusian Monastery near his estate. He discovered that the monks had bred an unusual herd of horses which were born black and gradually turned white as they grew older. When they were fully mature, they achieved the uncommonly tall height of eighteen hands, or 72 inches at the shoulder. In southern Spain, the horses were called Cartusian after the monastery.

General Terry brought several of the horses back to his Andalusian estate and began his own breeding program. Eventually, Philip V saw one of the magnificent horses owned by General Terry and suggested that Terry present several of them to the Archduke Charles of Austria. Philip hoped that a gift of the horses would help to soothe any resentments harbored by Charles in the wake of the War of Spanish Succession. Not wishing to offend the king who had given him so much, General Terry sent several of the horses to Vienna. Archduke Charles immediately established the Spanish Riding School and called the horses the Lipezaners. During the course of the next few centuries, they became famous throughout the world for their precision movements in formation.

The Irish merchants were particularly beneficial to Spain considering the decline in the Spanish economy during the 17th and 18th centuries. Not only did they noticeably add to Spain's commercial activity in general and stimulate particular areas of its economy, but there were times when the emigres exclusively could maintain economic activity which was barred to native Spaniards. When because of war or changed political or military alliances Spain was unable to trade with a particular country or its colonies, the Irish emigre merchants were often able to use their international clan connections to get around trade bans against Spain, and thereby continue to maintain some level of trade with these countries. Thus, the Irish merchants in Spain brought some stability to economic activity and relations in a time when international commerce was tentative and unpredictable.

THE PRESIDENT OF THE COUNCIL OF MINISTERS

Although there were many Irish emigres and their descendants who influenced commerce, medicine, education and military affairs in Spain, none was more important to Spanish society than Leopold O'Donnell. In the mid-19th century, he became the head of the Spanish government. As President of the Council of Ministers, he played a critical role in the reform movement which led to the development of a constitutional monarchy in Spain.

Leopold was a direct descendant of Red Hugh O'Donnell, the clan chieftain who had fought alongside the O'Neill in the 16th-century Irish rebellion known as the Nine Years War. After English soldiers defeated the rebels, Red Hugh fled to Spain, where he and his sons entered the Spanish army, thus beginning the O'Donnell tradition to pursue military careers. Leopold's grandfather, José, had commanded the Ultonia Regiment and risen to the rank of general; his father, Carlos, was a general in command of Spanish artillery; and his two uncles were infantry generals. Leopold began his military service in 1819, at the age of ten, as a cadet in the Ultonia Regiment.

Leopold O'Donnell's began demonstrating his extraordinary leadership capabilities in 1833 during a war to determine who should wear the crown of Spain. In that year, King Ferdinand VII died after rescinding a law which prevented a woman from ruling Spain. This enabled his infant daughter, Isabella, to succeed him. Ferdinand's brother Carlos, who would have become king under the old law, marshaled an army to contest the right of the new queen to rule. Far more was at stake than the succession to the crown. Isabella and her mother, the Queen Regent María Christina, believed that the common people of Spain should have greater say in government. Carlos was supported by the nobles and grandees of Spain who saw their traditional position threatened by the progressive Queen Regent and her liberal followers.

Initially, Carlos pinned his hopes of becoming King on two generals of Irish descent, José O'Donnell, Leopold's grandfather, and Pedro Sarsfield y Waters. Because of his military exploits in the 1808 uprising against the French occupation and subsequent leadership of Spanish troops in North Africa, O'Donnell had great prestige in the Spanish military. His support would insure that most of the Spanish army units would side with Carlos. Sarsfield commanded the Army of Observation which had been stationed to guard the Portuguese border since the close of the Napoleonic Wars, despite the fact that Portugal no longer posed any military threat to Spain. At the time, this Army was the finest fighting force in the Spanish army. Carlos assumed that both generals would support him because they frequently counseled the government against implementing democratic reforms too rapidly. In addition, he believed that no self-respecting Spanish general would accept the leadership of a woman.

To the surprise of Carlos, General O'Donnell and General Sarsfield committed their forces to the infant Queen Isabella and her mother, the Queen Regent María Christina. They felt that the radically conservative programs advocated by Carlos, which included reestablishing the Inquisition, would add more fuel to the anarchist movement which was growing stronger in Spain. Their decision was also prompted by their Irish and Celtic heritage which raised no objection to women rulers. They saw no compromise to their honor in pledging their loyalty to a queen. Despite receiving no support from O'Donnell and Sarsfield, Carlos ordered troops loyal to him to depose the Queen, initiating a conflict which became known as the Carlist War.

At the outbreak of the Carlist War In 1833, Leopold, the grandson of General José O'Donnell, was a newly commissioned young officer. In skirmishes and battles against the Carlists in northern Spain, he served with such distinction that he rapidly rose in rank. As a colonel in 1838, he was placed in charge of the defense of San Sebastián, a major port city on the Bay of Biscay. After repelling an assault on the city by a superior Carlist force, he earned promotion to the rank of general. The war concluded a year later when General Espartero, the commander-in-chief of Isabella's forces, agreed with the Queen's approval to recognize the noble titles granted by Carlos to the officers who sided with him. This induced substantial numbers of his officers to defect to Isabella's side, taking their troops with them. Abandoned by much of his forces, Carlos left Spain.

Much to the dismay of Leopold O'Donnell and many other Spaniards, General Espartero took control of the government and began to behave like a military dictator. In 1840, the young Queen Isabella and her mother fled to France to escape being made prisoners in the royal palace by Espartero. Leopold O'Donnell helped to arrange for their escape and accompanied them to France. Three years later, liberal supporters of the Queen overthrew Espartero and drove him into exile. O'Donnell returned to Spain with Isabella and resumed his interrupted army career. As a reward for his faithful service her, Isabella appointed him Governor-General of Cuba.

Soon after her return to Spain, Isabella established a legislative assembly called the Cortes composed of a Senate and a General Assembly. Some of the senators were appointed by the crown and some were appointed by towns, universities and the Church; while members of the General Assembly were elected by the people. The General Assembly appointed Ministers, usually the leaders of the political party which had gained a majority, who formed a Council to run the government. The Council then elected one of its Ministers as its President. This President was the head of state. The role of the monarch in this governmental scheme was limited to granting noble titles, appointing Senators, and calling for new elections. All other governmental activities were left to the Cortes and the Council of Ministers.

In 1847, when Leopold O'Donnell's tour of duty in Cuba ended, he returned to Spain. In recognition of his able administration of the colony, Isabella made him the Count of Lucerna and appointed him Senator. In order to devote his full attention to his new duties as Senator, O'Donnell turned down another military command. When he began attending the Cortes, however, he quickly discovered that many Senators and members of the Assembly were corrupt and indifferent to the social and economic problems of Spain, using their position primarily to increase their wealth. O'Donnell advocated the gradual introduction of democratic reforms, fearing that continued governmental corruption would serve only to alienate conservatives while encouraging radicals.

At the time, the Count of San Luís was the President of the Council of Ministers, and as such was head of the government. He passed laws and regulations requiring that the Cortes in Madrid make virtually all decisions formerly made locally by mayors, provincial councils and provincial governors. This was an attempt to shift meaningful political power away from the merchants and landowners who elected local officials to the Ministers and other politicians in Madrid. With the Ministers appointed by the Cortes in control of even the lowest level of government, all tax revenues and administrative requests from private citizens—which were often accompanied by bribes—would pass through the hands of the Ministers and their agents. Although San Luís claimed to be a liberal, many Spaniards believed his policies were as oppressive as the policies of Isabella's father, the absolute monarch Ferdinand VII, or the dictator Espartero. Opposition to the government from trade unions, merchants, and farmers grew intense, and many people refused to follow the decisions made by the government in Madrid. The ability of San Luís and the Council of Ministers to rule Spain was further undermined by the anarchist movement which was gaining many followers among the factory workers in Cataluña, the most industrialized province of Spain. Incidents of bombings, assassinations and strikes increased, and because the government in Madrid did not have the cooperation of local officials, it could not suppress the anarchists.

By 1854, civil war again threatened to erupt in Spain when anti-government rioting broke out in Madrid. Large crowds of anarchists carrying muskets, swords and pitchforks converged on the building where the Cortes was housed. Because many army officers did not support the corrupt government, no order was issued to suppress the rioting. Although Leopold O'Donnell was also strongly opposed the policies of the government, he feared that the rioting might encourage conservatives to seize power, depose Isabella from the throne, and restore an absolute monarchy. So he made his way through the rioting mob to the camp of a regiment stationed on the outskirts of Madrid and returned with the regiment to the streets of the city where the soldiers restored order.

The rioting forced San Luís and the other Ministers resigned, leading Isabella to call for new elections for the General Assembly of the Cortes. When Isabella asked O'Donnell to become a Minister in an interim government until the elections could be held, he readily agreed. He resigned as Senator and became the Minister of War. While serving in the interim government, he founded and organized the Liberal Union Party. Because of his prestige as the hero of San Sebastián, his role in suppressing the rioting in Madrid, and his reputation for honesty and commitment to the Queen, the Liberal Union Party attracted many followers. When the elections were held in 1856, the Party won a majority of the seats in the General Assembly, and most of the Ministers appointed by the General Assembly were Liberal Unionists. The Ministers then elected O'Donnell as the President of the Council of Ministers.

As head of the new government, O'Donnell convinced both liberals and conservatives to adopt a compromise plan that restored local control to government in cities and provinces, but left the Cortes in overall supervision of their activities. Because the Carlist wars and the corruption which followed had left Spain impoverished, O'Donnell invited foreign capitalists to invest in Spanish industry by having the government give them land on which they could build factories. Under his direction, the government also gave land to railroads to stimulate the growth of the Spanish rail system.

By the time O'Donnell retired in 1865, most of the Spanish people no longer doubted that a constitutional monarchy with an elected assembly was the best means to effectively govern Spain. The reforms and policies that he established helped steer Spain not only through a governmental crises, but also helped to lay the foundation for the future economic development of the country. A year after he left office, he died at his estate in Biatriz. The Spanish government brought his body back to Madrid, buried him by the church known as Las Salesas on the Plaza de Santa Bárbara, and erected a statue of him to commemorate his contributions to Spanish society.

The career of Leopold O'Donnell was an example of the strong influence that the Irish emigres and their descendants had on the development of Spanish culture. Because of the contributions of many generations of Irish emigres to education, commerce and the military, the Spanish people did not hesitate to entrust their government to a descendant of Irish emigres. Once in office, he demonstrated the adaptability, loyalty and talent for compromise characteristic of the Irish emigres in Europe.

CHAPTER 7

In The Service Of France

War battered dogs are we,
Fighters in every clime;
Fillers of trenches and graves,
Mockers bemocked by time;
War dogs, hungry and grey,
Gnawing a naked bone.
Fighters in every clime,
Every cause but our own.

—Emily Lawless, *With The Wild Geese*

THE FLIGHT OF THE WILD GEESE

On a cool day in the December of 1691, an Irish Colonel named Patrick Sarsfield arrived in France at the head of twelve thousand veteran Irish soldiers fully armed with their muskets and sabers. But this was no army of invasion bent on conquest. Instead, it was a migration of Irish to continental Europe on an unprecedented scale. As the soldiers disembarked from the French ships that had transported them from

Ireland, Sarsfield ordered his officers to muster them to demonstrate that even on foreign soil they remained a disciplined fighting force.

By the mid-18th century, these soldiers led into exile by Colonel Patrick Sarsfield plus thousands of others who left Ireland to join them in France in the following decades were known in Ireland and throughout Europe as the "Wild Geese." The first recorded description of them by this name is in an early 18th-century poem by Sean ó Cuinnegáin. With this image, ó Cuinnegáin evoked the romantic notion that like the migrating geese, the soldiers would one day return to their homeland after a flight to a distant foreign place. There is another, comparatively prosaic, origin for their name which is offered by some Irish historians. This explanation for term refers to the way the many individuals desiring to join the exiled Irish soldiers in France circumvented Irish laws preventing emigration. Because many of the emigres going to Europe were joining the armies of England's enemies in order to fight against English oppression in Ireland in this indirect way, the Lord Lieutenant of Ireland made it illegal for men with military experience to leave Ireland. To get around the law, Irish fighting men desiring to join the armies of England's enemies hid in the cargo holds of French merchant ships bound for French and other European ports. On their manifests, the ships' captains would record these hidden Irishmen as "wild geese." The ruse worked because the French routinely imported large numbers of such birds from Ireland as delicacies for the nobility. The French captains and crews were readily willing to play their part in the scheme since it helped to supply capable and enthusiastic fighting men for their armies in their perennial contest with England for supremacy in Europe. Whatever its origins, the name "Wild Geese" came to be applied to the defeated Irish troops led by Sarsfield who went into exile on that cool December day in 1691 and the many Irishmen who left Ireland by subterfuge over the following decades to join them.

Patrick Sarsfield and the Wild Geese found themselves in exile not because they rebelled against the kings of England like so many of their forbearers. Ironically, the reason they came to France was because they supported James II, the Catholic King of England who had been deposed in 1688 by the Protestant, William of Orange. William was supported by the Protestant majority in England who were opposed to the pro-Catholic policies of James II. To escape capture by William, James II fled to Paris and was welcomed by the king of France, Louis XIV.

Because William of Orange was the leader of a coalition of nations known as The League of Augsburg allied in a war against France, Louis feared that England would also declare war on France. To keep the English armies away from European soil, Louis devised a clever strategy. He persuaded James to go to Ireland with a small French army as a first step to regaining his lost throne by force of arms. If enough Irish soldiers serving in the English army joined James and he was successful, Louis would have England as an ally. But even if James was unsuccessful, he would weaken English forces in battle so they could not attack France.

In March of 1689, James landed at the Irish port of Kinsale with a few French regiments behind him. Irish Catholics— civilians as well as entire regiments of Irish soldiers in the English army—flocked to his banner, swelling the size of his force. The joint Irish-French army marched north toward Dublin, clashing with an English army near the Boyne River. King William's valor during the battle inspired his troops, and the English swept the Irish-French army from the field.

During the battle when William's victory appeared certain, James panicked and fled to Dublin and eventually to France. Despite James' cowardice, Patrick Sarsfield organized an orderly retreat from the Boyne. He led the remnants of the Irish and French forces towards the walled city of Limerick on the western coast. During the long march, the rear guard was led by Michael Hogan, who had become known as The Galloping Hogan for his extraordinary feats of horsemanship. Using the traditional Irish tactics of ambush and maneuver, he harassed the pursuing columns of English soldiers. His skirmishers became known as Rapparees, taking their name from the half-pike called a rappaire that they favored in combat.

The retreating Irish and French army eventually reached Limerick. The English army following closely behind laid siege to the city. The siege dragged on for several months with neither side achieving a breakthrough. To end the stalemate, William offered terms to the Irish guaranteeing freedom of religion and property ownership for Catholics. But William also required that all the Irish soldiers who served in the army of James II choose between pledging their loyalty to William or going into perpetual exile. After consulting with his men, Patrick Sarsfield accepted the terms of peace which became known as the Treaty of Limerick.

In accordance with the terms of the treaty, the Irish Catholic regiments which had been in the English army prior to enlisting in the cause of James II were forced to choose between exile in France or serving England. On the day the treaty went into effect, the royal banners of France and England were placed in a field outside Limerick. The Irish Foot Guards were the first to march out of the city, and without hesitation, they marched to the standard of France. They knew this meant permanent banishment from their homeland, yet they could not submit to William and the ascendancy of the Protestant religion he represented. By the end of the day, twelve thousand soldiers had decided to accept exile in France rather than serve England.

A few days after the signing of the Treaty of Limerick, a French fleet which had not heard about the Treaty sailed up the Shannon laden with troops and supplies to reinforce the defenders of Limerick. Sarsfield honored the agreement and did not resume the struggle. He forbade the French to land. Instead, he used their ships to transport some of his regiments to Europe. The Irish soldiers who did not sail with these French ships marched to Cork where they embarked for France a few weeks later. Scarcely a man of them ever set foot in Ireland again. After the army of Ireland had disbanded, after its best swordsmen were exiled to foreign lands, the English Parliament repudiated the Treaty of Limerick, leaving the oppression of Catholics in place. Had England abided by its terms, Ireland in the ensuing centuries would have been a far happier place; and new generations of Irish emigres would not have had to emigrate to Europe to enjoy the freedoms denied to them in their homeland.

THE IRISH BRIGADE

Patrick Sarsfield had been to France before. Twenty years before his arrival with the Wild Geese in 1691, he had received his initial military training as an officer in the French army's Dillon Regiment, made up entirely of Irish soldiers. After a large number of Irish soldiers fled to France in 1645 following defeat by Oliver Cromwell's Puritan army, the Regiment had been formed under the command of Edmond Robert Du Wall, whose brother Michael had been appointed general of the "entire foreign army" serving in France during the Thirty Years War. This unit became known as the Dillon Regiment in 1653 when it was commanded by Viscount Dillon, and it kept that name for the next century and a half. By the time that Patrick Sarsfield and the Wild Geese arrived in France, the soldiers of Ireland already had a reputation for exceptional courage among the French army.

The Dillon Regiment was not the only exclusively Irish unit in the French army in 1691. A year before, in order to repay Louis XIV for the loan of French troops to invade Ireland, James II had sent the Irish Regiments of Viscount Mountcashel and Lord Clare to France after they defected to James' army in Ireland. Immediately, the regiments of Clare and Mountcashel joined with the Dillon Regiment to become a separate unit of the French army called the Irish Brigade. The Brigade was sent to Savoy to fight against the League of Augsburg.

When they arrived in France, the Wild Geese were incorporated into the Irish Brigade which added new regiments. This was a measure which satisfied the different, but inter-related, interests of various groups of individuals. The Brigade gained the military skills and experience of the thousands of Irish soldiers, which made it an even more formidable fighting unit. Patrick Sarsfield was given the rank of brigadier general by the French and placed in command of the considerably enlarged Brigade. The Brigade pledged their loyalty to James II and his heirs with the hope that the Stuart family would one day regain the throne of England and end the English oppression of Ireland. They also gave their allegiance to King Louis XIV of France, who they saw as an ally in their struggle against England and champion of the Catholic faith.

Besides the military and political motives for incorporating the Wild Geese into the Irish Brigade, there were also considerations regarding the exiled Irish soldiers as individuals. The Wild Geese had been unexpectedly sent from Ireland. Joining this band of fellow Irish soldiers on French soil gave them a way to ease the pangs and regret of their sudden, Draconian exile from their homeland. Since France was an enemy of England, joining the Brigade also allowed them to express their undiminished opposition to England and its harsh exploitative policies in Ireland. This gave them the prospect of once again meeting English forces on the field of battle to exact revenge for the continuing injustices to their countrymen and women. Like the Irish emigre soldiers before them, the Wild Geese looked upon their regiments of the Irish Brigade as their new clan and their officers as their new clan leaders. With the loyalty of the members of the Irish Brigade to one another and their fighting spirit kept burning by the hope of battle against the English, the Brigade became a modern-day example of the mythic *fianna*, the Celtic oath-bound warrior band.

Until the Treaty of Ryswick in 1697, almost all of the soldiers who came to France in 1691 remained on active duty in the military. Nominally, the Brigade was in the service of James II, but it fought against the enemies of Louis XIV, whether English or Dutch or German. In 1697, England and France signed the Treaty of Ryswick, which contained the provision that James no longer maintain his own private army. Under the terms of this Treaty, the Irish Brigade should have been disbanded. Louis XIV, however, was reluctant to part with the services of such dependable fighting men. He ordered the Brigade transferred into the French army, but reduced its size in order to comply with another provision of the Treaty, requiring a reduction in the size of France's standing army. Despite their wish to continue in the service of France, many of the emigres of the Irish Brigade were discharged. Some entered civilian life. But many others considered themselves professional soldiers and spread out across Europe in a second migration of Wild Geese to join the armies of Austria, Poland and Russia. None returned to Ireland, where new acts of Parliament had insured that their religion would make them pariahs in their own nation. But throughout Catholic Europe, they were welcomed as equals and could rise to positions of importance and recognition.

After the Treaty of Ryswick, the Irish Brigade consisted of the three original regiments, which became fully integrated into the French army. The integration was in keeping with the role of the Brigade for both the Irish and French. For the Irish, the existence of the Brigade demonstrated to the English kings and their ministers that many Irish would not passively accept laws designed to destroy their culture. For the French, the Brigade was a highly effective military unit that could be entrusted with crucial battle missions. Its officers were properly pedigreed Irish nobles who could keep the occasionally rowdy troops in line. So the Irish Brigade became an institution in 18th-century France, fighting in over eighty-seven engagements. It was largely due to the success of the Irish Brigade that the French army was open to creating independent emigre units that would ultimately lead to the formation of the Foreign Legion in the 19th century.

In 1702, the Irish Brigade earned the respect of the entire French army during the Battle of Cremona in Italy during the War of Spanish Succession. After the French had occupied the city, Prince Eugène of Savoy launched a surprise night attack to retake it. In the dark and confusion, the French troops were unable to muster an effective defense. Eugène's troops poured into the city after capturing the gates of St. Margaret and All Saints. Before daybreak, most of Cremona was in Eugene's hands. His soldiers had even captured the French commander, Marshall de Villeroy. But then the Austrians came upon the soldiers of the Irish Brigade near the Po Gate.

Awakened by the clamor of shot and rattling sabers, Major Dan O'Mahoney roused his men from their sleep. Clutching their pistols and their swords, they rushed into the battle wearing only their nightshirts. O'Mahoney's men formed an unmovable barrier by the Po gate that became a rallying point for the French. Although the Austrians made repeated assaults on the position, they were repelled. To Prince Eugène, it seemed as if the half-naked Irishmen shouting and waving sabers were not made of the same blood and bone as other French soldiers. When enough French and Irish soldiers had gathered at O'Mahoney's rallying point, he counterattacked, recapturing a battery of 24 gun. By dawn, he swept the Austrians from Cremona.

Two centuries after the battle, Sir Arthur Conan Doyle wrote a fanciful poem about the engagement which ended with Marshall de Villeroy asking Major Dan O'Mahoney how the Irish heroes should be rewarded.

"Why then", says Dan O'Mahoney, "one favor we entreat.
We were called a little early and our toilet's not complete.

We've no quarrel with the shirt,
But the breeches wouldn't hurt,
For the evening air is chilly in Cremona."

In reality, Major O'Mahoney was rewarded not only by permission to don his trousers. He brought the news of the victory to Louis XIV at the palace at Versailles, insuring that he would receive royal recognition for his part in the battle.

Most of the Irish soldiers serving in the Brigade had left their wives and lovers in Ireland. Only several hundred women accompanied the Wild Geese in 1691, and very few Irish wives later joined their husbands. So eventually many of the Irish soldiers married French women, creating a considerable number of Irish-French families whose descendants would be very active in all areas of French society. Yet the process of full assimilation into French culture was slow for the members of the Irish Brigade during the 18th century. They continued to speak the Irish tongue and live by Irish ways within the Brigade, and only the officers interacted with French society outside of it. Any of their French-born wives who joined them as camp followers were expected to live like Irish women and follow the customs and traditions of their husbands.

This cultural separation from the mainstream French army enabled the Irish Brigade to largely avoid the decline in efficiency that plagued the military after Louis XV became king in 1715. For the first half of the 18th century, France had the largest army in Europe, but its troops were poorly trained and had too many officers who owed their rank to patronage rather than personal skill. In contrast, the Irish controlled their officer's promotions below the rank of general and insisted that all soldiers receive adequate training in military skills. Emphasis on efficient training and organization enabled the Irish Brigade to win many battles.

In 1701, France abrogated the Treaty of Ryswick which limited the size of its army. The Irish Brigade grew from its original three regiments which were named Mountcashel, Clare and Dillon to six regiments of infantry named Clare, Roth, Dillon, Lally, Berwick, Bulkleys after their commanders; and one regiment of cavalry named Fitzjames. Their numbers were augmented not only by the sons of Irish emigres born on French soil, but also by fresh recruits who kept coming from Ireland to escape oppression. The Brigade dispatched official recruiters to Clare and Galway and Cork to secretly spread the message of a life of dignity and adventure under the French flag. Occasionally, retired officers from the Brigade would return to Ireland to operate clandestine schools which taught military skills to young men to prepare them for service in the French officer corps. These recruiters and clandestine military educators faced death by hanging if they were discovered by the English overlords. There are no official figures or reliable documentation on how many Irishmen served in the Brigade during the 18th century. Estimates based on the number of troops exiled from Ireland in 1691, subsequent emigres leaving Ireland on their own or enlisted by the recruiters, and male children of these groups joining the Brigade range from 100,000 to 500,000.

The Battle of Fontenoy in 1744 was the only major engagement where all of the Irish Regiments fought together on the same field. The French used all of their Irish troops because they knew that an unusually large British force was opposing them. For the Irish, the battle was a chance to fight the historic foe and avenge the long-standing wrongs.

On the field of battle, the French were badly outnumbered. They the Irish Brigade in reserve under the command of Viscount Clare to counterattack if the French lines broke under an English assault. At midday, the Coldstream Guards advanced from the English side, firing their muskets with devastating accuracy. They soon penetrated the center of the French position to dominate the field. But then came the order for the Irish Brigade to attack. With cold visions of vengeance for the broken Treaty of Limerick, they fixed their bayonets and charged, shouting, "Remember Limerick and the treachery of the English!" A short while later, Irish steel and courage turned the tide of battle. The shattered remnants of the Coldstream Guards staggered back toward the English lines.

Henry Skrine, the leading English authority on Fontenoy, gave a clear picture of the Irish Brigade's boldness with the comment: "Among French infantry regiments those of the Irish Brigade stood first. Their desperate valor was a factor of great importance in our disaster." When the English king, George II, heard the news of his army's defeat because of the Irish, he muttered in despair, "Accursed be the laws which deprive me of such subjects".

In her poem about Fontenoy, Emily Lawless followed the Clare Regiment during the battle and captured the vision of vengeance which inspired such reckless courage from all of the soldiers of the Irish Brigade.

"In this hollow, star-pricked darkness, as in the sun's hot glare,
In sun-tide, in star tide, we starve for Clare!
Hark, yonder through the darkness on distant rat-tat-tat
The old foe stirs out there, God bless his soul for that!
The old foe musters strongly, he's coming on at last,
And Clare's Brigade may claim its own wherever blows fall fast.
Send us, ye western breezes, our full, our rightful share,
For Faith and Fame and Honor, and the ruined hearths of Clare!

If any regiment of the Irish Brigade deserved special recognition for their efforts, it was the Lally Regiment. It led the counterattack under the command of Colonel Thomas Arthur Lally, the French-born son of an Irish officer named Gerard O'Mullally who shortened his name to Lally after arriving in France with the Wild Geese. After the battle, Colonel Lally was presented to Louis XV, who immediately made him a brigadier general.

By the second half of the 18th century, the Irish Brigade was considered one of the best fighting units of the French army; and its officers were considered among the best as well. During the Seven Years War, this reputation for superiority led to an unfortunate end for General Lally. In 1856, because of his well-known hatred for the English, General Lally was chosen over other politically-connected senior officers to lead a French military expedition to India to challenge England's attempt to control the sub-continent. When he arrived in India, in the French colonial city of Pondicherry, Lally soon came into conflict with the corrupt civil administration and even some military officers who were enriching themselves by pilfering military supplies. After many travails in trying to fulfill his mission in India, Lally returned to France where he was brought to trial in 1766 on false charges and condemned to death. Lally was eventually exonerated by his son who exposed widespread corruption and incompetence throughout the French army during the reign of Louis XV. Not only was Lally's honor and reputation restored, but the Irish Brigade, his former command, was looked to as the model for the rest of the French army.

When Lally first arrived in Pondicherry, the corrupt administrators and officers offered him a part in their scheme. Lally angrily refused to join their criminal enterprise, and he told the administrators and officers that he was going to bring charges against them after he completed his mission. Lally was determined to try to fulfill his mission even though the corrupt officials, with the complicity of Paris bureaucrats, had stolen much of the supplies for the expedition. Besides weakening the expedition in this way, the officials refused to help Lally obtain maps of the area where he would be leading his troops or local native workers to help transport the expedition's military equipment and remaining supplies.

Although his expedition was severely weakened, Lally nonetheless set off on a two-hundred mile march along the humid east coast of India to the English-controlled city of Madras, a major trading center. Lally's force included his Regiment from the Irish Brigade as well as other regiments of the French army. By the time Lally's troops arrived at Madras, the English had enough warning to make defensive preparations. Although critically short of gunpowder and food, Lally laid siege to the city. But with the arrival of an English relief force, the French withdrew. After a number of battles and skirmishes with the English in which he was hampered by lack of supplies, Lally retreated to Pondicherry, which was then besieged by the pursuing English troops. Before long, Lally was forced to surrender to the English.

Lally's surrender at Pondicherry ended the French attempt to check English ambitions in India. The expedition led by Lally was a complete failure, and Lally was targeted for blame. When he returned to France, Lally was accused of conspiring with the English, despite his long record of outstanding service to France. In a hastily-arranged trial, Lally was found guilty of treason and executed soon after. Lally had become a scapegoat for the corrupt French officials in India and Paris who had seriously undermined his mission by stealing his supplies and refusing to help him.

The officials' corruption guaranteeing that Lally's expedition would fail and their role in the false charges brought against Lally would have gone undiscovered except for the determined efforts of Lally's son and his friend, the philosopher and historian, Francois de Voltaire. They caused a scandal by exposing the full extent of the corruption and incompetence which had set into the French army. When King Louis XV learned of the false charges brought by corrupt officials which led to Lally's execution, he exclaimed, "They have assassinated him!" He ordered a full investigation into the corruption and incompetence that he believed not only crippled Lally's expedition to India, but also was a major factor in France's defeat in the Seven Years War resulting in the loss of European and colonial territory.

The organization, training and military skills of the Irish Brigade were the model for the reforms demanded by King Louis XV when the decay of the French army became evident. During the next three decades, many Irish officers were promoted to general and assigned to other French units to supervise their reorganization. Their influence spread through the entire army, shaping the ideas about tactics and training methods followed by future French military leaders such as the Marquis de Lafayette and Napoleon Bonaparte.

After the Republican revolutionaries who stormed the Bastille in 1789 gained full control of the French government, an extremist wing of the movement instituted the Reign of Terror. Virtually everyone who had served the deposed King Louis XVI in any capacity was marked for execution on the guillotine. Yet despite the loyalty of most of the Irish Brigade to the monarchy, they suffered remarkably little during the Reign of Terror. In fact, the revolutionaries made special efforts to spare members of the Brigade—exemplified by an episode involving Father Donovan, the Brigade chaplain, shows. Father Donovan was imprisoned in the Bastille because he continued to offer spiritual counsel to any aristocrats seeking him out even though aristocrats were being hunted down and executed by the Republican extremists. Father Donovan was placed in a large cell containing many prisoners, including seven other members of the Irish Brigade.

As Father Donovan and the other prisoners were awaiting their fate, the Committee for Public Safety governing France after the revolutionaries deposed the monarchy issued an order that the lives of any native Irish imprisoned with other monarchists were to be spared in recognition of the Irish Brigade's contributions to French society. To insure that only Irish prisoners would go free, the jailers read the Committee's order in the Celtic-Irish language—which naturally came out very garbled. Nonetheless, Father Donovan, along with the seven other Irish prisoners, were able to figure out what the guards were saying, and thus stepped forward to be freed.

Although the Committee gave no reasons for its decision to spare any Irish men or women, it was probably motivated by international political considerations. In 1792, France was at war with England, Spain, Austria and Prussia which had formed an alliance which became known as the First Coalition to restore the monarchy to France. The new regime of France was encouraging republicans in Ireland who were themselves considering a revolution against the English overlords. The wholesale slaughter of Irish emigres in France would undermine republican support for France's Revolution in Ireland and thereby benefit England.

Immediately after the Revolution, the soldiers of the Irish Brigade faced a conflict between their loyalty to King Louis XVI, who had been their benefactor, and the Republican ideals of equality and democracy. Because most members of the Irish Brigade believed that their pledge to the King was inviolable, they sided with the monarchist forces still fighting the Republicans from the eastern provinces of France and the German states. These monarchist forces were too small to mount a major offensive against Republican France and were further hampered by a lack of funding. In 1792, the monarchist forces were disbanded, including the Irish Brigade, which by then had shrunk to the Regiments of Dillon, Berwick and Walsh. The final breakup of the Brigade came at a formal ceremony conducted by the Count de Provence, who became King Louis XVIII after the restoration of the Bourbon monarchy in 1816. He presented a banner to the three remaining regiments bearing an Irish Harp and the legend "Semper et Ubique Fidelis—1692-1792."

A few of the veterans of the Brigade who had been promoted to general prior to the Revolution sided with the Republicans. Because of the oppression visited on Ireland by the English aristocrats, they strongly sympathized with the plight of the peasantry and the bourgeoisie in France. When the extremely radical Committee for Public Safety collapsed in 1794 and was replaced by a five member Directory in 1795, many Irish generals found themselves in positions of great influence under the new government. Their sudden rise was due not only to their own talents, but to the shortage of experienced officers in France in the wake of executions and emigration during the Reign of Terror.

The most popular and influential of the Irish generals serving in the army of the Republic was Charles Kilmaine. He had come to France in 1765 as a student, but saw that he had greater opportunity for adventure as a soldier than as a scholar. After training as a junior officer in the Irish Brigade, he was part of General Rochambeau's invasion of Georgia and unsuccessful siege of Savannah to support George Washington during the American War for Independence. During France's military campaigns in northern Italy, he achieved the rank of general. Because the continued survival of the newly-formed French Republic depended on the success of its soldiers in thwarting the nations who sought to restore the Bourbon monarchy, experienced generals like Kilmaine were extremely influential among the members of the Directory. His principal rival in determining the shape that the military strategy of France should take was Napoleon Bonaparte, a young general who had achieved great fame for leading a successful campaign against the Austrians in northern Italy. Both Kilmaine and Bonaparte advocated taking the offensive in the war against England which had begun in 1792. However, they differed as to which kind of offensive campaign would be most effective. Kilmaine favored striking directly against England with a cross-channel invasion. As an alternative to this, he called for an invasion of Ireland which would stimulate an Irish rebellion against England. Bonaparte, on the other hand, believed that the best way to force England to sue for peace would be to attack its overseas empire.

Because both Kilmaine's and Bonaparte's strategies corresponded to the standard military doctrine for French forces established with the reorganization of the army in 1763 emphasizing aggressive operations, the Directory was disposed to approve of offensive strategies. The Directory opted for Kilmaine's strategy of invading England—and it ordered the formation of the *armée d'Angleterre* to accomplish this. Bonaparte was given command of the *armée*, with Kilmaine appointed as his assistant. Although Kilmaine's strategy was the one chosen by the Directory and an army was being prepared to execute it, Kilmaine, with the support of other Irish generals, pressed for swifter action against England. One of the Irish generals who supported Kilmaine was Henri Clarke; Clarke virtually ran the Ministry of War, although his official title was Chief of the Topography and Geography department.

The continued appeals from their highly-regarded Irish generals persuaded the Directory to send a fifteen thousand man contingent of the *armée d'Angleterre* to Ireland in 1796 under the command of General Hoche. But foul weather prevented a landing, and the soldiers returned to France. Bonaparte seized the opportunity presented by this failure to convince the Directory that the *armée d'Angleterre* should invade Egypt. The Directory agreed and sent a large portion of the troops to Egypt with Bonaparte, where they met disaster a battle against British forces. Kilmaine took command of the portion of the *armée d'Angleterre* remaining in France, and in 1798, the Directory allowed Kilmaine to make a second attempt at an Irish invasion. A small unit under General Humbert did land in Ireland, but the main force under the Irish emigre general Hardy was intercepted by British ships in Lough Swilly and captured.

Although the Irish generals were often not successful in the field of battle during the period of the Directory, their constant seizure of the initiative kept France's enemies off balance. The First Coalition against France collapsed in 1795, and only England refused to make peace with republican France. Because England could not be certain where the armies of France would appear next and had to guard the coasts of both its homeland and its far-flung empire it could not mount an offensive directly against France. The French military strategy gave the Directory and the republicans of France time to consolidate the sweeping political and social changes initiated by the Revolution.

The contribution of the Irish Brigade to French society was not limited to its example and successes in military affairs. During the 18th century, the Brigade was like a beacon which attracted Ireland's most talented people. Denied educational, economic or professional opportunities in their own land by oppressive English rule, many Irish saw the Brigade as offering the chance to pursue their desires in these areas. The Brigade was always looking for new Irish recruits to maintain its strength when its ranks were reduced from retirements, battle casualties and resignations. After joining the Brigade for a brief tour of service, many Irish emigres left for civilian life, where they became bankers, doctors, scholars, and merchants throughout France. In this way, they and their descendants had an influence on all areas of French society through the generations.

Because of the Irish Brigade, Irish emigres had a greater influence on French society than any other in Europe. This influence was broad and steady—and continues in myriad ways down to today.

SMUGGLERS AND ADMIRALS

During the 18th century, many Irish emigres in France were attracted to seafaring as an opportunity to gain great wealth. Some of these Irish mariners operated merchant ships, carrying goods between France and its colonies. Trade with other European nations and their colonies, however, was often prohibited by restrictive trade laws and taxes imposed by those nations. To trade with these closed markets, Irish merchants in France often became smugglers who used fast sloops to outrun foreign naval vessels and land their cargos in secluded coves. Other Irish emigres joined the French navy, which was considered the finest in the world for much of the 18th century.

One Irish smuggler in France who stands out is Anthony Walsh. Although he was born in Nantes in the early 18th century, he was very familiar with the rocky coastline of western Ireland from sailing on his father's sloop during smuggling runs when he was a boy. From these trips, young Anthony Walsh learned the business from the bottom up. On their voyages to Ireland, the Walsh family usually carried wine, molasses and rum. Sometimes they also carried a priest trained in France who was returning to Ireland to preach to Catholics in secret. On the return voyage, they carried Irish wool and butter to France. With cunning and skilled seamanship, they would avoid British naval vessels patrolling the coastline; and they often dropped anchor in secluded coves in western Ireland.

Smugglers like the Walshes had become an important aspect of French commercial activity because of English Navigation Acts prohibited trade in certain goods in order to protect products from English colonies and manufacturers in England. For instance, the Acts prohibited the import of French molasses and rum into any English territory to eliminate foreign competition for the molasses and rum from English plantations in the colony of Jamaica. To protect the supply of wool for the textile manufacturers in England, the Acts prohibited the export of wool from Ireland. Because of the smuggling enterprises of Walsh and other Irish emigres, the French were able to buy and sell goods in Irish and English markets that were legally closed to them by the Navigation Acts. Because of the important benefits of smuggling for their economy, the French regarded smuggling as practically an ordinary import-export business.

After Anthony Walsh inherited the family business, he expanded it by adding more French products to export. One new product he began smuggling to Ireland was wines from vineyards owned by other Irish emigres. Among these were La Hourange from the Bordeaux vineyard owned by John O'Byrne and Chateau Lagrange from the Bordeaux vineyards of the Brown family. When Richard Hennessy opened a distillery to make cognac after retiring from the Irish Brigade, Walsh was one of the first smugglers to carry this product to Ireland. Because of Walsh's activity, the Irish-owned vineyards prospered. When many Frenchmen who owned vineyards saw the success the Irish owners were having, they wanted Walsh to smuggle their wines to the foreign markets.

In the 1730's, Walsh decided to take his business to a new level by joining the ranks of the French privateers; who by royal approval were permitted to capture merchant vessels of the enemies of France. After being granted permission by King Louis XV, Walsh sent relatives of his to the town of St. Malo on the Normandy coast to build a brig swift enough to stay out of the range of the cannons of an English warship, yet strong enough to carry the arms and crew to capture a merchant vessel. When this ship he named *Duteillay* was completed, Walsh sailed the waters around both England and Ireland preying on English merchant ships.

For France of the 18th century, privateers were a valuable political and commercial asset. Because the English navy was so large and powerful, the smaller French navy had difficulty protecting its ports and coastline. To augment the French navy, enterprising privateers like Anthony Walsh intercepted English merchant ships for plunder and deprived England of the goods on board. In addition, privateers provided a means for taking direct action against the expanding English empire encroaching on French colonies in Canada and India. Many of the generals, diplomats and councilors to the king felt that diplomatic maneuvering alone would not halt English expansion and recommended confrontation both on land and on the sea. During times of peace, privateers could continue to challenge England with minimal political repercussions.

The successful activity of the Irish emigres in both smuggling and legitimate shipping to the French colonies encouraged other French merchants and adventurers to enter the trade. This reduced France's dependence on Dutch and British merchant ships that carried most French exports. During the Seven Years War from 1756 to 1763, the growing fleet of Irish merchant vessels proved vital to the economic survival of France. With the defeat of both the Atlantic and the Mediterranean squadrons of the French fleet by the English navy, Britain had achieved overwhelming command of the seas. After these disasters, with France no longer able to protect its merchant vessels and its major ports blockaded by English warships, overseas trade fell precipitously to about one-sixth of its pre-war level. Also, the French colonies were cut off from financial and military aid. During this bleak time for France, only the privateers with their small, swift ships could successfully run the English blockades. The merchant fleets built by the Irish emigres like the Walshes and the MacCarthys were instrumental in preventing the complete collapse of trade and communication with France's overseas empire. During the Seven Years War, many Irish merchants became very wealthy by supplying the sugar and spices that became scarce in France. The fortunes they made enabled them to enter other fields of business. The Routledges of Dunkirk were one such merchant family. They used their wealth acquired by providing scarce goods to France during wartime to establish a banking house in the 1760's which financed many French manufacturing ventures. In so doing, the Routledge bank played a part in laying the foundations for the Industrial Revolution in France.

The most influential of the firms engaged in both banking and shipping was Waters & Sons. It had been operating in Paris since the late 1600's. During the reign of Louis XIV from 1643 to 1715, costly wars against the

League of Augsburg, the War of Spanish succession and lavish architectural projects like the Palace at Versailles kept the royal coffers low. The Waters family agreed to finance the King so he could support his armies and continue his extravagant ways. But they discovered that a monarch can easily repudiate a debt shortly after Louis XV became king in 1715, and the firm entered bankruptcy. Waters & Sons was not able to recoup from this until they resumed their very profitable smuggling ventures during the Seven Years War.

Although the Irish emigre shipping firms prospered in 18th-century France, most of the reign of Louis XV—from his accession to the throne in 1715 to the conclusion of the Seven Years War in 1763—was a period of general decline in the French navy. Because service as a naval officer was prestigious, it attracted aristocrats even though they had scant enthusiasm for a life at sea and no interest at all in the day-to-day tasks of a ship's captain. In addition, there were an insufficient number of ships to patrol French coastal waters while simultaneously protecting France's overseas empire. French naval vessels were frequently defeated when they faced the better-trained and aggressively-led crews of British men o' war.

The relatively few Irish emigres who became naval officers demanded a higher degree of capability from their crews than was common in the French navy at this time. Like their counterparts in the Irish Brigade, they stressed training and aggressive tactics. During the War of Austrian Succession, Jean-Baptiste Macnemara achieved one of the few French naval victories of the conflict. He had been born in Ireland as John MacNemara and was one of the few children to accompany the Wild Geese to France in 1691. In 1707, he entered the navy as a midshipman, and rose through the ranks. In 1745, commanding the ship *Invincible*, he attacked four English warships, putting them all to flight. For this and his other exploits, he became known as one of the best tacticians in the French navy.

In 1763, when the French army came under scrutiny in the corruption scandal after the execution of Lally, the navy was also called to task for its poor showing during the past two decades. The number of ships was increased and the aggressive tactics used by Jean-Baptiste Macnemara were widely studied by midshipmen and officers in an effort to improve their performance in battle. Although the reforms were not sufficient to allow the French to wrest control of the seas away from the English, better training increased the effectiveness of the fleet. This was demonstrated during naval engagements in support of the American War for Independence when French ships were frequently able to defeat English men o'war. In the waters off North America, Jean-Baptiste's nephew Claude matched his uncle's famous exploit by capturing four British privateers and a 28-gun frigate while in command of a ship of the line named *Frippone*.

The influence of Irish emigres and their descendants on the French navy continued into the 19th and 20th centuries. During the Napoleonic Wars, Armand de MacKau (McCoy) gained fame for his daring exploits at sea as much as for his fiery affair with Napoleon's sister, Elisa. After the Bourbon Restoration of the monarchy in 1816, he achieved the rank of full Admiral, one of only thirteen French naval officers ever to do so. Later, he became the Minister of Marine and began to guide the French navy through its difficult transition from sail to steam, which required not only new ship designs, but also a complete change in battle tactics. In World War I, Commandant O'Byrne conducted a daring submarine raid on the Austro-Hungarian naval base at Pula on the Adriatic coast of Croatia. Because the Austro-Hungarians feared losing more ships to submarines, they increased their anti-submarine defenses and kept their vessels in port for the remainder of the war.

As with Spain, the maritime activities of numbers of Irish emigres and their descendants in France benefitted their adopted land in diverse ways from naval prowess to commercial growth. With their practical abilities, openness to new knowledge and search for adventure and heroic activities, they readily took to seafaring once they realized that it offered a palace for them in their adopted country.

IRISH SCHOLARS

The Penal Laws enacted by England during the early 18th century deprived the Irish of a right to Catholic education by making the operation of an Irish school or university a crime. But no act of a distant and remote Parliament in London could undo Irish desire for learning. Many young men and women of Ireland emigrated to France to get an education denied to them in their homeland. Because employment in law and government was forbidden to them in Ireland, most of them stayed in their adopted land to follow the careers that they had chosen.

The large majority of Irish going to Europe to receive an education in the early 1700's attended the Irish Colleges which were associated with major universities in Paris, Nantes, Toulouse, Bordeaux, Rouen and other cities throughout France. The largest of these Colleges was in Paris attached to the University of Paris. The first Irish students to study in Paris were six seminarians attending the Collège de Montaigu. They arrived in 1578, sponsored by John Lee, a prosperous merchant of Waterford. By 1605, there were enough Irish students attending different Colleges at the University of Paris for them to petition the University for an Irish College to be attached to the University's Collège des Lombards. The petition was refused. Despite this, Irish students came to Paris in increasing numbers in the early 1600's.

It wasn't until after the Irish students gained widespread attention for their position in the Jansenist controversy causing strife within the Catholic Church that they were finally permitted to form an Irish College in Paris. In an incident which became known as l'Affaire des Hibernois, twenty-seven Irish students signed a declaration denouncing Jansenism, a position taken by the Dutch theologian Cornelius Jansen that the Catholic Church had strayed from St. Augustine's doctrines of the 5th century which had always been claimed to be the foundations of the Church. In the days when the Catholic Church was still trying to stop the spread of Protestantism, Jansenism was seen as a serious threat by the Church hierarchy, including the Pope, and by the secular rulers, such as Louis XIV in France, who were Catholic and wanted their societies to remain Catholic. By the 1600's, the Catholic Church no longer emphasized Augustine's doctrine that divine intervention in the form of grace was essential for a person to achieve salvation. Another fault of the Catholic Church according to Jansen was its neglect of Augustine's idea of predestination, which the Church viewed as resembling the tenet of predestination which was the foundation of the Protestant sect of Calvinism.

The twenty-seven students signing the declaration were quickly joined by many other Irish students in denouncing Jansenism. This prompted students and faculty at many other universities in France to take positions in support of or in opposition to Jansenism. To try to abate the tension between the two sides of the religious conflict, the Academic Council of the University of Paris accused the Irish students of sophomoric insolence for passing judgement on complex and subtle theological matters that even theologians and bishops continued to have differences on. The Academic Council told the students they would be expelled unless they recanted their denunciation of Jansenism.

The students refused to recant. In a measure to avoid expulsion, they appealed the decision of the Academic Council to the Paris City Council. By this time, the Jansenist controversy had spread beyond the universities to the population and secular authorities, including the King and his ministers. So the City Council was familiar with the controversy and had an interest in it. The City Council issued an order that no action was to be taken against the students. Since the Academic Council could not expel them, it did take the action of appointing four doctors of theology to watch the obstinate Irish students for deviations from Church doctrine in their statements and writings by which the Council might bring charges against them.

The Jansenist controversy continued to grow, causing disturbance and concern in the Church and in many cities and regions of France. In 1653, Pope Innocent X tried to put an end to the controversy by issuing a Papal Bull titled *Cum Occasione* denouncing Jansenism. With this Bull written by the Pope, the Catholic Church officially took the position the Irish students had taken in 1643. The controversy had become heated, however, with each side becoming so intransigent that it did not die down for another century.

In recognition of the Irish students' opposition to the challenge of Jansenism, King Louis XIV granted a new petition to form an Irish College in 1677. In a royal edict, the King granted the students the right "to live in full possession of the Collège des Lombards and to enjoy all the privileges, rights and exemptions which colleges founded in favor of the native French enjoy." The Collège des Lombards had gotten its name from the region in Italy which sent priests to study at the College when it was established in 1330. Ignatius Loyola and Francis Xavier were students there in the 16th century. During the 17th century, Irish seminarians made up a large majority of its students. The Collège des Lombards became known as the Irish College in 1685, a few years after Louis XIV had granted the College to the Irish students. A decade later, in reaction to the increasingly oppressive policies of the English in Ireland, the Irish College changed its rules to admit lay students. Recent Acts of the English Parliament prohibited Irish Catholics from establishing universities, and they were denied admission to Protestant universities.

This change in the student body led to a change in the Colleges' curriculum. Secular subjects were added. In a short time, law and medicine replaced theology and other religious studies as the primary fields of study. In broadening its curriculum, the Irish College soon attracted students from throughout France and other parts of Europe, as well as Ireland. By 1730, the Irish College of Paris was a truly democratic and basically secular institution. It drew Irish emigres with diverse backgrounds from all parts of Europe to pursue studies in many fields. Irish attended the College in such numbers that an unknown French satirist was moved to remark, "with hungry looks and minds on whimsies nursed, gaunt troops of Irish through the door burst." Perhaps he had in mind the off-duty members of the Irish Brigade who attended classes at the College to learn more about the sciences and the humanities. The varied student body prompted the College to coin the slogan "the laymen will fight, the ecclesiastics will pray" to support their efforts to raise funds for the school from the French people.

During the 18th century, the Irish College in Paris and the others founded in Nantes, Toulouse, Bordeaux and Rouen became important centers of Irish society in France. They were places where emigres could visit a community where the Irish tongue was spoken and many of the customs of their homeland were maintained. In addition, some of the scholars teaching at the Irish Colleges wrote books to help Irish emigres acquire knowledge about their heritage. While teaching at the Irish College in Paris in 1728, Hugh MacCurtin wrote a widely-used Irish grammar book titled *The Elements of The Irish Language*. The Irish College also sponsored the printing of the first *English-Irish Dictionary* in 1732. Thirty-five years later the volume was revised and renamed the *Irish-English Dictionary*. In 1743, a retired chaplain from the Irish

Brigade named Abbè MacGeoghegan wrote a three-volume *History of Ireland* while residing at the College.

The Irish College in Paris and other French cities took the lead in education that reflected the ideas, perspectives and inquisitiveness of the Enlightenment. The traditional openness of the Irish to different ideas and their investigation of these ideas by inquiry and debate had an affinity with the rationalism and the critical spirit which marked the Enlightenment. The new scientific studies, political and social philosophies, and the emergence of fields such as economics complemented the interest in medicine, the practical tendency, the conception of community and other long-standing aspects of Irish culture. The movement of the Enlightenment also appealed to the Irish sense of the inter-connection of intellectual concepts and practical skills.

Besides the general role of the Irish Colleges in presenting ideas and subjects of the Enlightenment, there were a number of Irish individuals who are recognized as leading figures of the movement for the originality of their work. Among them was Richard Cantillon. For his essay *On The Nature of General Commerce* published posthumously in 1755, Cantillon was given the title Father of Political Economy. A banker in Paris, Cantillon and his business partners had each made a fortune by speculating in the shares of the Mississippi Company which had been organized under the direction of John Law to exploit the resources in French territory along the Mississippi River. In exchange an exclusive right to these resources from the French government, the Mississippi Company agreed to issue shares in the Company as payment of government debts to bankers and other creditors of the government. This so severely depleted the finances of the Company that it went bankrupt—but not before Cantillon and the other principle shareholders had sold their shares at a large profit. Although this venture profited Cantillon, he saw how the monopolistic policies of mercantilism followed by most European nations of the time caused the collapse of the Mississippi Company. He came to believe that prohibitive tariffs, control of exports, and other means of governmental oversight and control of a nation's economy hampered commerce and the efficient development of colonial resources. In his essay, Cantillon outlined an economic system in which the state did not interfere with natural economic forces.

Influenced by Cantillon's essay, French economic policy-makers gradually eliminated tariffs and other trade restrictions to bring about economic activity resembling the free-market system of today.

In the field of medicine, Gerard Fitzgerald's study and treatment of uterine ailments met with indifference from his fellow physicians. In the late 18th century, medical problems relating to women in particular were considered best left to midwives by all physicians. Fitzgerald, however, believed that ailments particular to women should not be excluded from the new methods of diagnosis and treatment devised in the 18th century. Despite the indifference of his colleagues, Fitzgerald persisted with his study and treatment of uterine ailments. He was a graduate of both the Irish College where he studied liberal arts, and the medical school of the University of Montpelier. Eventually, however, his treatments for women were adopted, and Fitzgerald was joined in his study of women's medical problems.

Education for women was another aspect of the Enlightenment in which Irish emigres were in the forefront. Accustomed as they were to the general equality between the sexes, Irish emigre women felt they should have the opportunity to get an education even through women in France could not attend universities. This proscription included the Irish colleges as well. Women could be educated by private tutors, and at some rare schools operated by nuns, such as the Poor Clare school in Dunkirk and the Visitation schools in several French cities. To increase the scope of opportunities for women to get a formal education, a few Irish emigre women founded independent schools. The faculty of these institutions was mostly nuns who had left Ireland after the Banishment Act in 1697 required all Catholic clergy to emigrate. The largest of these schools for women was in Ypres, run by the Irish Dames of Ypres, an offshoot of the Benedictine order. It was established by the emigres Alexia Legge and Mary Ryan in 1682, and enjoyed the sponsorship of the wife of Louis XIV, Mary of Modena. The school of the Dames of Ypres taught French as well as Irish students and was a model for other educational institutions in France for women. Although formal education for women was introduced into France in the 17th century from the efforts of Irish women, it wasn't until the 19th century that French universities allowed women to enroll as students.

The Irish educational institutions in France benefitted both the Irish emigres and French society. Because education in the sciences, theology, medicine and philosophy was denied the Irish in their homeland during the 18th century, the Irish Colleges in France became primary centers for Irish intellectual achievement. The education they provided enabled the Irish to contribute to the Enlightenment in the fields of engineering, medicine and political science. The Irish Colleges also allowed an Irish university faculty to remain in existence during a time of severe oppression in Ireland. Many of these faculty members returned to Ireland after the Penal Laws prohibiting Irish education were relaxed in the 1790's to found schools such as St. Patrick's College at Maynooth in 1796. The Irish Colleges in France continued the Irish tradition of education during a time when Catholic education was prohibited in Ireland and benefitted French society by providing educational opportunities to emigres who became French soldiers, diplomats and merchants.

PRESIDENT OF THE THIRD REPUBLIC

Of all the Irish emigres and their descendants, none had more impact on the history of France than Marshall Marie-Edmé-Patrice de MacMahon. In 1878, he became the first President of the Third Republic of France. He came from an Irish-French family that could trace its ancestry back to Mahan, the older brother of Brian Boru and founder of the clan. His grandfather came to France in the 1740's to study medicine at the Irish College in Paris and the medical school at Rheims, where he became a protégée of Jean-Baptiste de Morey, a counselor of the King. After de Morey's death in 1748, he married de Morey's widow and changed his name to honor his benefactor, becoming Jean-Baptiste de MacMahon. His son Maurice, Marshall MacMahon's father, was made a Count by Louis XVIII after the Bourbon restoration in 1816 for his loyalty to the monarchy.

Patrick MacMahon, as the Marshall preferred to be called, served in the armies of Louis Napoleon, President of the Second French Republic who dissolved the Republic in 1851 by proclaiming himself Emperor. A few years later, MacMahon distinguished himself in the Crimean War, and eventually he rose to the rank of Marshall.

At the outbreak of the Franco-Prussian War in 1870, MacMahon was placed in command of an army corps stationed in the city of Sedan. He was given orders from Louis Napoleon to hold Sedan against advancing Prussian forces. In ordinary circumstances, the commander of an army corps would have free rein to devise his own strategy to accomplish the assigned objective. But Louis Napoleon, who had by then proclaimed himself Emperor, was in Sedan to lead his army—and he fancied himself a masterful tactician, the equal of his renowned uncle, Napoleon Bonaparte. Louis Napoleon ordered MacMahon's corps to stand fast around the city, fighting a defensive battle against the advancing Prussian forces. Despite these orders, MacMahon did not contemplate a static defense of the city. When he saw his subordinates ordering their troops to dig trenches he shouted, "What, entrenching! But I do not intend to shut myself up. I mean to maneuver."

For MacMahon, maneuver and ambush was not only a part of his heritage as a member of an Irish emigre military family, but it was also doctrine taught at the French military academy at St. Cyr. But before MacMahon could convince Louis Napoleon to change his orders and allow his troops to take the offensive and engage the advancing enemy at its weakest point, the Prussians struck. From three sides, they bombarded his position using an advanced type of rifled artillery. In one of the first salvos, MacMahon was severely wounded and turned his command over to his subordinate, General Ducrot. After a valiant defense and frightful carnage, Sedan fell to the Prussians. When the Emperor Louis Napoleon was captured by the Prussians, a revolution broke out in Paris deposing him—and the French government collapsed.

Patrick MacMahon recovered from his wounds, and the people of France regarded him as one of the few heros of the disastrous war. When an Assembly was elected to write a new constitution for France, its representatives asked him to be President of a provisional government. MacMahon accepted the position despite the enormous difficulties he would face as President during this period of political instability. The vast majority of people, including MacMahon himself, wanted a restoration of the Bourbon monarchy. But a few years before, a violent minority had rioted in the streets of Paris, calling for the formation of a new Republic. Although the Parisian rioters had been put down by the military, extremist republicans continued to threaten violent insurrection if the monarchy was restored. MacMahon could maintain internal order in France only by balancing the competing monarchist and republican forces. He offered compromise to delay militant activists on both sides while the constitutional delegates bickered and feuded. After the Assembly finally came to an agreement in 1875, the Third Republic of France was born.

The new government had two bodies, a Chamber of Deputies and a Senate; Deputies were elected by the people, while Senators were appointed by provincial officials. Both the Chamber of Deputies and the Senate would then elect a President for a seven-year term. The President would appoint a Premier, subject to final approval by only the Chamber of Deputies. The Chamber of Deputies and the Senate overwhelmingly voted for MacMahon for President. This system satisfied the republicans while the monarchists felt that a President with wide powers was very close to the concept of a king, and if France should agree to restore the Bourbon monarchy, MacMahon would not hesitate to step aside. MacMahon's Irish heritage was certainly a key factor in his open support for a Bourbon restoration. Since arriving in France more than a century and a half before, the Irish had often behaved as if they were in fosterage to the kings of France. MacMahon himself bore the title Duc de Magenta which had been granted for his battlefield exploits, although it had little meaning in the new Republic.

The first general elections under the new Constitution were held early in 1876. The new members elected to the Chamber of Deputies were strongly republican in their political beliefs. When MacMahon nominated Premiers who were conservative monarchists, the new Chamber of Deputies refused to accept them, as was their right under the new constitution. They also objected to the expansive powers granted to the President under the terms of the Constitution, which included the right to dissolve the Chamber of Deputies and call for a new election. They feared that MacMahon could easily use his authority as President and his prestige as a battlefield hero to muster enough military support to crown a king with or without their approval. In 1879, the Chamber of Deputies demanded that MacMahon dismiss a number of monarchist officials he had appointed to government posts. Rather than risk the political battle that would further polarize the republican and monarchist factions if he refused to comply with the Chamber's demand, MacMahon resigned in disgust. It was a crushing blow to monarchist aspirations. The Chamber of Deputies and the Senate never again elected a strong President who would exercise the full authority granted to the office under the Constitution.

Although MacMahon's Presidency was turbulent, his prestige and influence provided a degree of stability during the critical first years of the Third Republic. The members of the Chamber of Deputies focused on their dispute with MacMahon rather than on their differences with each other. Once he left office and the position of President became almost completely ceremonial, the Deputies began four decades of bickering which led to crisis after crisis for the French government. Nevertheless, they remained committed to the form of democracy embodied in the constitution that Patrick MacMahon helped implement when he was President of the Third Republic.

At the time of his resignation in 1879, Patrick MacMahon was seventy-one years old. He retired to his family chateau at Sully, a 12th-century castle in the Saône Valley which had been enlarged into a country manor. After his death in 1893, the French people honored him by naming a major boulevard in Paris after him, the Rue de MacMahon. The Third Republic of France that he helped guide through its turbulent birth lasted until 1940 when it collapsed after the Nazi invasion of France.

From the time Columbanus founded his monastery in the 6th century until MacMahon served as President of the Third Republic in the 19th century, Irish wanderers have played a part in all areas of French society—from religion to politics, from education to military service, from medicine to commerce. Even today, at the close of the 20th century, the Irish College in Paris and many monasteries founded by Irish monks are still active. There is no country in Europe where the wanderers had a more extensive and continuous influence than France.

CHAPTER 8

The Irish in Portugal

"Let us all gather here and fight in the service of God and to defend our lands, for it is right that we should have a good understanding and that we should help one another for that purpose."

—Red Hugh O'Donnell, address urging the Irish residing in Portugal to prepare for an invasion of Ireland, 1605

IRISH MERCHANTS OF LISBON

The expanding business opportunities arising from the extensive Portuguese explorations during the close of the Middle Ages drew Irish merchants to Lisbon. Throughout the 15th century, Portuguese explorers sailed far into the Atlantic, discovering the Azores, the Canary Islands and the Cape Verde Islands. They also sailed south along the African coast, rounding the Cape of Good Hope in 1488 and reaching India in 1497. From trade outposts in these newly-discovered lands, exotic goods flowed into Lisbon; where they were then distributed to the growing market for them in France, Spain, England, Italy and other parts of Europe. The Irish merchants became involved in this 15th-century trade, and they prospered. With their success, the merchants set up permanent operations in Lisbon, and encouraged other Irish to come to Lisbon to start businesses or take part in the adventure of Portuguese exploration. After the Protestant Reformation of the 16th century, Portugal was even more attractive to the Irish because it was a Catholic country where they could freely practice their religion after leaving Ireland to escape the English laws suppressing it. The emigres concentrated in Lisbon, which was the only major city and area of worthwhile commercial activity in the small country of Portugal at the time. As their numbers in Lisbon grew and their wealth increased, the influence of the Irish in Portugal also grew.

The blossoming relationship between the Irish and the Portuguese at the beginning of the early modern period was not an extension of a medieval tradition, as it was in Spain or France. Prior to 1143, when Portugal gained its independence from the Kingdom of Castile, it was considered a province of Spain by everyone in Europe, including the Irish. During the Middle Ages when wandering Irish monks came to Spain, few of them actually lived in the territory that would eventually become Portugal. In the 1400's, Irish merchants became interested in Portugal as the Portuguese built a large fleet of ships for exploration and trade under the leadership of Prince Henry, called "the Navigator" for his keen interest in maritime affairs. In Galway, Cork and Waterford, the sight of Portuguese ships was common. Irish merchants purchased the Madeira wine and blocks of cork that the Portuguese crews offloaded onto the quays. Then the Irish paid the ship's captain for the transport of their own butter, wool and beef to the vessel's next port of call.

As Portugal discovered new lands and established colonies around the world, Lisbon grew into a bustling commercial port. It attracted a polyglot assortment of adventurers and merchants from all over Europe. A record exists from 1462 granting permission to reside in Lisbon to Richard May, Geoffrey Galway, and the brothers John and Dominic Lynch, all born in Ireland. They were merchants acting as agents for Irish importers, most likely in the wine trade. Some of the Irish in Lisbon also entered royal service because they had impressed the Portuguese rulers with their learning. In the 1450's, Prince Henry sent a captured African lion to Galway as a gift for an unnamed Irish retainer who had left the Prince's service and returned to his homeland.

By the middle of the 16th century, there was a thriving Irish community in Lisbon. Because all of the goods from the vast Portuguese Empire had to first pass through Lisbon on their way to other European ports, Irish merchants could eliminate the need for a Portuguese broker by establishing permanent offices in the city. Usually they sent their younger sons to Portugal to act as agents for the family import-export business. These Irish agents bought spices from Asia, teak wood from the Amazon Basin and other exotic goods, and arranged for their shipment not only to Ireland, but also to other European ports for distribution throughout the continent. Lisbon also provided commercial opportunities for Irish emigres who had only limited capital. A relatively small investment in a Portuguese overseas voyage could reap an enormous profit if the ship successfully returned laden with goods from the Far East or the Americas.

The Irish merchants residing in Portugal became increasingly important to the country's economy after the Protestant Reformation of the 16th century. Since the Irish remained Catholic, they were acceptable in Portuguese society. But because the Irish were technically English subjects, they could trade more easily with the Protestant nations of Europe. This was crucial for Portugal's economic relationship with England and the Netherlands. As England prospered, its demand for Madeira wine, spices from the Orient and other items from Portuguese colonies increased sharply. The Dutch cities of Antwerp and Bruges were also vital to Portuguese commerce because they provided access to the markets of central Europe for imports from the Portuguese colonies. During times of war with Portugal, the English and Dutch ports were closed to Portuguese ships. Even during times of peace, religious and economic rivalries could prevent Portuguese merchants from selling their goods in important northern European markets. But as "Englishmen", the Irish of Lisbon were readily granted permission to dock and offload their cargos in the ports of England and other Protestant nations.

Like their counterparts in Spain, France, and the other countries of Europe, the Irish merchants living in Portugal were never isolated from the people and culture around them. They intermarried with the Portuguese, weaving an intricate pattern of family relationships. One series of marriages linked Christopher Columbus with Patrick Sarsfield, the leader of the Wild Geese. Columbus married a Portuguese woman when he lived in Lisbon to try to interest King Joao II of Portugal in his project for sailing the Atlantic. When he moved on to the court of Aragon in pursuit of his dream, he left his children behind. His descendant Catalina Colón, as the surname Columbus was spelled in Portuguese, married James FitzJames Stuart in the early 1700's, the illegitimate son of Patrick Sarsfield's widow, Lady Honoré Sarsfield.

The Irish merchants in Lisbon also took part in the Great Armada launched by Spain in 1588 to invade England. Eight years before, the death of King Sebastao without an heir left Philip II of Spain with a claim to the Portuguese throne since he was Sebastao's cousin. He quickly annexed Portugal, making it a part of the Spanish Empire. The change of monarchs and political structure had little impact on the business affairs of the Irish merchants living in Portugal. When the call went out for pilots and interpreters to sail with the Armada, many Irish merchants volunteered. Spanish records listed the master gunner John Lynch, the mariners William Brown and Cahill MacConnor among the Irish who sailed on the flagship of the Duke of Medina Sidonia, the commander of the expedition. As seamen and merchants, the emigres were familiar with both English and Irish waters. Although their native tongue was Irish, many were fluent in the English language, which would be useful for the planned Spanish invasion of England. With the addition of the services of the Irish emigres in Lisbon, Philip II felt that his preparations to invade England were complete. Few of the emigres could have guessed that the mighty Spanish fleet would be turned back by the English navy. Ironically, a few of the Irish volunteers found themselves shipwrecked in Ireland when a storm drove some of the ships of the Armada onto the rocks of the Irish coastline.

At the time of the Flight of the Irish Earls in 1605, Portugal's fortunes were waning. The land was a province of Spain, distinguishable from other Spanish provinces only by the dialect spoken by its inhabitants. Many of the other nations of Europe had established colonies around the world, depriving Portugal of its virtual monopoly over the exotic spices and goods from its Asian and South American colonies. Yet Lisbon remained an important Atlantic port for distribution of goods from Portugal's Asian and American colonies.

Despite the ability of the Irish to freely move between both the Protestant and Catholic marketplaces of Europe, they were not numerous enough to stem Portugal's gradual economic decline in the 17th century. The Irish merchants of Lisbon did, however, help to keep alive a Portuguese tradition of international commerce which proved essential to the economy of the tiny nation when it regained its independence in 1640.

THE IRISH DIPLOMAT

In 1640, a group of Portuguese nobles staged a coup d'etat in Lisbon and arrested the Spanish governor. They then declared Portugal to be once again an independent nation and invited the Duke of Bragança to reign as King Joao IV. Spain did not immediately challenge the revolution. At the time, the province of Cataluña was also in rebellion, and Spain did not have the military forces to fight two wars on its home territory. So by default, Portugal achieved its independence.

The task facing King Joao IV was formidable. After sixty years of Spanish rule, Portugal no longer had an army, a navy or even an efficient method of collecting taxes. At any moment, Spain might resolve its dispute with Cataluña and march its army towards Portugal. To be prepared for this possibility, the new king made each region responsible for raising a military force and collecting revenues for the central government in Lisbon. Concerned that the forces he was raising might not be equipped or trained in time to challenge any Spanish invasion, in 1648, King Joao sent an Irish priest, Father Daniel O'Daly, O.P., on a secret mission to Ireland to try to recruit Irish soldiers with experience in fighting the English to form the nucleus of the Portuguese army.

Daniel O'Daly was a well-known Irish emigre figure in Lisbon, where he was known by his Portuguese name of Frei Domingo de Rosario. He was an active member of the Dominican order of monks who founded the monastery of Corpo Santo as well as an Irish College in Lisbon. O'Daly also became the confessor of Joao's wife, Queen Luisa. In those days, confessors were more than spiritual advisors. In the royal palace of Lisbon, O'Daly often discussed matters of state with Luisa. So when the King decided to recruit Irish soldiers for the Portuguese Army, Father O'Daly naturally came to mind.

Daniel O'Daly arrived in Ireland at a time when Oliver Cromwell's war against Irish Catholics was devastating the country. Famine and pestilence followed in the wake crop burnings and livestock slaughtering by Cromwell's armies. The defeated Irish soldiers hiding in the countryside were eager to join the service of England's enemies abroad. Even so, O'Daly did not attract a large number of Irish with his recruitment drive. The pay scale that he could offer was far lower than the wages for service in the armies of France or Spain. When Portugal regained its independence, there was no royal treasury and King Joao depended on a tax on imports and exports for most of the funds necessary to rule the nation. Revenues from the import-export trade dried up because Spanish markets were closed to Portugal; and because the Netherlands was at war with Spain and continued to regard Portugal as a Spanish province. Portuguese merchants were forbidden from trading in Bruges or Antwerp. So O'Daly could entice the Irish soldiers only with the promise of glory and the hope of eventual financial rewards. When the small number of Irish recruits he attracted arrived in Portugal, they were scattered throughout the army as junior officers and drill sergeants. O'Daly did manage to convince the experienced field commander Murrough O'Brien, Lord Inchquin, to accept a general's commission in Joao's army. But when he arrived in Portugal, O'Brien quickly grew dismayed by the state of the army and returned to Ireland.

King Joao IV considered O'Daly's mission a success even though he did not persuade many Irishmen to join the Portuguese army. The small number of Irish soldiers who did join the Portuguese army were given the task of training the inexperienced Portuguese troops in the tactics and strategy the Irish had developed in their conflicts against the English. The Irish military trainers taught the Portuguese the flanking maneuvers they used against enemy formations so the Irish could bring their superior swordsmanship into play. This tactic had helped the Irish overcome the English advantage in having artillery batteries and the most advanced muskets. The Irish also stressed the use of cavalry to break up enemy formations or to reinforce weak positions. This instruction and drill by the Irish was appropriate for Joao's incipient Portuguese army because, like the Irish fighting the English, the Portuguese did not have the funds to be able to purchase the latest artillery, muskets and other military equipment.

By following the tactics and strategy taught to them by their Irish trainers recruited by O'Daly, the Portuguese army would be able to be an effective fighting force on the battlefields of 17th century Europe. Under the Irish instruction, the Portuguese army was turned into a fighting force that would deter Spain from believing that it could easily reclaim Portugal—which was King Joao's primary aim for O'Daly's mission.

A few years after O'Daly's return to Lisbon, Joao IV entrusted him with another diplomatic mission of great importance to the survival of Portugal. O'Daly was sent to France and the Netherlands to try to obtain international recognition for the independent status of Portugal and, if possible, establish military alliances. Because France and the Netherlands were at war with Spain and regarded Portugal as a province of Spain, Portuguese ships were denied access to French and Dutch ports. Once Portugal achieved international recognition, Joao IV could then make treaties which would allow the goods from Portuguese colonies to be delivered in markets closed to Spain.

At the time of O'Daly's mission to France and the Netherlands, only England accepted Portugal as a sovereign nation because of a treaty signed in 1642 by Charles I in one of his last acts in office. The treaty was ratified by the new English government after Charles I was deposed by Cromwell. England hoped to benefit from an alliance with Portugal by using Lisbon as a naval base. With England recovering from many years of civil strife, however, Joao IV could expect little military assistance if Portugal was attacked by Spain in an effort to win back its wayward province.

In 1656, O'Daly went to Paris for talks about forming an alliance against Spain with the Prime Minister of France, Cardinal Mazarin. O'Daly strongly urged Mazarin to take the lead in forming a league among Portugal, France and the Netherlands against Spain. O'Daly proposed that this league would include Portugal as a full ally of France and the Netherlands, but would not require that Portugal declare war on Spain unless attacked. Such a league would not only gain recognition for Portugal from two major European powers, but would also allow Portugal to trade with France and the Netherlands as well as provide military assistance if attacked by Spain. Although France was already at war with Spain, Mazarin initially told O'Daly that he saw no advantage to France from such a league because he believed that continued Portuguese independence depended on Joao IV, and would not endure if the King should die. Mazarin changed his mind, however, after Joao IV died in November of 1656 and the crown passed to the King's young son with Queen Luisa as regent without provoking a rebellion or an attack from Spain. Mazarin granted O'Daly a partial alliance by agreeing to provide military aid to Portugal, but on the condition that Queen Luisa took the initiative and attacked Spain. Since Portugal did not have the resources to challenge Spain, the compact had very little substance as a military alliance, but it did gain French recognition of Portugal's sovereignty and open French ports to Portuguese shipping. Other nations quickly followed the lead of France, including the Netherlands with its markets that were essential for the Portuguese economy.

O'Daly traveled on to Rome, to the court of Pope Alexander VII. There he obtained official papal recognition for the independent state of Portugal. In staunchly Catholic Portugal, the approval of the Pope was necessary to defuse a growing conflict between the civil government and the Portuguese Inquisition. Before his death, Joao IV attempted to reduce the severity of the methods used by the Inquisition, which retaliated by questioning his authority to rule. Papal recognition would restore some of the support that the Portuguese government had lost because of the frequent challenges of the Inquisition. In order to gain the Pope's recognition, however, O'Daly had to assure the Pope that the new Queen Luisa had no intention of continuing Joao IV's policies of interfering with Church matters in Portugal.

A few months later, in 1657, Spain sent its army across the Portuguese border to reclaim what it still regarded as a rebellious province and captured the city of Olivença The invasion caused a crises in the high command of the Portuguese Army, and for a time it appeared as if Spanish soldiers would soon be marching through Lisbon. But France, England and the Netherlands were also at war with Spain in a dispute over economic and territorial interests in the Caribbean. The threat to Spain's holdings in Flanders and the West Indies, and the possibility of invasion along its northern border with France limited the number of Spanish troops available to fight on the Portuguese front.   Spain eventually lost the war with France, England and the Netherlands, and the victorious allies insisted that Spain abandon its claim of sovereignty over Portugal and recognize it as an independent nation. Spain acquiesced, withdrawing its troops from Portuguese territory.

During the first two decades of Portuguese independence, Daniel O'Daly's Irish heritage opened diplomatic doors that might have been closed to someone of Portuguese birth. The Irish emigres in Europe, particularly in France and the Papal States of Italy, had a reputation for honoring their word. Many of O'Daly's fellow emigres were in positions of power in the French government and were certain to have smoothed his negotiation with Mazarin. The international relationships that O'Daly forged for Portugal were critical for the nation's commercial and political survival. For these accomplishments, Daniel O'Daly entered Portuguese history as a key figure in maintaining the independence of his adopted land.

THE GALLOPING HOGAN

In the early 18th century, the Irish emigre Michael Hogan played a key role in a crucial moment of Portuguese history. Leading a brigade of Portuguese cavalry, Hogan drove a Spanish invasion force from Portuguese territory. In accomplishing this, Hogan employed tactics that he had used successfully against the English in Ireland. In Ireland, Hogan's extraordinary skill as a horseman had earned him the name the "Galloping Hogan." His skill and leadership were especially evident after the Irish defeat in the Battle of the Boyne in 1690. Hogan led the rear guard protecting the retreat of the defeated Irish to Limerick, keeping the retreat from becoming a rout. During the subsequent siege of Limerick by the English army led by King William, Hogan led a daring midnight raid on the English artillery train approaching the city. While the artillerymen were bivouacked for the night, Hogan attacked the English camp, captured or drove off the English soldiers, and blew up the cannon. This prevented the English from using their artillery to destroy the walls of Limerick. Eventually, however, the Irish were forced to surrender. Hogan was a member of the body of Irish troops who chose exile rather than take an oath of loyalty to King William and became known as the Wild Geese. In 1691, Hogan went to France where he became an officer in the Irish Brigade and was promoted to general after distinguishing himself in several battles in Flanders.

Hogan's duel with a fellow officer of the Brigade in 1705 was the incident which led to his going to Portugal. Although Louis XIV had issued an edict in 1679 prohibiting dueling, the nobility flaunted the law and continued to duel whenever they believed their honor was compromised. Because dueling was such a common practice in French society and involved many prominent nobles, despite his ban, Louis XIV frequently granted pardons or reduced the punishments of surviving duelists. In the military, there were additional regulations against dueling to prevent soldiers of lower rank from challenging their superiors, thereby undermining military discipline. Hogan's opponent in the duel was Captain James Conway; whom Hogan later discovered was his cousin. When they faced each other with pistols, Hogan mortally wounded Conway, causing a scandal in the Irish Brigade. In 1706, a court-martial tried Hogan and demanded his resignation from the army, but ordered no additional punishment. Since Hogan's duel had also violated the King's edict against dueling, he faced civil charges as well. But Louis XIV decided to grant Hogan a pardon because of his exemplary service in the Irish Brigade while in Flanders. His career as an officer in the French army was at an end, however. Louis XIV suggested to Hogan that his military skills and leadership could be put to good use in Portugal, and gave Hogan a letter of recommendation to King Joao Vl.

Following the King's suggestion, Hogan went to Lisbon in 1708 to present himself to King Joao V. Recognizing Hogan's value to his own inexperienced army, the King immediately gave him a commission as Brigadier General in the Portuguese army. As a sign that he now considered Portugal his home, Hogan changed his name to André Miguel Hogan.

Hogan arrived in Portugal during the War of Spanish Succession. In this conflict, an alliance of England, the Netherlands and Austria was trying to preserve the European balance of power by preventing the new Spanish King, Philip V, from also becoming the King of France. Although Portugal was not a part of the alliance against Spain, King Joao V was nonetheless concerned that Spain might find the war against the other European powers an excuse to try to annex parts of Portugal.

Hogan's first assignment as Brigadier General was the command of a cavalry brigade stationed along the border with Spain in central Portugal. Although it was not until the war was almost over that Hogan's brigade came into combat, it was not idle in its defensive position. For more than three years, Hogan had been teaching his cavalry troop the hit-and-run tactics he had used so effectively against the English in Ireland. Hogan especially emphasized the night maneuvering and attack the English found difficult to defend against. Such nighttime tactics for a fairly large force were based on stealth and silence and on the ability of the force to stay together in the darkness. Such tactics were rare in the warfare of the early 1700's. This training proved its worth in the closing stage of the War of Spanish Succession when Spain made a bold, forceful attempt to seize a portion of Portuguese territory in order to strengthen its position in the peace negotiations which had opened in Utrecht in Belgium.

The Marquis de Bey of Spain led the attack on Portugal. During this invasion, his savagery toward both soldiers and civilians earned him the title "The Scourge of Portugal." The sole barrier between the Marquis and Lisbon and the court of King Joao V was the fortified town of Campo Maior garrisoned by a small infantry unit under the command of the Count de Riberia. As the Spanish approached, de Riberia sent a courier to Hogan at the headquarters of the Portuguese cavalry requesting reinforcements. Although dusk was gathering when the news arrived, Brigadier General Michael Hogan mustered a force of 500 men and led the mounted troop through the darkness in a ride reminiscent of his raid on King William's artillery train during the siege of Limerick. Hogan's men reinforced the garrison at Campo Maior at dawn; and although badly outnumbered, Hogan's troops and de Riberia's garrison repulsed the Spanish assault.

Not only as a dramatic military feat, but also as a model of advanced tactics, Hogan's nighttime maneuver and role in the defeat of the Spanish invasion force became a part of military history. Hogan's feat became so noteworthy that the historian John O'Callaghan was prompted to include it in his *The History of the Irish Brigade in the Service of France*, not only because of Hogan's one-time service in the Brigade, but also as an example of the fighting spirit and innovative tactics typical of the Brigade.

The last affair of arms in this war between Spain and Portugal occurred in the campaign of 1712, under circumstances so creditable to an Irish officer as to deserve notice here, though that gentleman was not of the Irish Brigade. Notwithstanding the negotiations for peace at Utrecht, no truce having taken place by September between the two peninsular kingdoms, the Marquis de Bey (styled "The Scourge of the Portuguese") appeared on the 28th, with nearly 20,000 men before Campo Maior in Portugal, and broke ground, October 4th-5th, the place being then in anything but a condition to make suitable resistance. As, however, it was of the utmost consequence to preserve it, the Count de Riveria and a gallant French Protestant engineer officer, Brigadier de Massi, contrived a day or two after to make their way into the town with 200 or 300 Portuguese grenadiers, and 400 or 500 more Portuguese subsequently succeeded in doing so likewise under an Irish Officer, Major General Hogan—apparently the same M. Hogan, Irlandaise Lieutenant Colonel in the Bavarian Guards tried by Court Marital in 1706 at Mons for killing a Captain and countryman of his own in a duel, and hence, most probably, obliged to enter another service.[*] Having assumed command of the garrison, the Major General took due measures for the defense. After battering and bombing the place from October 4th with 33 cannons or mortars, the Marquis de Bey ordered a grand assault to be made on the 27th, in the morning, by 15 battalions, 32 companies of grenadiers and a regiment of dismounted dragoons, under Lieutenant General Zuniga.

"By help of a prodigious fire from the cannons and small arms, observes my English narrative of the *Compleat History of Europe for 1712*, with respect to the enemy, they made a descent into a part of the ditch that was dry and gave 3 assaults with a great deal of fury; but they were as bravely repulsed by the Portuguese under Major General Hogan, and forced to retire after an obstinate fight that lasted 2 hours, though the breach was

[*] At the time of Compo Maior, Hogan was a Brigadier General

very practicable, and so wide that 30 men might stand abreast in it. Their disorder was so great they left most of their arms and 6 ladders behind. This action cost them 700 men killed and wounded, whereas the Portuguese loss did not amount to above 100 killed and 87 wounded, and such was their ardour that they pursued the enemy into their very trenches without any manner of order (notwithstanding the endeavors of Major General Hogan to put a stop to them), which might have proved very fatal to them, if the enemy had courage to improve the opportunity."

The next day, the Spanish lifted the siege and moved back into Spanish territory, ending the threat to Portugal. A short time latter, the delegates to the peace conference in Utrecht signed a treaty and the War of Spanish Succession ended with Portuguese territory intact. King Joao recognized Portugal's debt to Michael Hogan by promoting him to Major General and awarding him a villa and an annual stipend. Hogan continued to serve in the army of Joao V teaching other officers horsemanship and cavalry tactics. He married a woman related to the royal family of Bragança and was a frequent visitor to the King's court in Lisbon.

Michael Hogan's night ride to Campo Maior became legendary in the Portuguese cavalry. From the success of this action, other army officers came to view cavalry as a highly mobile strike force that could quickly be sent to the point of greatest threat. As obvious as relying on the mobility of cavalry may seem today, it required Hogan's extraordinary achievement to make the tactic a part of Portuguese military operations.

IRISH CONFLICT WITH THE PORTUGUESE INQUISITION

In both Portugal and Spain, the Irish rarely became targets of the Inquisition. Nearly all of them were devout Catholics. In addition, since they were considered refugees from Protestant persecution, they were given a higher status by the clergy than individuals who has not suffered for the sake of their Catholic beliefs. But as the 18th century unfolded, a series of events occurred that placed the Hogan family in direct conflict with the Portuguese Inquisition.

On the basis of his important role in the War of Spanish Succession, Michael Hogan came to have considerable influence on the political affairs of Portugal as well as its military affairs. His brother John, and a relative, Jacob (probably a cousin) also rose to the rank of general. Like Michael Hogan, they married women with ties to the royal family of Bragança. Portuguese historical records encapsulating the patrimony and achievements of the Hogans also hint at the reason the Hogan family came into such a serious confrontation with the Portuguese Inquisition.

An entry from a document in the Portuguese National Archives in Torre do Tombo concerning Dennis Hogan, the son of Michael Hogan, reads:

> Dennis (or Dionysius) Hogan, 30 years old, Irish, native of Vilanova county of Tipperary, lieutenant of cavalry in the Alcantara regiment, resident of Janelas Verdes {Green Windows}, parish of Santos. This Dennis Hogan came to Portugal in 1724 and was appointed cavalry lieutenant on November 5, 1734, in recognition of services rendered to our country during nine years, by his uncle John Hogan; ... Dennis Hogan became a Mason in 1737.

The incidental notation that Dennis Hogan became a Mason discloses the cause of the Hogan family's troubles with the Inquisition. The Masonic brotherhood was a particular target of the Portuguese Inquisition during the 1730's. The secret society embraced atheism and republicanism, concepts that the Catholic Church believed undermined its authority. The Masonic Order began during medieval times as a guild of builders who recognized no religion and paid homage to no king. Despite their controversial nature, because of their unique architectural skills, the Masons were welcomed by the nobles in the major cities of Europe to build cathedrals and universities. The society flourished and used its wealth to influence kings and nobles by making secret loans to finance military campaigns. The growing political power of the Masonic Order attracted ambitious men who had little to do with construction, but hoped to benefit from the powerful, yet clandestine brotherhood. By the 18th century, its members were known as Freemasons and the order was growing rapidly. It was becoming popular particularly among the aristocracy and political leaders of Catholic nations who resented the interference of the Church in civil affairs. In a time when oaths were taken very seriously, the vow to secrecy taken by each Freemason was intended to prevent infiltration of the organization by agents of the Catholic curia. Recognizing the Freemasons as a dangerous movement, Pope Innocent VIII strongly condemned them in the 1720's.

Dennis Hogan was attracted to the Freemasons because of their desire to limit the power of the Catholic Church in Portugal. For centuries, the Catholic clergy maintained a political grip on Portugal by using the Inquisition to accuse even the highest-born nobles of heresy whenever they attempted to interfere with Church laws or property. Like many other Irish in Portugal, Dennis considered this Catholic religious oppression little different from the Protestant religious oppression in Ireland.

The Holy Inquisition was a Church institution created by Pope Gregory IX in 1231 to discover and punish heresy throughout Europe. A special branch of the Holy Inquisition was created in Spain and Portugal by papal decree at the close of the 15th century. The Catholic hierarchy of the Iberian Peninsula believed that the large number of Moslem Moors and Jews residing in their land increased the possibility that Christians would hear and respond to heretical teachings. Rooting out and eliminating the Jewish and Moslem religions required sterner measures than were usually employed by the Holy Inquisition in other parts of Europe. This was the origin of the infamous Spanish Inquisition, which was intended to insure conformity with Catholicism. It terrorized not only the Moors and Jews, but also many Christians of Spain and Portugal until the 19th century.

Dennis Hogan knew that the methods used by the Inquisition in Portugal were as terroristic and brutal in Portugal as they were in Spain. Regardless of social rank, a man or woman could be arrested by the Inquisition on the faintest suspicion of heresy and subjected to torture if they did not immediately confess. If the prisoner confessed, his or her life might be spared, providing it was a first offense. If prisoners failed to confess to heresy, or if it was a second conviction, they were turned over to the civil authorities for execution because the Catholic Church prohibited the clergy from carrying out a death sentence. To demonstrate their support of Catholic doctrine, government officials organized public burnings of heretics, which the Portuguese termed the *auto de fé*, the act of faith. Sometimes the men and women sentenced to death were kept in prison until the authorities had enough condemned people to stage a mass execution. These public spectacles were meant to warn others of the consequences of deviating from Catholic doctrine. Afterwards, all of the property of the executed heretic was confiscated by the Church, thus creating a financial incentive for the Inquisition.

Along with many other educated Portuguese, Dennis Hogan believed that the activities of the Portuguese Inquisition unreasonably harmed innocent people and severely hampered the economic development of the nation. Foreign merchants from Protestant lands hesitated to invest in Portugal for fear that their agents would be arrested and their goods confiscated. Special permission was required from the Inquisition for a Protestant foreigner to live in Lisbon, but they were not immune from arrest if they spoke an ill-considered word that conflicted with Catholic teachings. Any native Portuguese who amassed wealth automatically came under the scrutiny of the Inquisitors. A single ancestor who was Moslem or Jewish, no matter how remote, could bring the charge that a person was a "lapsed Christian" who secretly practiced another religion. The activity of the Inquisition in northern Portugal, where Dennis Hogan lived, was especially virulent in the 1730's. So many people were arrested that whole towns were deserted and prosperous business were ruined by neglect and mismanagement following confiscations.

Although Dennis Hogan opposed the Inquisition, he did not take the dangerous step of taking the Freemason's oath until after the great *auto de fé* in Lisbon in 1737. At this spectacle, twelve people were burned at the stake and thousands of others were stripped of their property and condemned to lesser punishments. All of the accused were from the northern province where Dennis lived, and among them were many of Dennis's friends and acquaintances. The population of his native city of Bragança and the surrounding region had been decimated by the Inquisition a few years before. Many of the aristocrats, including his stepmother related to the royal House of Bragança, felt that there should be an end to the Inquisition, but few of them dared speak their thoughts openly. By joining the secret society of Freemasons, Dennis Hogan was able to collaborate with others opposed to the injustices of the Inquisition.

Before long, Dennis Hogan was named as a Freemason to the Inquisition. He may have been named by one of the many informers the Inquisition had throughout Portugal; or by someone in the hands of the Inquisition hoping for mercy by giving the Inquisition the names of other heretics. Hogan was arrested on the ecclesiastical charge of heresy and the civil charge of treason. At the same time, the Inquisition arrested seven other Irish military officers for the same crimes. To save himself from torture, Dennis immediately confessed and gave lengthy depositions in which he claimed ignorance that the Pope in Rome had outlawed Freemasonry.

During the time of Dennis' imprisonment, his father, Michael, worked tirelessly to obtain his release. Michael knew he was placing himself in jeopardy since any persons who tried to help those accused by the Inquisition were themselves automatically suspect. But Major General Michael Hogan was well into his sixties and had never before succumbed to his personal fears. When his political connections at the royal court proved powerless to intervene, he tracked down the Scotsman named Gordon who had recruited Dennis and the other Irish officers for the Freemasons. Gordon gave him a signed statement showing that Dennis agreed to an addendum to the Mason's oath that guaranteed his loyalty to the King of Portugal and to the Roman Catholic Church. Perhaps this document conveyed the truth. Perhaps it was a crafty invention by a frantic father. Whatever Dennis actually swore to was never known since Michael arranged for Gordon to flee from Portugal to prevent any further testimony. Yet this statement combined with the prestige of the three Hogan generals and the royal house of Bragança secured the release of Dennis Hogan. The young Lieutenant returned to military service with no apparent prejudice to his career. He eventually advanced to the rank of Major General by the time he retired.

The brief misadventure of Dennis strengthened the Hogan family's resolve to support any movement to loosen the grip of the Inquisition over the Portuguese people. This resolve was rooted in their oath as military officers to defend the monarchy and the nation against internal enemies as well as foreign ones. By the 1740's, the Hogans, along with many other leaders of Portuguese society, viewed the Inquisition as a threat to Portugal. The Inquisition not only undermined their authority, it also threatened them personally with arrest, imprisonment and confiscation of their property. The Hogan generals became part of a secret group of government ministers and military officers who met to plan the best way to limit the power of the Inquisition. A prominent member of the group was Sebastian Cavalho e Mello, the Marquis of Pombal, who was related to Dennis Hogan by marriage. Although this group failed to agree on any specific plan, the members agreed to support one another if any opportunity arose to challenge the authority of the Inquisition.

It was several years before circumstances presented themselves so that the group was in a position to take effective action toward their aim of curtailing the Inquisition's power. During the 1740's, the Marquis of Pombal was Portugal's ambassador to England, and then Austria. While in England, he gained a reputation as a liberal statesman for his regular assurances that Portugal was ready for the economic and political reforms which would make it attractive for investments. While posted in Vienna, he observed that the Catholic monarchy of Empress Maria Theresa remained popular, strong, and effective without oppressing Protestant sects and other religious minorities. In 1751, the Marquis returned to Lisbon to be appointed Prime Minister. One of his first acts after his appointment was to order that all prison sentences imposed by the Inquisition had to be confirmed by the civil government. The Marquis put himself at risk of being charged with heresy by the Inquisition. But the Marquis was able to take this risk because he had the full support of the Army. By this time, Dennis Hogan had risen to the rank of Major General. Dennis informed the leaders of the Inquisition that he would use his troops to protect the Marquis from arrest, and he used his influence among other generals to persuade them to back the civil government's challenge to the power of the Church. Faced with defiance from both the government and the military, the Inquisition agreed to accept the Marquis' order to allow its prison sentences to be confirmed by the government.

The Marquis de Pombal continued to issue decrees to end the power of the Inquisition in Portugal. But the Inquisition was so entrenched in Portuguese society that in many areas local civil authorities continued to approve executions of heretics for another ten years. It was not until 1771 that the government was able to permanently outlaw the public burning of religious dissenters. Dennis Hogan played an important part in curtailing the power of the Inquisition. His encouragement of the Marquis de Pombal and his open support of the Marquis at the critical hour in 1751 helped Portugal shed the yoke of religious oppression.

In other European countries, Irish emigres influenced societies in specific areas such as education, military affairs, or agriculture. But in Portugal, the Irish had a direct and identifiable involvement in shaping events that affected all parts of Portuguese society. Daniel O'Daly secured international economic and political ties for Portugal in a time when its survival as an independent nation was in doubt. The markets he opened and the alliances he established benefitted all of the people of Portugal, from the peasant plowing a field to the dragoon patrolling the border. Michael Hogan helped preserve Portuguese independence. Dennis Hogan helped to alter the course of Portuguese society by curbing the abuses of the Inquisition, an institution which hampered the economic and intellectual development of the nation and unjustly killed thousands of Portuguese citizens. The Irish in Portugal were able to play such a prominent role in the development of Portuguese society because the nation was small, allowing their actions to have an immediate, widespread effect.

CHAPTER 9

Irish Resistance to Assimilation in Europe

We hold the Ireland in the heart
More than the land our eyes have seen,
And love the goal for which we start,
More than the tale of what has seen.

—AE (George Russell)

HOPE OF RETURN AND EMIGRE AMBIVALENCE

Although their Celtic heritage gave the Irish a penchant for migration, when they began to emigrate from Ireland in considerable numbers in the 1500's to escape English oppression, they emigrated with the hope that they might one day return to Ireland. The monks of the late Middle Ages had been inspired to leave Ireland by the concept of the White Martyr, which was based on the pangs of leaving brethren and countrymen for missionary work in foreign lands. Although motivated by the concept of the White Martyr, the monks left Ireland voluntarily and accepted that they were never to return. But the later emigres were not devout religious persons following a divine calling, but were individuals from all walks of life seeking to escape political and religious oppression. They were farmers, craftsmen, merchants, dispossessed nobles, teachers, physicians and others from all parts of Irish society.

By the 1100's, Celtic society had been long established in Ireland; and it had prospered removed from the imperialism of Rome, barbarian invasions and other historical currents flowing across continental Europe. Not only was there no place left to emigrate to once Celts reached Ireland, but the fertility and small population of the island allowed Celtic culture to flourish. With Celtic culture finding space to grow distant from any threats to it and the Celtic people of Ireland becoming more attached to it with each generation, the migrating penchant of the Irish abated. For the Irish, Celtic culture and the land of Ireland became intertwined in a way that was new in Celtic culture. Thus when the English came in force to conquer Ireland in 1169, rather than emigrate, the Irish responded militarily. For three centuries afterwards, the Celtic Irish and the English struggled for political and cultural supremacy over Ireland. Only in the 1500's when England fully subjugated the Celtic Irish did migration of the Irish resume. Many of these later emigres were among the Irish who resisted English domination; and when the Irish were defeated in battle, they were among the first to emigrate. Many of them left relatives and other family members behind. Rather than submit to defeat and compromise their Irish culture under English oppression, the later Irish emigrated—but it was under the duress of oppression.

This phase of emigration did not arise sheerly from the migratory tradition of the Celts or from a practical motive such as avoiding a threat by establishing Celtic culture elsewhere—for there was nowhere to emigrate to where Celtic culture could be reestablished. Ireland was the only place the Irish felt they could enjoy their culture as they had been accustomed to it. This later emigration prompted by English oppression was regarded as a way to preserve Irish culture so that it could be reestablished in Ireland when English domination was overthrown. The yearning for an Ireland free of English domination tempered the emigres' understanding of their position in the countries they went to. As long as they held the hope that they or their descendants would return to Ireland in the near future, they did not become reconciled to becoming entirely integrated into their new countries.

This hope was not unfounded. It was based not only on the intentions of the members of each generation of emigres, but on changing historical conditions in Ireland. Ever since England had instituted its rule over Ireland, there had been recurring rebellions and other types of subversion. In the 14th century, the Irish had rallied behind Edward the Bruce's attempt to drive out the English and create an independent Irish kingdom. The near success of the 16th-century Irish rebellions which became known as the Geraldine Wars and the Nine Years War and the 17th century rebellion of the Confederation of Kilkenny encouraged the emigres to believe that someday a rebellion might be successful.

The hope of returning to an Ireland free of English oppression was also bolstered by historical events in England and Europe. After Charles I was deposed and beheaded by Oliver Cromwell in 1648, his sons, Charles and James, lived in exile in France. They promised to change English policies oppressing Irish Catholics in return for the support of Irish emigres in the efforts of the royal brothers to regain the English throne for Charles. After the Restoration of Charles II in 1660, he ended some of the oppressive Irish policies established by his predecessors. When he died in 1685, James II accelerated the process of restoring Irish-Catholic civil liberties. For a brief time, it seemed to many emigres that the hope of returning to an Ireland free of repressive laws might become a reality. In 1688, however, William of Orange deposed James II and three years later, defeated James' Irish-French army at the Battle of the Boyne. James then established a court-in-exile in France. Since James had already demonstrated that he favored religious and political equality for the Irish, the emigres remained loyal to his cause. For the next fifty years, the Stuart Pretenders to the English throne encouraged the Irish emigres to believe that conditions in Ireland would improve enough to allow them to return to their homeland if the Stuarts could regain the English throne. In 1745, the grandson of James II, Charles Stuart, invaded Scotland as a prelude to conquering England. He was accompanied by elements of the Irish Brigade, and the expedition was partly financed by wealthy Irish emigres such as Anthony Walsh and the Routledges. Although the Highlanders of Scotland flocked to Charles' banner, his army was defeated at the Battle of Culloden in 1746. This defeat marked the end of the Stuart cause, yet the Irish emigres continued to hope that historical events would eventually free Ireland of English rule.

Besides these historical events, there were some individual emigres who kept the hope of return alive and sought support for an Irish rebellion from various European monarchs. Such individuals were especially active during the Reformation when England redoubled its oppression of the Irish. In the 1570's, James Fitzmaurice petitioned France, Spain and Pope Gregory XIII for funds to raise an army to invade Ireland. In 1578, Pope Gregory granted the petition and helped Fitzmaurice raise an army of 6,000 Italian mercenaries and bandits. Fitzmaurice dispatched 2,000 soldiers under the command of Thomas Stukeley to Lisbon to set up a staging point for the invasion of Ireland. But as soon as Stukeley's contingent arrived in Lisbon, King Sebastao of Portugal impressed it into the Portuguese army and sent them on a disastrous invasion of Morocco. The preparations to invade Ireland collapsed shortly afterwards when Pope Gregory withdrew his financial support. In 1601, Red Hugh O'Donnell, one of the rebel leaders of the Nine Years War, went to Spain after the English defeated Spanish forces that had invaded Ireland at Kinsale. His mission—which was common knowledge among the Irish emigres—was to urge Philip III of Spain to mount another invasion of Ireland. O'Donnell was poisoned in 1602, most likely by an English agent. In 1605, Hugh O'Neill, the rebel leader of the Irish during the Nine Years War, came to Europe seeking aid from the King of France and the Pope to establish an invasion force. In 1618, another rebel leader of the Nine Years War named Donal O'Sullivan Baere was planning to return to Ireland from Spain with a small contingent of Irish emigre soldiers who would act as the nucleus for an Irish uprising. But before he could carry out his plan, he was assassinated in Madrid by John Bathe, an agent of the English government. As late as the 1790's, Irish emigre generals in the French army—including Generals Charles Kilmaine and Henri Clarke—advocated an invasion of Ireland in support of an Irish republican rebellion. If successful, such an invasion would serve both French and Irish interests by freeing Ireland from English rule. A small force under General Humbert landed in County Mayo in 1798, but was quickly defeated by English troops.

After this failure of the French invasion of Ireland, the hope of the return rapidly faded among the Irish emigres in Europe. After having been sustained for two centuries and with many attempts to fulfill it having been dashed again and again, the hope of return inevitably waned.

Not only the disappointments of each generation of emigres, but also changing historical considerations in Europe played into the waning of the hope. The rivalry throughout Europe between Catholicism and Protestantism led monarchs and segments of the populations of Catholic countries to support for the idea of a return by the emigres to Ireland. The monarchs of the Catholic countries deplored the dominance of English Protestantism over a country that was traditionally strongly Catholic. But with the diminution of the rivalry over time, the support of the Catholic monarchs correspondingly diminished. Besides, in the growing tides of democracy in Europe during the 18th century, the monarchs no longer had the standing or authority to provide meaningful encouragement or support to the Irish in their wish to return to their homeland. Europe was being shaped by the tendencies of democracy and secularism. In the changes, the basis of support for the Irish died away.

The shift of Irish emigration from Europe to America and Australia in the late 1700's was another reason for the waning of the hope of return—although there was a brief resurgence of it in the United States after the Civil War. The much greater distance from Ireland made the hope seem impracticable. Because of this shift in the pattern of immigration, the number of emigres going to Europe dropped off considerably and no longer helped keep the hope alive.

By the beginning of the 19th century, the European emigres' hope of a victorious return to Ireland had passed away. For over two centuries, it had been sustained because it appealed to the Irish image of the heroic. But with their penchant for migration, capacity for adaptation and practical viewpoint, the Irish eventually abandoned their dreams of returning to free Ireland from English rule.

Although the Irish maintained the hope of returning to Ireland in the near future during the 17th and 18th centuries, they were nevertheless able to have an influence on their new lands because of their concept of shape-shifting. Shape-shifting was not only a spiritual experience that was a part of Celtic religion or characteristic of Celtic mythological figures, but was a principle which was a part of the psyche of every Irish person. It was this concept of shape-shifting which allowed them to adapt so readily to new situations and to become involved effectively in new circumstances while not becoming firmly rooted in them. Because of the hope of returning to Ireland held by the emigres, their understanding of their position in their new societies was ambivalent. But because of the concept of shape-shifting which was a part of their culture, the Irish were suited to acting effectively in new circumstances.

THE IRISH IDEA OF COMMUNITY

Their ambivalent standing allowed the emigres to maintain their Irish identity. This identity was important to them. Many of the emigres had resisted the English invasion and rule; and a prime reason many of them left Ireland was so their Irish identity would not be threatened or subverted by English oppression. But although the Irish had a strong attachment to freedom, this identity was not based on a sense of individuality. The basis of this identity was the community an individual belonged to, i.e., his or her clan. The Irish emigrated in such numbers not from a desire to maintain their "individuality," but because the community to which they were attached was being ruined by English government and English oppression of Irish traditions such as Catholicism, clan ownership of land and the Celtic system of farming. There was no guarantee, of course, that emigres could retain their traditional communities by going to Europe. But no matter what their future held, they would at least not be accepting English dominance or serving English masters. With the hope of returning to Ireland one day, emigration seemed the way to try to preserve this community.

With their strong sense of community based on the clan, the Irish had little sense of identity or of the purpose of action except in relation to the community they belonged to. Although Irish emigres went to Europe in large numbers, their numbers were not so large that they established ghettos where they could survive largely indifferent to the surrounding culture. Besides, a good proportion of emigres scattered to the countryside where they could continue the farming or crafts they had been engaged in Ireland. Moreover, it was simply not in the Irish nature to deliberately separate themselves from the larger communities which they entered by emigration.

It was not only because of the vestiges of Celtic culture in Europe that the emigres were able to have such an influence, but also because they were accustomed to acting in the context of the extensive community of the clan. Leaving Ireland partly to preserve this concept of community that was suffering under English rule, once in Europe the Irish recreated this sense of community as best they could. The best and readiest way they could recreate it was by giving their loyalty to the monarchs of the countries they went to. The monarchy was seen as a substitute for the clan an emigre left behind, and the monarch was like the clan chief. By loyally serving a monarch, the Irish emigres' actions were meaningful to them.

Besides the clan tradition accounting for the way the Irish established themselves in their new countries, there was also the tradition of Irish emigres becoming involved in European societies in helpful, constructive ways. This tradition started with Columbanus and his band, the first monks who came to Europe toward the close of the Dark Ages. The monks had taught local populations agricultural practices, animal husbandry, metalworking, and other skills which had improved their lives tangibly and immediately. Although the emigration of monks dropped off dramatically when Viking raids increased in northern Europe, the works of the monks and their place in local culture, and in some cases individual monks, became a part of the folklore of an area. Moreover, although fewer Irish monks journeyed to Europe to settle in the late Middle Ages, they continued to have a regular presence because of attendance at Church councils held in various places in Europe and pilgrimages to monasteries or holy sites. To reach their destinations, the monks would have to travel through other parts of Europe, which would also help to keep the memory of them alive among the people of Europe.

Familiarity with the Irish continued also by their involvement in the religious controversies of the early Middle Ages. Celtic Christianity vied with Roman Christianity to determine the nature of Christianity in Europe. Roman Christianity had advantages and resources which left little doubt that it would win out over Celtic Christianity; among these were a historical affiliation with Europe from its association with the Roman Empire and its assertion that its ecclesiastic authority was derived directly from the apostle Peter. Nonetheless, Celtic Christianity did offer doctrines and practices which appealed to the Europeans, and some of these were adopted by Roman Christianity. Until the time of the Carolingian Renaissance, the Irish monks were continually involved in the councils and convocations debating Christian doctrine. A few individuals from Ireland became leading figures in this ferment in which the fundamentals of Christian doctrine were decided. John Eriugena was widely regarded by scholars as one of the major theologians of the Middle Ages. Many of the Irish followed the teachings of Pelagius, although these teachings were considered heretical by the Roman Christians. Thus, even though there were no longer large numbers of Irish monks coming to Europe in the late Middle Ages, the involvement of Irish monks in central doctrinal issues of the Catholic Church—the dominant cultural force at the close of the Middle Ages—helped to keep the Irish prominent in Europe.

The long benign and beneficial presence of monks from Ireland largely erased any reluctance populations of Catholic European countries might have had to the Irish being a part of their societies. Although during the Renaissance there were much larger numbers of Irish emigres, there were never so many that they threatened the position of other groups or political factions. There were not that many Irish in any one field, such as the military or education, that they could dominate it; and the ideas and activities of Irish emigres who became leaders in certain fields were supported by the country's monarch or were plainly advantageous to the society. During most of the centuries that the Irish were emigrating to Europe, there was no such notion as "immigration" or "national identity." The Irish became accepted in a country largely by being accepted by the monarchy and aristocratic class. This simplified their involvement in the different societies. In any event, with their Catholic religion and their activities in education, the military, and agriculture, the Irish were ordinarily accepted by the commoners in the various countries where they settled. When national identities began to form in the 1500's and 1600's, the emigres and their descendants began to be affected by this movement and became leaders in the different countries. Over the long course of their emigration, because of their Celtic origin which gave them an affinity with most Europeans, their adaptability, their practicality, and the qualities and skills they offered, the Irish emigres were always able to become a part of the countries they favored by relatively simple and natural social processes. This allowed them to sustain their Irish identities while receiving the appreciation and in many cases the praise of a country's rulers and leaders and its population.

CHAPTER 10

Italy and The Papal States

People so beset with saints, yet all but vile and vain:
Wild Irish are as civil as the Russies in their kind:

— George Turberville, 1568

THE IRISH AND ITALIAN CIVILITY

In most cases, the Irish were accepted into the countries they emigrated to not only because of their allegiance and competence, but because of their Catholic religion which they shared with the large proportion of the population of these countries. An exception to this was Italy, however. Italy was the Catholic country of western Europe where the Irish emigres had the least effect. The basis of this went back to the difference between the Celtic Christians and the Roman Christians during the early days of Christianity. Even at this early time, Rome had been the center—and virtually the origin—of Roman Christianity. Roman Christianity eventually became the dominant religion throughout western Europe; but nowhere was the Pope's political and spiritual power stronger or more immediate than in the Italian peninsula. After the Protestant Reformation of the 16th century, the city-states and petty kingdoms of the peninsula identified with the Catholic religion and the Pope, encouraged papal sovereignty over territory in central Italy, and regarded themselves as protectors of Catholicism.

While the differences between the two early versions of Christianity were the general, deeper reason for the very limited effect the Irish emigres had on Italian society, there were also a number of specific historical and cultural reasons for this. The principle historical reason for this limited impression was that Italy lagged behind the other major countries of western Europe in the formation of a comprehensive national state. By the early Renaissance, when large numbers of Irish emigres began arriving in Europe, France, Spain and other lands were well along in the process of creating nations from diverse peoples and widespread provinces. The Italian peninsula, however, was still divided into many small kingdoms or city-states ruled over by autocratic leaders and dynastic families. These numerous political entities were made of homogenous populations composed for the most part of the descendants of various peoples who had migrated to Italy at the time of the collapse of the Roman Empire and had not mingled with one another to a great degree. In the process of the forming nations during the 16th and early 17th centuries, monarchs and the majority of their populations became used to inter-acting with varied types of people, accommodating their customs and viewpoints, and seeing their talents and characteristics as elements in the development of the nation. The small kingdoms and the city-states of Italy, however, remained closed systems in which outsiders were not welcome. The early Renaissance was the time of Machiavellian machinations and stratagems in the courts of the Italian rulers—and the Irish emigres going to Italy found no place for themselves in such intrigues and power struggles.

Besides the political fragmentation of the Italian peninsula and the Italian political practices of the time, the notion of "civility" in Italian culture was another reason Irish emigres did not play a substantive or noteworthy part in Italian society and history. The Italians regarded themselves as the most civilized people of Europe. This perspective transcended the differences and contests among the diverse kingdoms and city-states. As the city of Rome had been the center of Roman civilization which had dominated Europe, it was now regarded as the center of

Western civilization. Because of their ancient connection to Rome, the city-states and kingdoms of Italy shared directly in this civilization. With Italian culture as the standard of civility, the farther away a country was from Italy, the less civilized it was. Since Ireland was distant from Italy, on the rim of Europe, the Irish were among the least civilized people of Europe. The Italians viewed the Irish as half barbarous.

The Italians saw the Irish primarily as rustics from a basically agricultural society. This view toward the Irish was shared by the Popes and the Catholic Church hierarchy, although they did recognize the value of the strength of the faith and the industry of the Irish Catholic clergy in combating Protestantism. But the Irish did not meet the Italian standard of civility because they came from a society whose cities would not compare with those in Italy in size, architecture or wealth. Compared with Florence, Milan and other leading Italian cities, the Irish cities were little more than large towns. Besides, the Irish seemed quarrelsome rather than refined or courtly. That the Irish had never been able to govern themselves with a monarchy or a hierarchal system such as the Roman Empire or Catholic Church was evidence of their inherent refractoriness which kept them from becoming civilized.

Italian scholars, writers and artists were leaders in the changes in Western society during the Renaissance. Many of them were sought out by monarchs and wealthy persons of other countries to engage in work under their patronage. Because of this self-awareness and recognition that their culture gave birth to the individuals and achievements representing the best of European culture, the Italians had no desire to change their society or political system. This led to a parochial outlook which left the many Italian states reluctant to adapt to the historical developments that were occurring throughout the rest of Europe—and which inevitably came to affect Italy. Unable or unwilling to adapt to the historical developments, the Italian states tried to defend themselves against change. When faced with the imperialism of other European powers that was a vein of their nationalism and the large, well-organized armies making use of the latest technological developments, Italian states would have to seek alliances with major European powers in order to prevent their conquest by a different European powers. While such an alliance would save an Italian state from conquest by one imperialistic European power, it would usually result in the virtual submission of the state to the European power it had allied itself with. Thus, in the two hundred years after the Renaissance, Genoa and Turin were controlled by France; Venice and Milan were controlled by Austria; and Naples and Sicily were controlled by Spain. Rome and the Papal States associated with it remained autonomous because no Catholic country of the time dared to attack or occupy the seat and symbol of Catholicism. It wasn't until King Victor Emmanuel I of the Italian city-state of Savoy, with the support of Giuseppe Garibaldi, led an Italian nationalist movement in 1859 that the patchwork of kingdoms and city-states of the Italian peninsula was swept away and in 1870, the peninsula became united into a modern nation.

As they had in other countries of western Europe, Irish emigres could have helped lead Italy into the modern world. With their ingenuity, skills and loyalty, Irish emigres could have served Italian rulers and made contributions to Italian society in the fields of medicine, military affairs, education, the status of women, agriculture and modern, democratic government. But myopically concentrated on maintaining the bases of the own power, Italian rulers failed to make use of the ideas and talents of the Irish emigres. Thus, the relatively small number of emigres who settled in Italy remained on the periphery of Italian society. Emigres who were members of the clergy, and were not sent back to Ireland to keep Catholicism alive there, found positions in the lower levels of the Catholic ecclesiastical hierarchy. Emigres who were farmers, merchants and artisans managed to establish themselves so they could maintain satisfactory lives. But the preoccupation of the Italians with their cultural achievements and with maintaining their power in the patchwork of petty kingdoms and city-states of the Italian peninsula resulted in an indifference, and sometimes a resistance, to the capabilities and ingenuity of the Irish emigres which relegated them to anonymity.

THE IRISH AND THE POPES

Nowhere was the patronizing attitude of the Italians towards the Irish more conspicuous than in Rome. The first of the Irish emigres to arrive in the city were Catholic clergy in the late 16th century. Like the Irish religious refugees arriving in France and Spain, they were searching for a place of refuge from Protestant persecution in their homeland. As

educated Catholic clergy, they expected to find employment in the service
of the Vatican.

The Popes received the Irish emigre clergy and praised their devotion
to the Catholic faith. But the Popes suggested that the Irish priests return
to their homeland in secret to help keep the Catholic religion alive. Many
of the Irish were promoted to bishops and sent back to Ireland. The few
who stayed in Rome were given only minor tasks to perform for the
Vatican curia. They also discovered how difficult it was to live in Rome
without the patronage of the Italian bishops and cardinals who controlled
all aspects of life in the theocracy of the Papal States. Their attempts to
establish an Irish College met with procrastination. It was not until 1625,
after fifty years of petitioning the University of Rome, before the Irish
received permission to form their own college affiliated with the
University.

The Popes and high-ranking clergy of the time were all Italian, and
they held the view prevailing in their society that the Irish did not meet the
Italian standard of civility. But this was not the only reason the Popes and
high-ranking clergy were cautious in their relationship with the Irish
clergy. Apart from this stereotype, the Popes and clergy believed that
there was a considerable political risk in giving unqualified support to the
Irish in their religious and political conflict with England. For living in
Rome at the close of the 16th century was an influential group of English
Catholic aristocrats who hoped to someday reestablish the Catholic faith
in England with the help of the Holy See. Because the Popes believed that
England was a more politically influential nation than Ireland, they were
more concerned with reestablishing Catholicism in England than
preserving the religion in Ireland. If the Popes openly supported the Irish,
the English emigres could see this as aiding and abetting political rebels.
So in dealing with Irish emigres the Popes often chose the middle ground
of neither fully supporting nor completely rejecting the Irish emigres.

The Italian notion of civility also colored the view of the Italian
hierarchy towards Irish Catholic theology and religious practices. Not
only were the Irish from a wild and barbarous land scarcely able to grasp
the principles of civilization, but also they had flirted for centuries with
religious deviance, and could not be trusted to have purged pagan beliefs
from their version of Catholicism. The Irish continued to venerate many

individuals they regarded as saints who had not passed the official process of Catholic canonization. Unusual practices that remained in Irish Catholic ritual seemed suspiciously pagan to the Italian clergy. Particularly suspect were outdoor services conducted near wells and small ponds with people walking in circles around the water as they prayed. In theological discussions, the Irish point of view persistently echoed Pelagianism, the heresy that an individual could find redemption without divine intervention in the form of grace. Although the Italian Popes never openly stated an official Church policy toward the Irish clergy, they kept close watch over Irish activities in Rome.

During the decade of the 1660's, the reservations of the Catholic hierarchy toward the Irish intensified when a movement among both native and emigre Irish denied that the Popes should exercise power over worldly affairs. This movement began with Charles II of England, the Stuart King who had recently been restored to the English throne after the English Civil War and the rule of Oliver Cromwell. Unlike earlier English monarchs, Charles II was not hostile toward the Catholics under his rule, including those in Ireland. However, Charles was aware that the Puritans and Anglicans who made up a significant proportion of his subjects and were influential in England believed that the rebellions frequently springing up in Ireland were encouraged, and perhaps even instigated, by the Pope. In order to counter this belief, and bring greater harmony to his realm, Charles II requested that the Irish Franciscan Friar named Peter Walsh draw up a document stating that the Pope had no authority to interfere with the English civil government in Ireland. The King picked Walsh to write such a document because Walsh was an outspoken loyalist who had written many letters to prominent Irish Catholics urging them to also openly pledge their loyalty to Charles. Walsh was well-known among Irish Catholics for exposing an attempt by Bishop Edmund O'Reilly to betray Irish soldiers to Cromwell's forces because O'Reilly believed that Cromwell's victory in Ireland was inevitable and Catholics would be more favorably treated if they supported the new English government. A considerable number of bishops and priests in Ireland and Irish emigres abroad agreed that the Pope should not interfere with the English civil government in Ireland. They supported the position stated in Walsh's document, which became known as the Irish Remonstrance of Peter Walsh.

Pope Alexander VII saw this position as a threat that could potentially weaken his authority in the civil matters of Catholic nations. Exiled Irish bishops and priests were scattered throughout the capitals of Europe. Many of them were the confidants of monarchs and statesmen who would like to free themselves from the tradition of papal intervention in the affairs of their governments. To discredit the Irish Remonstrance, the Pope gave approval for the Archbishop of Armagh to call a synod to denounce Walsh and the position he had taken. The synod ordered Peter Walsh to go to the Franciscan priory at Louvain in France so his brother friars could watch him to insure that he caused no further trouble for the Pope. Walsh complied with the synod's order, but other Catholic countries began to reject papal involvement in their civil affairs. For Alexander VII and his successors, Walsh's challenge to papal authority, which spread across Europe, further demonstrated how wild and unpredictable the Irish could be.

Because the hierarchy of the Catholic Church was dominated by Italians, the disdainful attitude of the Italian Popes and Cardinals towards the Irish trickled downward into the Catholic clergy in Europe. Although the Irish were well-educated and staunchly Catholic, they did not contributed a cadre of clergymen who strongly influenced the doctrines and political development of the Catholic Church in early modern Europe. Only in the monastic orders which operated quasi-independently from Rome and could set their own internal rules did Irish monks and priests achieve positions of influence and leadership. The Irish clergy, however, was very successful in influencing Catholics as parish priests and as Jesuit, Dominican and Franciscan educators.

The attitude of the Catholic hierarchy towards the Irish often spilled out of the religious arena and into politics. Perhaps the most notable Irish emigre to be caught in the indecisiveness of the Vatican policies was Hugh O'Neill, the Earl of Tyrone. In 1605, he left Ireland along with several other nobles in what became known as the Flight of the Earls. For many years, he had been engaged in rebellion against England. With the aid of Spanish arms and soldiers, he had almost succeeded in winning political freedom for Ireland. But many of the other Irish lords became impoverished during the protracted rebellion and abandoned his cause. O'Neill ended his rebellion in exchange for a pardon from Queen

Elizabeth just before her death. Despite the pardon, the government of the new English King, James I, continued to harass O'Neill with lawsuits challenging the title to his lands and spies who openly watched his every move whenever he left his home. When O'Neill was summoned to London to appear before James I to answer false charges brought against him claiming that he had plotted to seize Dublin Castle, O'Neill hastily fled to Europe rather than risk being imprisoned or even executed by the King if he could not refute these false charges. In the dark of night, O'Neill, boarded a ship in a Lough Swilly harbor, sailed to France, and then traveled overland to Belgium, which was under the control of Spain at the time. He was accompanied by his sons, John, Hugh and Henry; and by the Earl of Fermanagh, who was also being threatened by English plots to seize his lands, and fifty other Irish men and women who feared similar reprisals for their part in the rebellion against England.

Although the monarchs of France and Spain considered O'Neill the leader of the Irish people, they were no longer at war with England and were reluctant to start another conflict for Irish interests alone. After a brief stay in Brussels, O'Neill, his son Hugh, and some of his Irish followers made their way to Rome to seek the assistance of Pope Paul V in forging a military alliance among the Catholic nations of Europe on behalf of the Irish. O'Neill expected that his reputation and his deeds in defense of the Catholic faith would receive serious consideration from Pope Paul V. At this time, however, the Pope was far more concerned with stifling the new movement towards separation of church and state in France, and saw little advantage in supporting Irish rebels.

The Pope gave O'Neill an annual stipend and arranged for the King of Spain to give him additional funds. O'Neill spent the remaining years of his life in Rome, ineffectively trying to win support of the political cause of the Irish among the Italian clergy that governed the upper echelons of Catholic hierarchy. His words fell on deaf ears. He died in 1616, embittered and puzzled by Pope Paul V's apparent indifference to Irish issues.

The people of Rome spurned the services of Hugh O'Neill and the other Irish emigres who accompanied him. As the center of western Catholicism, the city was thronged with foreign pilgrims, religious refugees and adventurers. The Irish were but one group among many. In addition, because of the notions of civility which classified the Irish as barbarous, the Italians gave them little opportunity to demonstrate how they could contribute to their adopted land. Most of the Irish who did come to Italy during the 17th and 18th centuries eventually continued their travels to pursue opportunities in other lands.

IRISH SOLDIERS IN ITALY

With so much of Italy under the control of Spain, France and Austria during the 17th and 18th centuries, many Irish emigres were temporarily in Italy serving as soldiers and government administrators for these countries. The Irish Brigade of France frequently saw combat in the northwestern Italian provinces of Piedmont and Savoy. Many of the Irish generals of Austria gained their initial experience in military campaigns during Italian battles and skirmishes. But the Irish soldiers and administrators were only temporary residents in Italy and left no permanent mark on Italian society. Their primary allegiance was to the nations which had sent them to Italy.

During the 19th century, a large number of Irish entered the Papal armies, but they too had little impact on Italian society. In 1859, Napoleon III of France and the Italian kingdom of Piedmont waged war on Austria, hoping to evict the Austrian Emperor, Franz Josef, from northern Italy and annex his lands. The coalition won the battles of Solferino and Magenta, but the threat of Prussian intervention on the side of Austria forced them to the negotiating table. The peace treaty coming from this made and Lombardy became part of Piedmont while Venice remained in the Austrian Empire. The war, however, had sparked Italian nationalism, with Piedmont assuming leadership in the Italian unification movement.

One of the primary forces opposing Italian unification was the Catholic Church. In central Italy, the Popes exercised direct political control over the territory known as the Papal States, as they had since the time of the Renaissance. In governing their lands, they behaved as any other ruler of their day, appointing administrators, collecting taxes and waging war. Shortly after Piedmont gained control of Lombardy, King Victor Emmanuel of Piedmont invaded the Papal States from the north, a group of republican revolutionaries led by Giuseppe Garibaldi marched on Rome from the south, and many people of the Papal States rose in rebellion against Pope Pius IX. The Pope refused to negotiate with King Victor Emmanuel and Garibaldi, scorning their suggestions of democratic reform. Victor Emmanuel's invading army quickly defeated Papal forces and surrounded the city of Rome, making the pope a virtual prisoner in the Vatican.

The momentum of the Italian unification movement alarmed the Austrian government. Piedmont, with the aid of its French ally, had defeated Austria and annexed the prosperous city of Milan. A unified Italy under the leadership of Piedmont, would place a strong nation on the southern border, another potential enemy for the Austrian Empire, which was already bordered by hostile nations. Besides, the Emperor Franz Josef was concerned with domestic problems and did not want to risk another war with Piedmont by aiding the Pope in hopes of thwarting Italian unification. So the Austrian Count Charles MacDonnell, the descendant of Colonel MacDonnell who had fought for Austria at Cremona in 1701, proposed a solution for Austria's dilemma. He suggested that he go to Ireland to recruit a battalion of Irish soldiers to fight for the Pope's cause. The troops would be financed and trained by Austria, but would be politically and militarily attached to the Papal States. A contingent of Irish soldiers in Italy would provide the Pope with badly needed military support and stimulate other nations to send forces to the papal armies. Both the Austrian Emperor and Pope Pius IX approved the plan, and in 1860, Charles MacDonnell was dispatched to his ancestral homeland.

MacDonnell appealed to the Irish as Catholics, asking them to fight in Italy for the sake of their religion. He received an excellent response from young men eager to escape the grinding poverty of farm life while advancing the Catholic cause abroad. In a short time, thousands of Irish volunteers arrived in Italy to defend the territory claimed by the Pope as his personal domain.

When the Irish volunteers arrived at the city Macerata in west-central Italy where they would be stationed, they faced a politically and militarily chaotic situation. The people in some of the cities and towns in the Papal States along with the remnants of the papal army defeated by Victor

Emmanuel's troops supported Pope Pius IX. The people in other cities and towns—sometimes only a few miles from cities and towns supporting Pius IX—believed that the Pope's temporal power should end and Italy become united under the leadership of Victor Emmanuel. Because of the revolutionary character of this conflict, the Irish could not know if the Italians around them were friends or enemies. To make matters even more complex for the Irish, Emperor Louis Napoleon of France had agreed to send French forces to help Pius IX maintain control of the Papal States, but had secretly instructed the French generals not to oppose Victor Emmanuel's invasion. Frequently the French troops and Italian supporters of Victor Emmanuel intercepted military supplies on their way to the Irish soldiers, creating critical shortages in ammunition and rifles.

Due to the rapidly deteriorating political and military situation in the Papal States, neither the Austrians nor the Papal army provided the Irish Brigade with suitable leadership or training. The men who were rustic laborers in Connaught and Munster lacked the discipline and experience to rapidly become effective soldiers. They found themselves on the field of battle armed with unfamiliar weapons and led by foreign officers indifferent to the loss of Irish lives. At the battles of Spoleto and Perugia, more than five hundred were taken prisoner. Out of frustration and anger, they mutinied at Macerata, rampaging through the town. In spite of the Irish efforts, the emerging nation of Italy eventually absorbed most of the Papal States except for the small territory of the Vatican. Disillusioned by their foreign adventure, the Irish volunteers returned home, their brief and hapless intervention leaving no imprint on Italian society.

Because of political conditions unique to Italy during the period of the Renaissance, when large numbers of Irish were emigrating to Europe, and the general disdain of the Italians toward the Irish because of their supposed cultural inferiority, the Irish had hardly any effect on Italian society or historical development. Most of the Irish who went to Italy during this era did not stay long, and resumed their travels after realizing that there was no worthwhile or productive place for them in Italian society. They continued on to join their fellow emigre countrymen in Spain, France and Austria—which held promise closed to them in Italy.

CHAPTER 11

Eastern and Central Europe

"I see none more competent..."

—The Empress Maria Theresa when
speaking of Francis de Lacy.

ON TO THE EAST

While most of the Irish emigres of the 17th and 18th centuries found
new homes in the Catholic nations of western Europe, a few journeyed to
the eastern nations of Europe. Some of them were professional soldiers
discharged from service in France or Spain when the dwindling finances
of monarchs could no longer support a large standing army. But other
Irish emigres chose to wander eastward for no reason other than their
desire to explore different lands. They were individuals who had
abandoned the romantic notion that they would some day be part of a
French or Spanish army sent to free Ireland. Without this hope, it made
little difference to them where they settled as long as the country tolerated
their Catholic faith.

The inhabitants of Austria, Hungry and even distant Russia had some
familiarity with Irish people and culture. During the Middle Ages, Irish

monks had settled in these lands; and their deeds became part of the local history and folklore of central and eastern Europe. In 17th-century Vienna, Irish emigres could visit the monastery founded in the mid 1100's by the Irish monk, Gille-na-Maemh, which came under the control of Austrian Benedictines shortly after the death of its founder. Any of the emigres hardy enough to travel to far-off Kiev would hear from local historians about the Irish monks of that city who made a dangerous escape to Christian Poland when they refused to submit to the Mongol invaders during the 13th century.

The aristocracy of central and eastern Europe welcomed the new wave of Irish emigres because they brought with them military, technical and agricultural skills sorely needed in these lands. A considerable number of the educated nobility recognized that lingering medieval customs and ideas were preventing their countries from prospering. In wars with neighboring countries, inferior armaments, inadequate logistics and outdated tactics were often disastrous for the armies of Austria, Hungary and Russia. Many armies relied on poorly-trained rural conscripts who were viewed as little more than cannon fodder by generals who had achieved their rank only because they were aristocrats and not for their personal skill. Because of their training and combat experience in the better-trained and better-equipped armies of western Europe, the Irish emigres were quickly entrusted with positions of high command in the military. The Irish also brought with them technical knowledge in banking, medicine, and engineering. Their agricultural knowledge proved particularly valuable when rapidly increasing populations led to food shortages in Austria and Hungary during the 18th century. Most of the crops were grown on feudal-like manors that could not produce sufficient surplus to feed the people living in the cities. Like the medieval Celtic monks, the influence that the Irish had on the nations of central and eastern Europe stemmed from their ability to teach their skills to others.

As they had proved in other countries, the Irish emigres in central and eastern Europe possessed a favorable combination of intellectual capabilities and practical skills which could help solve social problems. As imaginative, relevant and effective as the activities of Irish emigres may have seemed to the people of eastern European countries, he Irish were just acting in ways they always had throughout their long heritage stretching back to the Celts of the Iron Age. This Celtic heritage enabled the Irish to act thoughtfully and effectively in new circumstances. This heritage was formed by adapting to new situations as the prehistoric Celtic clans ranged over Western Europe, simultaneously imposing their own ways on other peoples they came into contact with and, in turn, assimilated new ways, until they eventually prospered on the remote island of Ireland.

In general, the farther east the Irish emigres went into Europe, the narrower their effects were on the nations and cultures they became active in. There are three major reasons for this. The first is that by the 18th century when the emigres arrived in this region and became involved in local affairs, the cultures and nations were much more defined than those of western Europe—France and Spain in particular. Not only were the cultures and nations of central and eastern Europe more defined, but they had absorbed as a part of their definition Mongol and Byzantine influences. These influences were quite foreign to the fundamentals of the cultures and nations of Western Europe, which were in many respects Celtic.

The second reason the influences of the emigres were relatively limited is that a smaller number of Irish emigrated to these areas. Those who did were guided by a sense of adventure, a wish to fill a role or gain a status which was already being filled by other emigres in the countries of western Europe, or a desire for a chance to regain wealth they had lost in the changing economic circumstances of western Europe.

The third reason the Irish emigres had a relatively limited influence in central and eastern Europe was that the activity of the small number who did go there was concentrated in a few areas. The small number stood out, and the most able among them were enlisted by the rulers of different countries to help solve social, political, or military problems they faced. As a result, many of the rest of the small number of Irish would follow into these areas and thus did not find their way into a broader range of fields as the Irish had in other countries of Europe. Whereas in Spain, Portugal, and France (and in later times in the United States and Australia), the Irish became involved in—and often became leaders in—areas as diverse as education, religion, commerce, military affairs, agriculture, and diplomacy, in central and eastern Europe, their activities were mostly concentrated in military affairs and statecraft. It was in these areas that the central and eastern European rulers found the services of the Irish most valuable. As important or crucial as it was, the Irish emigre influence in these areas was limited because their activity was focused on a particular pressing problem facing a ruler.

With their small number, their involvement in only a few activities and no successive groups of emigres following them, the Irish emigres of central and eastern Europe did not have the wide and continuous influence of the emigres in other parts of Europe. However, the role of the Irish in dealing with the immediate problems was usually effective and in some cases crucial. It was in the Austro-Hungarian Empire where the emigres played their most important role in central and eastern Europe. They also played distinctive roles in Russia. But they did not venture into the lands that are the modern nations of Yugoslavia, Rumania, Bulgaria or Greece. During most of the early modern era, these lands were controlled by the Ottoman Turks who had built a Moslem Empire which the Irish believed offered little opportunity for Christians. Because the freedom to practice their Catholic religion was so important to the Irish emigres, they chose to settle in lands where they knew it would be accepted.

PETER DE LACY AND CZAR PETER OF RUSSIA

At the close of the 17th century, most Europeans considered Russia a land of medieval barbarism. Its feudal social structures had changed little for centuries. Serfs were tied to the land they tilled, and nobles were despots. To govern effectively, the Czar had to rely on the goodwill of the nobles and the continuing support of his personal regiment of bodyguards, the Strieltsy. The science and technology transforming Europe during the Renaissance and the Enlightenment had only a small effect on Russia. All foreign ideas and viewpoints were shunned as the work of the devil, as potential threats to the existing social order ordained by God.

When Peter Romanov became Czar at the close of the 17th century, he resolved to use his power and authority to lift Russian society out of its medieval lethargy. He overcame the resistance of the Russian nobles to foreign ideas, and he was so effective in modernizing Russia that he is remembered as Peter the Great. He began by ordering his nobles to trim their shaggy hair, shave their long beards and wear western style jackets and breeches. The nobles grumbled, but obeyed. When Peter decided to travel abroad, it caused a scandal among the conservative nobles of Russia. But travel he did, learning as much as he could about the science and technology in Germany, Holland and England. During his journeys, he enticed a number of European scientists, artisans and military leaders to join the small group of foreigners who lived in Russia under his protection. Peter hoped to use their knowledge and skills to revamp Russian society.

In 1698, while in Poland to see the Polish monarch, King Augustus II, about the alliance they had formed to wage war against Sweden, Peter met a Polish army officer of Irish origin named Peter de Lacy. Czar Peter and de Lacy struck up an immediate friendship based on their mutual enthusiasm for carousing through the night in seedy taverns and houses of prostitution. Czar Peter also saw that de Lacy had military experience and skills that he might be able to make use of in his plans for modernizing Russia.

Emigrating from Ireland in 1691 as one of the Wild Geese, de Lacy saw service in the Irish Brigade of France. Being discharged in the reduction of French forces after the Treaty of Ryswick in 1698, de Lacy went eastward because the Polish Count de Croy, who de Lacy had met in France, had told him that the King of Poland would welcome experienced Irish officers in his army. When he arrived in Poland, de Lacy was given an officer's commission with the rank of major.

When Peter the Great continued his tour of Europe by traveling to Vienna, De Lacy secured leave from the Polish army to join the Czar's entourage. While Czar Peter was preparing to visit Venice, a messenger from Moscow brought news that the regiment of troops that was his personal bodyguard, the Strieltsy, were plotting to crown Peter's son Alexis as Czar of Russia. This plot stemmed from the resistance to change among the conservative nobility. As he hurriedly prepared to return to Russia, Peter persuaded de Lacy to join him. De Lacy agreed, and Peter made him a major in the Russian army.

When Czar Peter arrived in Moscow, he found that the Strieltsy had been arrested by army forces led by a Russian noble named Schien who was loyal to him. To strike fear into the hearts of the nobles who had secretly supported the Strieltsy plotters, Czar Peter personally tortured and executed many of the members of his former bodyguard in a public square near the Kremlin. Peter invited de Lacy, as well as some of the other foreigners who had returned with him to Russia, to take part in the hangings and beheadings. But when Peter held out an executioner's sword for de Lacy, de Lacy declined it. The Czar did not press it on him, but kept the sword and went back to his grisly work.

In the days following this harsh introduction to Russian society, Peter de Lacy received his assignment from Peter the Great. Along with other European officers recruited by Peter, De Lacy was to train the Russian army in the techniques of European warfare, which included rapid loading and firing of muskets, and hand-to-hand combat with bayonets. But De Lacy ran up against the inertia of centuries of Russian military custom requiring the use of sword and cavalry instead of shot and cannon. He encountered resistance from many Russian officers who believed that foot soldiers were ignorant brutes capable only of overwhelming an enemy by their sheer numbers. Their traditional tactics called for launching wave after wave of soldiers at the enemy. If the attacking units found themselves outnumbered, or if they sustained heavy casualties, they usually broke and ran. The inertia of the Russian military leaders was so ingrained that even with the active support of the Czar, de Lacy was able to train only one battalion of soldiers in modern tactics. This battalion—called the Grand Musketeers—was formed particularly for De Lacy to command and composed only of Russian nobles. These nobles later became officers of other units after serving under de Lacy, thereby gradually extending the influence of his training methods throughout the Russian army. Because of the battlefield successes of the Grand Musketeers in the war against Sweden, in 1708 de Lacy was placed in command of the Siberian Regiment of Infantry. At the Battle of Poltava, the Siberian Regiment distinguished itself by repelling the main Swedish attack.

In 1700, Russia and its Polish ally declared war on Sweden in what came to be known as The Great Northern War. King Charles XII of Sweden proved to be a masterful tactician, and the war went badly for Russia. With a smaller army, Charles defeated the Russians and their

Polish allies at every encounter. The Czar's poorly-trained and ill-equipped army could not prevail against the iron discipline and the rifled muskets of the Swedes. By the spring of 1709, Charles had advanced deeply into the Ukraine and was confronting a Russian army near the fortress-city of Poltava, a strategically important point on the main road between Kiev and Moscow. Although the Swedes were heavily outnumbered, they were relying on the usual tactic of an artillery barrage followed by a bayonet charge to cause panic among the poorly-trained Russian soldiers. But one of the regiments facing the Swedes at the point they chose for their main attack was de Lacy's Siberian Regiment. He ordered his troops to hold their fire until he gave the command. During the Swedish artillery barrage, de Lacy's troops stood firm. When the cannon fire stopped and the Swedes were charging towards the Russian lines with bayonets bristling, the Siberian Regiment held their fire. Only when the Swedes were almost at the Russian line did de Lacy order his men to shoot. The concentrated musket fire from de Lacy's regiment caused such heavy Swedish losses that the entire Swedish attack foundered. A Russian counter-attack defeated the Swedish army, and Charles XII fled the battle, never to threaten Russian lands again.

In recognition of Peter de Lacy's services, the Czar made him a general and a count. Because he had been so successful at Poltava and now had a noble title, other officers in the Russian army took a greater interest in the European methods of training and tactics that he was introducing. For the next two decades, the Russian army retrained and rearmed, largely under de Lacy's direction. He taught both officers and enlisted men the fundamentals of European warfare of the day. In 1736, he was promoted to Field Marshall.

The few Irish emigres who came to Russia after de Lacy also followed military careers. They include Count John O'Rourke in the army of Catherine the Great and his nephew, Major General Joseph O'Rourke, who led Russian troops against Napoleon. Peter de Lacy, however, was the Irish emigre with the most renown in Russian history and culture. Despite his prominence and his rank, he never became fully at ease with Russian society. Its customs seemed too foreign, its traditions seemed too alien from his Irish heritage. When his son, Francis, was old enough, he sent the lad to Austria to become a cadet in an army regiment. Since

Francis stayed in Austria and Peter had no other sons, future generations of the de Lacy family were Austrian. The internal structural changes in the military that Peter de Lacy helped set in motion continued to influence Russian training and tactics throughout the 18th century.

THE IRISH GENERALS OF AUSTRIA

Russia was not the only eastern European country whose military forces were outdated. Austria's defeat in 1735 in its war with the Ottoman Empire had exposed Austria's weaknesses in facing an army employing modern tactics and equipped with modern arms. Although smaller than armies in previous centuries, the modernized armies of the 1700's were composed largely of professional soldiers, and they were thus more effective fighting forces. Conscription was used only in times of national emergencies. Logistics had also become an important factor for a modernized army so that troops in the field would not have to depend on scavenging the countryside for food.

Austria's humiliating defeat by the Ottoman Empire offered opportunities for advancement into the high ranks of its army for a number of Irish emigres familiar with the latest developments in military administration, strategy and tactics, and logistics. The modernization these Irish generals effected for the Austrian army proved its worth in Austria's war against France, Spain, Prussia and Bavaria, called the War of Austrian Succession.

The war began shortly after a young and beautiful woman inherited the throne of the Austrian Empire in 1740. The new Empress was Maria Theresa von Hapsburg—the heiress of an imperial dynasty founded almost five centuries before when the Swiss Count Rudolph von Hapsburg was elected as the Holy Roman Emperor in 1273. There were many in Austria who felt that Maria Theresa was not capable of governing the Empire because of her inexperience and because she was a woman. Her cousin, Prince Charles Albert of Bavaria, immediately challenged her right to wear the crown. He was supported by France, Spain and Prussia, all of which saw the conflict between Charles Albert and Maria Theresa as an opportunity to destroy Austrian military and political power in central Europe. This led to the War of Austrian Succession, which lasted eight long and bitter years.

The War started when King Frederick of Prussia invaded Austrian territory. The King thought it would be easy to conquer Austria now that it was led by the twenty-three year old Maria Theresa who, Frederick believed, was surrounded by feeble and impotent ministers. In December of 1740, he sent an army of thirty thousand battle veterans into Silesia, an Austrian province ordering Prussian territory. He was certain that his army would shatter all resistance and would soon be marching through the streets of Vienna.

But Maria Theresa was far more capable of governing Austria than any of her enemies supposed. When Austria was invaded, the first act was to seek the advice of her ministers and generals to decide how to deal with the Prussian threat. She knew that her Empire was in disarray because of bureaucratic abuses during the reign of her father. The army's actual strength was far less than the 100,000 claimed by its generals, and army pay was more than two years in arrears. Many of the Empress's advisors suggested the cautious route of political compromise as the solution to the threat facing Austria. But a small group of Irish emigre generals and colonels urged defiance to Prussia and any other nation that sought to invade Austria to annex its territory or topple its monarchy.

Maria Theresa heeded the advice of her Irish military experts, not only because they believed they could achieve victory against Prussia and its allies, but also because their past service to Austria merited confidence in them. This group included men like Field Marshal Oliver Wallis, whose grandfather, Oliver Walsh, came to Austria in 1666 and changed his name to Wallis to make it easier for German-speaking people to pronounce. For three generations there had been a General Wallis leading the troops of the Austrian army. Another was General MacDonnell, whose father had led Prince Eugene's attack on Cremona in 1701 and personally captured the French commander, Marshal Villeroy. The most ardent advocate of resistance to Prussia was Maximillian Browne.

At the age of thirty-five, Browne was one of the youngest field marshals in the Austrian army. He strongly supported Maria Theresa's desire to keep her throne and protect her empire from foreign incursions. His father had received a colonel's commission in Austria after he was discharged from the Irish Brigade of France due to its reduction in size in 1698. Maximillian was born in 1705, and at the age of five, his parents sent him to stay with relatives in Limerick so he would not loose his connection to his Irish heritage. But his mother, who was a Fitzgerald of the Desmond branch, soon regretted her decision to send her son to live amid the strife in Ireland created by the newly enacted Penal Laws. After a short time, the Brownes recalled Maximillian and sent him to live with his uncle George Browne, a Colonel of Hungarian infantry. Young Maximillian Brown quickly discovered that his uncle George was a highly-respected officer who was the author of drill books and the military code of justice used by the Hungarian army. He watched his uncle transform the unseasoned Hungarian troops into an effective fighting force. To follow in the footsteps of his father and uncle, Maximillian resolved to pursue a military career.

In 1725, Browne returned to Austria and received a Colonel's commission in the Austrian army. He was given this high rank in recognition of the administrative training he had received as a cadet in his uncle's Hungarian regiment. This administrative background made Browne stand out even among the other Irish officers of the Austrian army. At the time, the Austrian army sorely needed officers with administrative skills to help the army modernize its organization. Given command of a regiment, Browne soon proved his leadership and organizational abilities by revising training methods and devising an efficient logistical support system for his regiment.

Austria's war against the Ottoman Empire in 1735 gave Browne the opportunity to demonstrate the proficiency of his regiment. Twenty years before, the Austrian army under the leadership of Prince Eugene defeated the Ottoman Turks at Peterswarden and the siege of Belgrade. Upon the defeat of the Turks, Austria was able to annex a good deal of territory belonging to Hungary and Serbia that had long been under Turkish rule. The second war grew out of the Turkish ambition to reclaim the disputed lands. In this second conflict, because of its neglect of training and logistics, the Austrian army met with defeat after defeat at the hands of the Turks. One of the few positive signs offering hope for the future in this disastrous conflict for Austria was the performance of the regiment commanded by Maximillian Browne. Although it was unable to turn the tide of battles it fought in, the good account it gave of itself demonstrated the effectiveness of Browne's training in maneuvering and modern fighting methods. Based on the outstanding performance of his regiment, Browne was given the rank of general and put in charge of several regiments. The war with the Turks ended, however, before the new methods Browne brought to the Austrian army could be put to the test. But even after the war, Browne continued with his modernization program by establishing a training routine for the entire army.

In December of 1740 when the Prussians invaded the Austrian province of Silesia at the start of the War of Austrian Succession, Browne—who was by then Field Marshall Maximillian von Browne—entreated the Empress Maria Theresa to let him lead an army of his modernized forces to challenge the enemy advance. The Empress readily consented. Because the Austrian army had shrunk in size during the 1730's and few troops were stationed in Silesia, Browne could muster a force of only 6,000 troops to meet a Prussian army five times this size. He knew that if his small army confronted the Prussians directly, they would be quickly overwhelmed. So Browne relied upon the traditional Irish tactics of ambush and maneuver he had learned from his father and uncle. Throughout early 1741, the Austrians raided and withdrew to delay the Prussian advance.

During the Silesian campaign, Browne introduced the new tactic of regiments of highly-mobile troops, which later became known as light infantry. These regiments were composed of infantrymen armed only with muskets, without the artillery, engineers or supply trains that normally accompanied infantry regiments. They took up positions on the flanks and ahead of a regular infantry column. Their purpose was to hold off advancing enemy forces until the larger main body of troops was able to shift from marching in a column to the line formation for battle, an involved and time-consuming process during which the main body was vulnerable. Browne's light infantry regiment was composed of Croatian sharpshooters who could slow down the approach of an enemy. After running into them in January and February of 1741 during his advance across Silesia, Frederick II of Prussia said they were the most dangerous opposition he had to face. Despite Browne's innovative tactics, he was unable to prevent the advance of Frederick's much larger army.

While Browne was defending Austrian territory in Silesia, Maria Theresa was assembling and equipping a force strong enough to try to drive the Prussian forces out of Austria. She would have led this force into battle herself except that German society prohibited women from taking part in warfare. When she spoke of her desire to fight alongside her soldiers, only her Irish generals and colonels offered her encouragement. For them, the image of Maria Theresa riding at the head of her army touched mythic chords from their Celtic-Irish heritage which revered female military leaders like Queen Maev and Queen Boudica. But other advisors to the Empress feared that Maria Theresa would loose the support of many of her conservative subjects if she strayed so far outside the bounds of female behavior dictated by traditional Germanic culture. So when her army marched north to engage the Prussians, she remained in Vienna.

In April of 1741, while Browne was still in Silesia, the Austrian army that Maria Theresa assembled met the Prussians on the field of Mollwitz on the border of Silesia and Austria. Although the Prussians carried the day, they took so many casualties that their advance into Austria was halted. Over the next few years, Austria unsuccessfully attempted to drive the Prussians out of Silesia. At the same time that Austria was fighting the Prussians, France had seized the Austrian-controlled province of Alsace, thereby threatening invasion across the northwest border of Austria. This threat from France was not eliminated until 1744 when England became Austria's ally and the two nations mounted a joint counter-offensive in Alsace. Although the province was not recaptured, France was prevented from occupying any additional Austrian territory. After the war dragged on for four more years with neither side gaining a decisive victory, the belligerents agreed to a peace conference in Dresden in 1748. Maria Theresa sent Maximillian Browne to this conference as the Austrian representative because his military exploits and his unswerving support of her right to rule the nation had made him one of her most trusted advisors. In order to secure a peace, he was forced to cede the economically important province of Silesia to Prussia and to grant independence to several smaller Austrian territories in Italy. Although Austria lost land, Maria Theresa gained her objective when she was confirmed as Empress of Austria as part of the peace settlement.

During the ensuing period of peace, Austrian generals taught their troops to protect regular infantry columns with regiments light infantry regiments. Prior to this time in European armies, the tactic of ambush and maneuver was used only at the discretion of a regimental commander whose unit was operating independently from the main force. There were no regiments specializing in the tactic. As word of the success of the Austrian light infantry spread, this type of specialized regiment was added to the armies of other nations. By the close of the 18th century, virtually every army in Europe was using light infantry units as skirmishers and flankers.

The War of Austrian Succession also led to the establishment of the military academy at Wiener Neustadt. During the long years of the war, Maria Theresa's armies relied heavily on the leadership talents of emigre military officers from Ireland, France and other nations. Once peace was made, she resolved to create an officer corps that was modern, efficient and made up of native-born Austrians. In 1752, she ordered the construction of a military academy to train Austrian cadets.

The academy was located in a citadel built during medieval times to keep watch for attacks from Mongols who had overrun neighboring Hungary. Many of its first instructors were Irish who were skilled veterans of the Austrian army. In 1771, it became known as the Theresian Academy to honor its founder, a name it still bears. To remind the young cadets of the heritage of honor and service they were expected to live up to, a series of portraits of Austria's prominent generals was hung in the Academy's great hall. Out of the thirty-seven faces looking down on the students, ten were men who were born in Ireland or who were descendants of Irish emigres. The Irish influence on Austrian military affairs became part of army tradition and culture, affecting to some degree every cadet who passed through the Academy.

In 1756, Austria became engulfed in the Seven Years War which broke out across Europe. The conflict grew out of the territorial ambitions of the major European nations in both Europe and the Americas. The former Austrian province of Silesia remained in the hands of Frederick II of Prussia, and he made no secret of his ambition to annex even more of Austria. When he learned that Maria Theresa was planning to form military alliances with France and Russia to both safeguard Austrian territory from Prussian aggression and to possibly regain Silesia, Frederick simultaneously attacked both Russia and Austria before this coalition against him could be formed.

Once again, Maria Theresa relied upon her Irish generals to defend her Empire. In one of the first battles of the war near Prague, Field Marshall Browne was mortally wounded when a cannonball crushed the bones of his leg. Theresa appointed Browne's cousin by marriage, Count Francis de Lacy, to replace Browne at the command of her armies on the Prussian front.

Francis de Lacy had shown the same outstanding, dependable military capabilities as Browne. De Lacy had a reputation for stressing the value of an efficient supply system for the units under his command so that the soldiers could concentrate on training and fighting instead of foraging for food. Because the officer corps of the day was still largely composed of aristocrats with little practical experience in supply or commerce, he often found himself teaching them matters ranging from overall logistic plans and to negotiating prices with farmers.

During the Seven Years War, De Lacy did not have the military resources to drive Prussian forces out of Silesia. With parts of the Austrian army occupied in other areas, he did not have enough troops. Furthermore, although Austria had made considerable progress in equipping its troops with the latest armaments such as the rifled musket, its weaponry was still not equal to that of the Prussians. Handicapped as he was, de Lacy was able to reach only a stalemate with the Prussians. Considering the disadvantages he had in this conflict, it required remarkable military skill for him to achieve this deadlock. Recognizing this, in commenting on de Lacy's achievement, Empress Maria Theresa wrote in a letter to her Chancellor, "I see no one more competent than de Lacy." When the War ended, the Queen made him President of the Council of War. In this position as head of the Austrian army, de Lacy continued to direct the gradual, costly process of modernizing the Austrian army's equipment, supply system and organization.

The part played by Irish emigres in the military and political affairs of Austria during the 18th century was important to Austria's survival and development as a nation. As a central European empire, the country was surrounded on all sides by nations who were potential enemies. Austria's military setbacks in the War of Austrian Succession and the Seven Years Wars had exposed the weaknesses of the Austrian army. Austria had lost portions of its territory and had to negotiate for peace from the weaker position. Irish emigre military leaders played important roles in saving Austria from total defeat. Although Austria had suffered setbacks, the Austrian monarchy was still in place and Austria was still a whole, independent nation. Austria had learned that a modernized army was fundamental in offering any hope of protecting its borders against the potentially hostile nations surrounding it. In the years after these two wars, Irish military leaders—de Lacy and others such as General Laval Nugent and General William O'Kelly—took the lead in improving training, logistics, armaments, and organization of the Austrian army so that Austria could effectively defend itself when attacked by another nation. From 1690 until the mid 19th century, Irish emigres and their descendants played central roles in the wars of Austria and the evolution of the Austrian army.

AGRICULTURE AND THE IRISH IN CENTRAL EUROPE

In the 18th century in Austria, Hungary and Russia, food production still depended on serfs working small plots of land owned by nobles who were entitled to a large portion of the crop. Surplus crops were ordinarily meager, however, because the farming tools used by the serfs were primitive, and it was the rare serf who had a horse or ox for plowing. The serfs were ignorant of the practices of crop rotation or fertilizing to keep the soil from being depleted. Instead, they planted the same cereal crops of wheat and sorghum year after year. Despite the arduous, thankless life of the serfs in toiling to produce meager harvests, they could not engage in any other kind of employment or move to a more fertile location without permission from the local noble. But a noble would hardly ever give such permission. Rather, with the surplus crops they sold in the markets being their main source of revenue, the nobles continually demanded higher production from their serfs.

In Austria, this farming system, antiquated as it was, managed to supply the population with enough food until there was a sudden increase early in the reign of Maria Theresa, about 1745. (The reasons for this increase in population are unknown to this day.) Since the serfs could not grow enough food for this increased population, a food crisis came upon Austria. The crisis touched the people of the country as well as the cities.

Many serf families grew so large that they could not even feed themselves. Out of desperation, whether they had the permission from their noble or not, legions of serfs abandoned their plots of land to make their way to the cities to try to find work. In Vienna, Linz, Prague or one of the other cities of the Austrian Empire, they lived under wretched conditions, and few found work. Not only were the uprooted serfs alarmed over the possibility of starvation, but they were faced with sharply rising food prices.

Austria's food crisis had a serious effect on the nation's military when the Seven Years War began in 1756. After a full day's drill, no matter how hot or cold the weather, soldiers could expect only a bowl of thin soup. They were often weakened from hunger when they went to battle with enemy forces. Many deserted just to look for food.

Faced with growing discontent in all parts of Austrian society, Maria Theresa directed her Chancellor Wenzel Kaunitz to seek a solution to the problem of low food production. She had appointed him Chancellor in 1753, and he had capably administered her government. She picked him for this task over her other advisors because he had a keen interest in agriculture and recognized that food production was essential to maintaining social harmony in Austria. Kaunitz belonged to a number of agricultural societies recently formed among the landed gentry to experiment with crop rotation and cultivation of plants from foreign lands. Since agriculture had become a gentleman's hobby in Austria as well as other parts of Europe, many other land owners also belonged to the agricultural societies. Kaunitz was particularly struck by the ideas of Viscount Nicholas Taaffe, an elderly Irish emigre prominent in both military and agricultural circles.

Taaffe had been interested in farming all of his life. His father, Francis, had been a gentleman farmer on his lands in County Sligo before immigrating to Austria in the 1680's. When the English Parliament passed an act forbidding Catholics from owning land, Francis was faced with a choice between continued prosperity if he converted to the Anglican faith and poverty if he remained true to his traditional religion. To escape this dilemma, Francis found a Protestant willing to buy his land and he left Ireland for Europe, where he wandered for a time before settling in Austria. He offered his services to the Austrian army, fought against the

Ottoman Turks and rose to the rank of general for his role in the relief of Vienna in 1683. But his main interest remained farming. With the funds from the sale of his Sligo estates, he purchased a manor in Silesia where he supervised the planting and cultivation of crops whenever he had time away from his duties to the army and the court in Vienna. Like his father, Nicholas pursued a military career—rising to the rank of general—while actively supervising the farming of his lands whenever his military duties would permit. Seeing that disease often struck the cereal crops that were planted year after year on the same ground, Nicholas wondered if the potato, the staple of his family's homeland that his father had grown before coming to Austria, would flourish in Silesian soil. At the close of the 1730's, he obtained some seed potatoes and instructed the peasants in potato cultivation—how to slice the seed potato to preserve the eye, how to shape a mound of soil around the base of the plant, and how to protect the plant's leaves from insects. At the end of the summer, these methods yielded an abundance of potatoes.

Taaffe's success did not spread bring an immediate end to the problem of food production in Austria. New ideas in farming spread only by the slow method of word-of-mouth, and were implemented only spottily and haphazardly. Besides, the start of the War of Austrian Succession interfered with any progress Austria might have made in food production. When the War ended, some of the landowners belonging to agricultural societies became interested in potato cultivation, including Field Marshal Oliver Wallis, an Irish emigre also involved in farming who followed Taaffe's lead by planting potatoes in the fields of his estates. So when Austrian food production could not keep up with the growing population in the 1750's, both Taaffe and Wallis began to work closely with Chancellor Kaunitz to inform farmers about their success in potato farming.

Taaffe and Wallis also joined with Kaunitz in advocating fundamental reform in the agricultural practices in the Austrian Empire. Following their advice, the government passed regulations to control the type of crops planted and to create market incentives for farmers to produce a surplus. The agricultural societies were used to educate other farmers in the most advanced farming techniques. Peasants and landlords alike were taught the value of crop rotation, fields left fallow for a season, and efficient pest control. The program was successfully implemented, but it took decades before the inefficient practices of a serf-based agricultural system were replaced with more modern farming methods throughout Austria. Year by year, food production increased until the specter of famine was lifted from the Austrian Empire.

In the second half of the 18th century, Nicholas Taaffe's success in convincing Austrian farmers to raise potatoes had an effect that went far beyond alleviating the Austrian food shortage. As the Austrian army increasingly relied on potatoes for its rations, other nations began to see the benefits of using the cheaply-produced and long-lasting potatoes as one of the staples in the diet of soldiers. By 1777, the War of Bavarian Succession—fought between Austria and Prussia to prevent the Austrian Emperor from inheriting the crown of Bavaria—was popularly called "The Potato War" because the troops of both sides depended so heavily on potatoes for their rations. By the Napoleonic era, the potato was as important to the French soldiers marching across Europe as their muskets and bayonets.

In Austria, Taaffe, Wallis and other Irish emigres played an important role in implementing changes in farming methods during the 18th century. They demonstrated that the soil could produce a much greater quantity of food. But even more vital were their efforts to educate farmers. Replenishing the soil with fertilizer, rotating crops, and cultivating larger plots was the core of their message. Because of their prominent social position in the court of the Austrian Emperors, they became the primary agricultural advisors. Irish emigre landowners, statesmen and soldiers in Austria influenced the government and farmers to meet the need for food for the growing population, thus helping Austria move into the modern age.

THE MYSTERY OF PRINCE RUDOLPH'S DEATH

In 1969, an elderly man named Edward Taaffe, who was known to his friends as "Yaxi", died in Dublin. He was a direct descendant of the same Nicholas Taaffe who helped to lead Austria out of its food crises in the 18th century. Although Yaxi was born near Vienna and inherited the Austrian title of Count, he had emigrated to Ireland in 1938 when of

Germany annexed Austria. Because of the Taaffe family's connections to the Hapsburg rulers of Austria, Yaxi's death rekindled a controversy concerning the suicide of Crown Prince Rudolph of Austria in 1889. Yaxi's grandfather, also named Edward, had been Prime Minister of the Austro-Hungarian Empire from 1879 to 1893. Many people believed that the Prime Minister had passed down to his grandson secret documents which contained information about Prince Rudolph's death.

Rudolph was the first-born son of Franz Joseph, Emperor of the Austro-Hungarian Empire in the late 19th century. To his father's dismay, Rudolph seemed more interested in gambling, drinking, and carousing with artists and anarchists than in the responsibilities of a Crown Prince. Although libertine behavior was characteristic of the Austrian royalty at the time, Emperor Franz Joseph considered his son's behavior disgraceful, and barred him from any role in public affairs. In 1881, Franz Joseph insisted that Rudolph marry the Belgian Princess Stephanie in the hope that they would produce a child better suited to become a monarch. Rudolph assented, but he found his new bride priggish and continued a number of affairs with women of the royal court.

Rudolph fell in love with one of his paramours, the Baroness Marie Vetsera. In 1889, he asked his father for permission to divorce Princess Stephanie. Franz Joseph postponed responding to his son's request while he considered the political consequences. If Rudolph divorced Stephanie, he would be ineligible for the crown and Rudolph's cousin, Franz Ferdinand, would become the Crown Prince of Austria. The Emperor consulted with his Prime Minister, Count Edward Taaffe, who strongly advised against granting a divorce. Although Taaffe believed that Franz Ferdinand would be a more suitable Crown Prince than Rudolph, he was concerned that liberals seeking to limit the power of the Emperor would use a divorce scandal to discredit the Emperor and his family.

Taaffe had earned the confidence of the Emperor for his years of devoted service to Austria. In 1867, as Deputy Minister President, he was one of the principle architects of the agreement with Hungry that created the dual monarchy of Austria-Hungary. This organized the Empire into a confederation, with Austria and Hungary as separate states that recognized the same monarch—Emperor Franz Joseph. The people of Austria and Hungary could elect their own legislators and decide most internal matters for themselves. But the arrangement left nationalist groups within the Austro-Hungarian Empire dissatisfied. As minorities, the Czechs, Croats, Serbs and Slovaks did not believe they were adequately represented in the legislators and clamored for as much autonomy from the Hapsburg Emperor as the Hungarians enjoyed. Nihilists, anarchists, and communists added to the political ferment in the Empire with their radical agendas.

After he became Prime Minister in 1879, Taaffe negotiated a compromise with Czech nationalists. The Czech language would be given equal footing with German in Bohemia; a Czech university was founded; and more positions in the government were promised to the Czechs. The other nationalities within the Empire responded by asking for similar concessions. Throughout the 1880's, Taaffe continued negotiating with the dissident ethnic groups hoping to achieve internal political stability for the Austro-Hungarian Empire while avoiding any incidents—such as a divorce in the royal family—that could ignite rebellion.

Although Taaffe knew that the conservative nobility, clergy and middle-class merchants of the Empire were already concerned that Rudolph was unfit to wear the crown, he advised the Emperor against granting Rudolph a divorce because the scandal would create misgivings about the Emperor and his family, and potentially alienate the Christian Socialists, the most important Austrian political party. These conservatives supporting the Emperor were termed the "Iron Ring", and Taaffe believed that the political stability of the Empire depended on their continued support. It was largely due to Taaffe's influence that Franz Joseph refused to grant Rudolph a divorce. But the problem of Prince Rudolph's outrageous behavior which making him unsuitable to wear the crown remained unsolved.

The dilemma was unexpectedly resolved in June of 1889 when Rudolph took Maria Vetsera to his hunting lodge at Mayerling so they could enjoy each other's company in seclusion. The next day, both Crown Prince Rudolph and the Baroness Maria Vetsera were found dead from gunshot wounds. Rumors of intrigue and assassination swept through Austria. Publicly, the Emperor declared that Rudolph had shot his lover and then killed himself. But privately, he instructed Count Taaffe to conduct a discreet investigation to answer questions that arose about the death of his son.

A few months later, Count Taaffe finished his report and delivered it to the Emperor. Franz Joseph read it and returned it to Taaffe with the order that it was to be kept secret. Taaffe was to safeguard the report, and it was to be passed down to the eldest son in each generation of Taaffe's descendants for perpetual safekeeping. Yaxi Taaffe was the last male descendant of the line and should have had these documents in his possession, but they were not found after his death in 1969. Some historians speculated that the documents were destroyed in 1916 when a fire ravaged the Taaffe estate in Ellischau, Austria. Because of several letters from Catholic bishops to Edward Taaffe referring to the documents, other historians believed that the papers were entrusted to the Vatican, sealed forever in its archives. Because these documents were not found after Yaxi Taaffe's death and because of the steadfast refusal of the Vatican to reveal if they have any Taaffe archives in their possession, the truth of the Mayerling affair will probably always be a mystery. But it did reveal the amount of trust and power that the Emperor placed in his Prime Minister, Edward Taaffe.

After Prince Rudolph's death, Edward Taaffe prevented the scandal surrounding the Prince's death from damaging the monarchy by granting additional concessions to ethnic minorities in the Empire. His policy of striking a balance between the liberals who desired to dismantle the Empire and the conservatives who desired to stifle all political reforms kept the Austro-Hungarian Empire intact. Despite Taaffe's keen negotiating skills, however, he could engineer no permanent solutions for the Emprie's ethnic and political rivalries. Taaffe retired in 1893. A little more than two decades after Taaffe's death in 1895 at his estate at Ellischau, the patchwork Austro-Hungarian Empire broke apart from internal social and economic stresses intensified by World War I.

Edward Taaffe was one of Franz Joseph's most trusted officials. This exemplifies the role of Irish emigres or their descendants in Austrian society. Because of their small number, their roles in crises of Austrian society—whether military threat, a food shortage or a scandal involving the monarchy—the contribution of Irish emigres and their descendants to Austrian society and history is especially evident.

CHAPTER 12

The Enduring Influence

All those far seas and shores that must be crossed,
They terrify me; yet
Go you, my son, swift be your cleaving prow
And do not quite forget

—Colman, c. 7th century

During the millennium covered in this book—from the 700's to the 1800's—men and women from Ireland had a steady influence on the formation of Europe. It was during this millennium that the origins of Western culture were laid in the Carolingian Renaissance, Christianity took root throughout Europe, universities were founded, the bases ofscience were established, nations were formed, democracy was established, and the various states of Europe became inter-related by diplomatic and economic activity. Irish emigres had significant, and in some cases major, parts in each of these developments in the formation of Europe.

The unusual aspect of this steady, multifarious and identifiable influence of the Irish is that they did not bring anything essentially novel to Europe. Irish lore and activities stimulated the seeds of Celtic culture which remained in Europe after the Roman Empire collapsed and during the barbarian invasions and rule. The re-emergence of fundamentals of Celtic culture in Europe from the influence of the Irish emigres was not so strong that these fundamentals supplanted aspects of Roman civilization and barbarian culture which had taken root. But the spirituality and knowledge the Irish related, the skills they taught and the effects of their activities ensured that Celtic culture, along with classical and northern barbarian culture, would play a permanent and central part in Europe's history and cultural development.

The remarkable influence of the Irish in Europe stemmed not only from the qualities the Irish emigres brought with them—qualities that were primarily reflections of ancient Celtic culture. It also stemmed rom the pattern of Irish emigration over this millennium, plus the numbers of Irish in this pattern. Although there were dips in this pattern of emigration—most notably the period from the waning of the Carolingian Renaissance (c. 900) until the late Middle Ages (c. 1300)—over the entire millennium, the Irish influence is seen as continual. Although the numbers of Irish emigres—almost all monks—fell markedly in the late 800's, the influence of generations of monks up until this time was such that it remained strong and formative despite not being regularly reinforced or extended by the fewer numbers of monks who came to Europe afterwards.

One of the principal reasons the monks journeying to Europe toward the end of the Dark Ages had such a long-lasting influence was the sturdy monasteries they built which became spiritual and educational centers for the surrounding populations. A number of these monasteries survive today, engaged in the same spiritual and educational work as they were in the time when they were founded. The early Irish monks determined the purpose and set the tone for these early medieval monasteries, establishing customs and observances continued by following generations of monks whether they were from Ireland or not. Another reason the influence of the early monks lasted beyond their time is that they taught the rudiments of practical activities such as growing crops and animal husbandry. During the Middle Ages, such practices continued virtually unchanged, so that the methods taught by the monks remained in use for centuries. A third reason why the influence of the monks persisted is that the monks influenced the spirituality, interests such as education, and other aspects of the manner of rule of petty kings in different parts of Europe. This manner of rule adopted by these petty kings in the period of change from the Dark Ages to the Middle Ages continued long into the Middle Ages, thus prolonging the influence of the early Irish monks.

Another important reason that their influence continued was that the Middle Ages were an embodiment of basic cultural elements that were strongly influenced by the monks, and in some cases were almost direct reflections of them. The monks had a strong influence on the development of the Christian spirituality which became bound in the Middle Ages. The closeness between the spiritual leaders and temporal rulers had its basis in the relationship between the Irish monks and the petty kings. But more than this, the monasteries founded by the Irish monks were the models for the manors upon which feudalism—the foundation of the Middle Ages—was based. Like the monasteries, the manors were meant to be self-sufficient. The manors were meant to provide for the spiritual concerns as well as the practical needs of the people involved in them. The variety of skills possessed among groups of monks who founded a monastery—such as stone masonry, woodcraft, animal husbandry—were possessed by the varied persons who belonged to a manor. The class structure with its reciprocal obligations by which a manor's self-sufficiency could be maintained was a more complex and explicit representation of the organization of a monastery. The influence of the Irish monks in the beginnings of the Middle Ages shaped the spirituality and way of life which came to be the main feature of the Middle Ages. Since the Middle Ages were a long period of stability during which there was no significant change in the spirituality or the way of life, the influence of the Irish lasted long beyond their appearance in Europe.

When Irish emigres again began arriving in Europe in appreciable numbers towards the end of the Middle Ages—in the 1400's—they readily adapted to the broad changes underway in the culture of Europe which was moving into the Renaissance and the modern era. Whereas the monks of the late Dark Ages and early Middle Ages had come to Europe primarily for spiritual motives, the later generations of emigres were soldiers, merchants, farmers, nobles, artisans and teachers, along with some priests and nuns. This diversity of positions and occupations enabled the later Irish emigres to integrate into varied positions in European societies when the feudal system was breaking up, cities were growing, ties between different regions and different countries were forming, and secularization was altering perspectives. Because the Irish had not been involved in the feudal system, they often brought fresh ideas and new practices to the fields they became engaged in; and some of the emigres became leaders in those fields. Apart from the ideas and practices the later emigres brought with them, they were accepted because of the favorable memory of the monks who had long ago preceded them and because like the monks, they touched vestiges of the ancient Celtic culture they shared with the Europeans.

New emigres and descendants of previous emigres from Ireland were involved in the trends shaping the Europe of the modern world during the Renaissance. The central movement shaping Europe at this time was the Protestant Reformation. Although Irish emigres and their descendants played only a small role in those European countries that largely became Protestant, the Irish helped Catholicism to remain vibrant and dominant in those European countries which resisted the Reformation. The numbers of Irish lay persons who were staunchly Catholic, along with the activities of Irish clergy, contributed to the strengthening of Catholicism in countries such as France and Austria which had sizeable Protestant minorities. Many emigres played roles in shaping the responses of these countries to Protestantism, which responses figured heavily into the nature of these countries in the modern world. For instance, in helping certain countries of Europe remain Catholic, the Irish also played a role in their secularization. The Irish had never been authoritarian, hierarchical or ceremonious in their practice of Catholicism. Yet they had always been defenders of Catholicism. In the close inter-relationship between Church and State in the Middle Ages, it had been bishops, cardinals and Popes representing Roman Catholicism, not Celtic Christianity, which influenced the kings and nobility that ruled a country. Even though many countries in Europe remained Catholic, despite the major historical movement of the Protestant Reformation, they were nevertheless inevitably much affected by the trends of secularism of the time. When such trends brought about the increasing separation of Church and State, the influence of the Irish emigres and their descendants grew.

Although strong Catholics, the Irish always had a more practical and democratic approach to daily life, political and social matters, as well as religious views. This practical and democratic approach was more in tune with the secularization of the era, and therefore the Irish often had considerable influence with a country's ruler and in the fields such as business and medicine which were developing as a part of the secularization.

Besides secularization, nationalism was another movement which emerged following the Middle Ages. The Irish, with their sense of individuality and concept of clan loyalty, played substantial parts in the nationalistic trends shaping a number of the countries of Europe. These parts were played not only by Irish counselors, diplomats, statesmen and government officials, but also by Irish military leaders and soldiers. The exploits of military units led by Irish officers or all-Irish military units helped Spain from being conquered by Napoleon's forces, Portugal from losing territory to Spain, and Austria from being defeated by Frederick the Great of Prussia. Such exploits not only epitomized the nationalistic spirit, but also led to the geographic shape of a number of the nations of modern Europe.

Although the Irish emigres had a capacity for adaptability which allowed them to cope with changing social conditions and historical developments over centuries in Europe, they also had a worldview which gave them a stability in particular circumstances and in the course of historical changes. The Irish had a holistic worldview that had its origins in Celtic culture. As with the ancient Celts, the Irish saw knowledge, spirituality, and practical abilities and skills as inter-related. This worldview enabled Irish emigres to offer solutions to the problems perceived by rulers and local populations of Europe. There were times when this solutions offered could seem almost visionary. But besides this practical dimension of the worldview, it also afforded the emigres and their descendants a position in the changing circumstances which kept them from adopting absolutist forms or radical ideas for dealing with the changing circumstances and problems they became involved in. Thus, while genuinely and firmly Catholic, the Irish never completely accepted the doctrines or the absolutist authority of the Pope. With their Catholicism, the earlier emigres were welcomed across Europe; and then when the influence of Catholicism began to wan with the Protestant Reformation, the Irish did not undergo a change in the principles or beliefs in order to play a role in the secularization of the countries which remained Catholic. They played their influential role without having to change the Catholicism they always practiced and by resisting the Protestant Reformation. This unique position the Irish would hold in historical changes occurring in Europe is perhaps best evidenced in the reliance of different European monarchs on the Irish as counselors and diplomats in the transition of their countries from kingdoms into nations and also as advisors and political leaders for reforms in response to the movement of democracy. While being mostly egalitarian and democratic from their Celtic roots, emigres nonetheless served rulers and nobility loyally and effectively. When democratic tendencies grew in European societies, the emigres were well suited to serve a country's monarchs by helping in their response to these tendencies. In these circumstances, the Irish acted on their inherent beliefs and principles without joining the revolutionary movements growing in the countries of Europe.

Despite their exceptional capacity for adaptability and their focus on particular problems or needs in various European societies at different times, the Irish worldview remained constant during the centuries of emigration. It had the effect of reinforcing the accomplishments and qualities of earlier generations of emigres, which substantiated the Irish influence on Europe.

Not only the pattern of the generations of Irish emigres, but their number accounted for their exceptional influence. Their numbers were not so large that they could not be absorbed by the countries they went to, but not so small that they were assimilated without a trace. Because their numbers were not so large and were spread out over the whole period of emigration and several countries, following generations of Irish were welcome in countries favored by the emigres. In these countries, since the numbers of previous emigres had been enough so that there was nonetheless an Irish presence, following generations of emigres were attracted to them. The intermediate number of emigres also enabled particular Irish who became distinguished in different fields to gain their prominent and influential positions. There were never so many Irish in any one country that its rulers and other leaders or its native population were concerned that Irish who rose to prominence were leading the way for an Irish takeover of a field.

The basis for the Irish influence was not only the inter-action between Irish emigres and rulers and populations of the countries they went to, but also the inter-action among Irish within a country and between generations of emigres. This basis can be illuminated by a comparison of the Irish with both the barbarian tribes of northern Europe and the Jews. The barbarians of northern Europe came to Europe in such numbers that they overturned the societies based on Roman administration and reflecting the Roman domination. They replaced this Roman system with their own hodgepodge of petty kingdoms. These kingdoms were basically warrior societies in which the crafts and arts slipped into desuetude and spiritual inclinations had no outlet. The culture and characteristics of the barbarians obviously dominated Europe. But the Irish never came to Europe, or to any part of it, in such hordes that they had such a totally transforming effect. Rather, the Irish were like waters of nourishment or were innovators in various fields, usually fields they were assigned to or allowed to enter by the rulers of a country.

When compared to the Jews, the Irish were present in greater numbers, and over a considerably broader range of fields. Thus, although particular Jews made notable or outstanding achievements in certain fields, these achievements were based on the particular qualities of the individual, not cultural attributes. Thus where Jews had exceptional influence over a field of the broader culture, this is seen as reflecting practices of the existing culture, not materially contributing qualities or capacities of Jewish culture to the traditional culture of a country. Jewish culture was just not compatible with the culture of Europe in the essential way that the Irish culture was with its Celtic roots. Besides, there were not following numbers of Jewish emigres to reinforce and substantiate the achievements of individual Jews.

Besides the qualities, enterprise and innovative spirit of the Irish emigres which were reflections of their culture of Celtic origin, their emigration pattern over the geography of Europe and the numbers of emigres spread over the centuries of emigration were factors in their identifiable, unique and enduring influence on European history and culture.

To note this exceptional influence of the Irish emigres on the formation of Europe as we have in this book is not to minimize or disregard the influence of national characteristics, ethnic traits, or other immigrant groups. To note this Irish influence, however, is to point to the common ground of Celtic culture from which thir particular influences arose. The story of the influence of outstanding Irish individuals and descendants and the numbers of Irish emigres is to bring to light a significant influence on the formation and nature of Europe; and it also discloses its foundation in Celtic culture and the reawakening and ongoing influence of this culture which was represented most clearly by the Irish.

BIBLIOGRAPHY

The Ancient Celts

Ailred. *The Life of Ninian*. Facs. Reprt. n.p.: Llanerch Enterprises, 1989.

Chadwick, Nora. *The Celts*. London: Penguin Books, rprt. 1991.

Cottrell, Leonard. *The Roman Invasion of Britain*. New York: Barnes & Noble, 1992.

De La Bedoyere, Guy. *The Finds of Roman Britain*. London: Batsford, 1989.

Ellis, Peter Berresford. *The Celtic Empire - The First Millennium of Celtic History, 1,000 B.C.-51 A.D*. Carolina Academic Press, 1990.

_____. *The Druids*. London: Constable, 1994.

Funck-Brentano, Fr. *A History of Gaul: Celtic, Roman and Frankish Rule*. trans. E.F. Buckley. New York: Barnes and Noble, 1993.

Gambutas, Marija. *The Civilization of the Goddess: The World of Old Europe*. ed. Joan Marler. San Francisco: Harper, 1991.

Green, Miranda. *Celtic Goddesses: Warriors, Virgins and Mothers*. New York: George Braziller, 1996.

Hart, B.H. Liddell. *Scipio Africanus: Greater Than Napoleon*. London: Greenhill Books, rprt. 1992, orig. pub. 1926.

Herity, Michael and George Eogan. *Ireland in Prehistory*. London: Routledge, 1973.

Hubert, Henri. *The History of the Celtic People*. London: Bracken Books, orig. pub. 1934, rprt. 1992.

Matthews, John. *Taliesin: Shamanism and The Bardic Mysteries in Britain and Ireland*. London: The Aquarian Press, 1991.

_____. *The Celtic Shaman*. Rockport MA: Element, 1991.

Rankin, H.D. *The Celts and The Classical World*. London: Croom Helm, 1987.

Ross, Anne and Don Robins. *The Life and Death of a Druid Prince*. New York: Summit Books, 1989.

Rutherford, Ward. *The Druids: Magicians of the West*. London: The Aquarian Press, 1978.

The Middle Ages

Bede, The Venerable. *Baedae Opera Historica*. vol 1. Cambridge, MA: Harvard University Press, 1930.

Brondsted, Johannes. *The Vikings*. Trans. Kalle Skov. Baltimore: Pelican, 1965.

Colum, Padraic. *A Treasury of Irish Folklore*. New York: Wing, 1992.

Condren, Mary. *The Serpent And The Goddess: Women, Religion and Power in Celtic Ireland*. San Francisco: Harper, 1989.

Delbrück, Hans. *Medieval Warfare*. trans. Walter J. Renfroe, Jr., vol. III, History Of The Art of War. Lincoln, NB: University of Nebraska Press, 1982.

De Paor, Liam. *Saint Patrick's World*. Dublin:Four Courts Press, 1993.

Ellis, Peter Berresford. *Celtic Inheritance*. New York: Dorset, 1992.

_____. *Celt and Saxon: The Struggle For Britain AD 410-937*. London: Constable, 1993.

Englebert, Omer. *The Lives of The Saints*. trans. Christopher and Ann Fremantle. New York: Barnes & Noble, 1994.

Giraldus Cambrensis. *On The Instruction of Princes*. trans. Joseph Sevenson. Dyfed, Wales: J.M.F. Books. Facs. Rprt. 1991.

246   BIBLIOGRAPHY

Herlihy, David. *Women, Family and Society in Medieval Europe: Historical Essays 1978-1991*. Providence, RI: Berghahn Books, 1995.

Kelly, Fergus. *A Guide to Early Irish Law*. Dublin: Dublin Institute For Advanced Studies, 1988.

Lehane, Brendan. *Early Celtic Christianity*. New York: Barnes & Noble, 1993.

Mackie, J.D. *A History of Scotland*. Baltimore:Penguin, 1964.

McCall, Andrew. *The Medieval Underworld*. New York: Dorset, 1979.

McManus, Damian. *A Guide to Ogham*. Maynooth, Ireland: An Sagart, 1991.

Minahane, John. *The Christian Druids*. Dublin: Sanas Press, 1993.

Otway-Ruthven, A.J. *A History of Medieval Ireland*. New York: Barnes and Noble, 1980.

Patterson, Nerys. *Cattle Lords & Clansmen: The Social Structure of Early Ireland*. 2nd ed. Notre Dame,IN: University of Notre Dame Press, 1994.

Richter, Michael. *Medieval Ireland: The Enduring Tradition*. Dublin: Gill and Macmillan, 1988.

Roche, Richard. *The Norman Invasion of Ireland*. Dublin: Anvil Books, 1979.

Roy, James Charles. *Islands of Storm*. Chester, PA: Dufour Editions, 1991.

Seymour, St. John D. *Irish Witchcraft and Demonology*. New York: Dorset, 1992.

Toulson, Shirley. *The Celtic Year*. Rockport, MA: Element, 1993.

The Renaissance

Berleth, Richard. *The Twilight Lords*. New York: Barnes & Noble, 1995.

Hale, John. *Civilization of Europe In The Renaissance*. New York: Atheneum, 1994.

Henry, Gráinne. "The Emerging Identity of an Irish Military Group in the Spanish Netherlands". R.V. Comerford, et. al. *Religion, Conflict and Coexistence in Ireland*. Dublin: Gill and MacMillan, 1990.

Kilfeather, T.P. *Ireland: Graveyard of The Spanish Armada* Dublin: Anvil 1967, rprt. 1979.

Morgan, Hiram. *Tyrone's Rebellion: The Outbreak of the Nine Years War in Tudor Ireland*. Woodbridge, England: The Boydell Press, 1993.

O'Malley, John W. *The First Jesuits*. Cambridge, MA: Harvard University Press, 1993.

The Seventeenth and Eighteenth Centuries

Anderson, M.S. *Europe In The Eighteenth Century*. London: Longmans, 1961.

Barbosa Suerio, M.B. *Um Inquérito da Inqusiçao No Século XVII*. Lisboa: Tipog. da Penitenciaria, 1930.

Boylan, Henry. *Wolfe Tone*. Dublin: Gill and MacMillan, 1981.

Braudel, Fernand. *Civilization and Capitalism: 15th   18th Century*. Vol. I. "The Strutures of Everyday Life." trans. Siân Reynolds. New York: Harper and Row, 1979.

Casway, J. "Irish Women Overseas, 1500-1800", Margaret MacCurtain and Mary O'Dowd, ed. *Women In Early Modern Ireland*. Dublin: Wolfhound Press, 1991.

Clear, Caitriona. *Nuns In Nineteenth Century Ireland*. Dublin: Gill and MacMillan, 1987.

Conway, James, report on death of in duel with General Hogan. Chérin 59, Folio 7. Départemente des Manuscrits, Bibliothèque Nationale, Paris.

Delbrück, Hans. *The Dawn of Modern Warfare*. trans. Walter J. Renfroe, Jr., vol. IV, History Of The Art of War. Lincoln, NB: University of Nebraska Press, 1982.

Dos Passos, John. *The Portugal Story*. Garden City, NY: Doubleday & Co., Inc. 1969.

Elliott, Marianne. *Partners in Revolution*. New Haven, CT: Yale University Press, 1989.

Feasa, Fergus [Liam Conaghon]. "Spain: The Inishown Connection." *Derry Journal*. 24 June 1986.

Fitzpatrick, Brendan. *Seventeenth-Century Ireland: The War of Religions*. Dublin: Gill and MacMillan, 1988.

Hargreaves-Mawdsley, W.N. ed. and trans. *Spain Under the Bourbons, 1700-1833*. Columbia, S.C.: University of South Carolina Press, 1973.

Henderson, Nicholas. *Prince Eugen of Savoy* London: The History Book Club, 1966.

Joao V. Appointment of M. Hogan to rank of Brigadier General, 4 May 1708. DS. Nacional Arquivo, Torre do Tombo, Portugal.

Joao V. Appointment of Jacob Hogan to Adjutant, 23 January 1709. DS. Arquivo Historie Militaire, Santa Appolonia, Portugal.

Joao V. Appointment of M. Hogan to rank of Lieutenant General, 30 April 1710. DS. Arquivo Historie Militaire, Santa Appolonia, Portugal.

Joao V to Joao Hogan, 12 November 1712. LS. Packet 141, No. 70. Nacional Arquivo, Torre do Tombo, Portgual.

Joao V. Appointment of Joao Hogan to Major General, 10 Aug 1713. DS. Nacional Arquivo, Torre do Tombo, Portugal.

Joao V. Appointment of D. Hogan to rank of Lieutenant, 14 August 1726. DS. Packet 72, No. 19. Nacional Arquivo, Torre do Tombo, Portugal.

Kee, Robert. *The Most Distressful Country.* vol I. *The Green Flag.* London: Penguin Books, 1972.

Kelly, James. *That Damn'd Thing Called Honour: Duelling in Ireland 1570-1850.* Cork:Cork University Press, 1995.

Lawless, J. Murphy "Images of 'Poor' Women in the Writing of Irish Men Midwives", Margaret MacCurtain & Mary O'Dowd, ed. *Women In Early Modern Ireland.* Dublin: Wolfhound, 1991.

Livermore, H.V. *A New History of Portugal.* Cambridge, England: Cambridge University Press, 1966.

Lynch, John. *Bourbon Spain, 1700-1808.* Oxford: Basil Blackwell, 1989.

Mac-Geoghegan, the Abbé. *The History of Ireland, Ancient and Modern.* New York: D. & J. Sadlier & Co., 1868.

Macrory, Patrick. *The Siege of Derry.* Oxford: Oxford University Press, 1980.

MacCurtain, Margaret. *Tudor and Stuart Ireland.* Dublin: Gill and MacMillan, 1972.

Magtochair. *Inishowen, Its History, Traditions and Antiquaries.* N.P: M. Haskin, 1867.

Marques, A. H. DeOlivera. *History of Portugal: From Lusitania To Empire.* Vol I. New York: Columia University Press, 1973.

Mareschal, M., King's First Surgeon, to Duke of Chartres, 2 March 1727. LS. Bibliotèque Nationale, Paris, France.

Murtagh, Harman. "Irish soldiers abroad, 1600-1800," *A Military History of Ireland.* ed. Thomas Bartlett and Keith Jeffrey. Cambridge, England: Cambridge University Press, 1996.

O'Callaghan, J.C. *The History of the Irish Brigades in the Service of France.* n.p.: 1842.

Ohlmeyer, Jane H. *Civil War and Restoration in the Three Stuart Kingdoms.* Cambridge England: Cambridge University Press, 1993.

250   BIBLIOGRAPHY

Roth, Cecil. *The Spanish Inquisition.* New York: W.W. Norton & Co., 1964.

Saxotte, Pierre. *Frederick the Great.* New Haven, CT: Yale University Press, 1942.

Simms, J.G. "The Irish on the Continent, 1691-1800". *A New History of Ireland.* ed. T.W. Moody and W.E. Vaughn. Oxford: Clarendon Press, 1986.

Swords, Liam. *Soldiers Scholars Priests: A Short History of the Irish College, Paris.* Paris: The Irish College, 1985.

Szabo, Franz A.J. *Kaunitz and Enlightened Absolutism 1753-1780.* Cambridge, England: Cambridge University Press, 1994.

Valaer, Peter. *Wines of the World.* New York: Abelard Press, 1950.

Verlinden, Charles. "Prince Henry in Modern Perspective As Father Of The Descobrimentos." *Portugal, The Pathfinder: Journeys From The Medieval Toward The Modern World.* ed. George D. Winius. Madison, WI: The Hispanic Seminary of Medieval Studies, 1995.

Williamson, James A. *A Short History of British Expansion.* New York: The MacMillan Company, 1931.

The Nineteenth Century

Bonner, Brian. *That Audacious Traitor.* Pallinskery, Ireland: Silesian Press Trust, n.d.

Coverdale, John F. *The Basque Phase of Spain's First Carlist War.* Princeton, NJ: Princeton University Press, 1984.

Grivot, Denis. *Le Chateau de Sully.* Lyon: Héliogravure Lescuyer, n.d.

Kern, Robert. *Liberals, Reformers and Caciques in Restoration Spain, 1875-1909.* Albuquerque, NM: University of New Mexico Press, 1974.

Macartney, G.A. *The Hapsburg Empire 1790-1918.* London: Wiedenfield and Nicolson, 1968.

Reál Cuerpo Colegiado de Caballeros Hijosdalgo de la Nobleza de Madrid. "Geneology of Leopold O'Donnell." Madrid, 1976.

Shapiro, J. Salwyn. *Modern and Contemporary European History.* New York: Houghton Mifflin Company, 1946.

Shirer, William A. *The Collapse of The Third Republic.* New York: Simon and Schuster, 1969.

General Historical Works

Cheetham, Nicholas. *A History of the Popes.* New York: Dorset, 1982.

Fair, Charles. *From The Jaws Of Victory.* New York: Simon and Schuster, 1971.

Hardiman, James, Esq. *The History of the Town and County of the Town of Galway.* Dublin: W. Folds and Sons, 1820, rprt. Connact Tribune Ltd., 1958.

Hayes-McCoy, G.A. *Irish Battles: A Military History of Ireland.* Belfast: The Appletree Press, 1990.

Hinsley, F.D. ed. *The New Cambridge Modern History.* Cambridge, England: Cambridge University Press, 1962.

MacManus, Seumas. *The Story of The Irish Race.* Old Greenwich, CT: The Devin-Adair Company, 1990.

Moore, Thomas Esq. *The History of Ireland.* London: Longman, 1835.

INDEX

Cúchulain, 20,26.
Cúl Dreimne, battle of, 54.

Dal Riada, 55.
deClare, Richard (Strongbow),
109-13,121.
De Divisione Naturae, 80.
De Gratia, 55.
de Lacy, Hugh, 99, 106.
De Lacy, Peter, 218-23.
De Lacy, Francis, 238-29.
de Ledrede, Richard, 103-05.
de MacKau, Armand, 167.
Dermot, High King, 54.
Dermot MacMurrough, 54,94-96.
Devorgilla, 94.
Diodorus, 18, 32.
Druids, 28-32,49,75.
Du Wall, Robert, 153.

education, 7-9,28,36, 167-73.
Edward II, King, 107, 109.
Edward III, King, 109-10.
Edward the Bruce, 108, 197.
Erasmus, 137.
Ermingarde, 35.
Eruigena, John Scotus, 79-81.
Eugene of Savoy, 154, 223-24.

Faughart, Battle of, 108.
Faustus, 48-49.
Felix II, Pope 66.
Fearghal, 68.
Fianna, 26.
Finian of Moville, 54.
Finn MacCumhail, 26.
Fitzgerald, Gerard, 172.
Fitzgerald, Lucy, 132-34.
Fitzgerald, Thomas, 114.
Fitzgerald, Tómas, 136-37.
Fitzmaurice, James, 197.

Fitzstephen, Robert, 95.
Fontaine, 6.
Fonetnoy. Battle of, 154-56.
fosterage, 22, 106.
French Revolution, 5.
Fridian, 83-84.

Gall, 62-63.
George II, 157.
Geraldus Cambrensis, 59.
Gergovia, seige of, 20.
Gerona, siege of, 30, 132-34.
Gildas, 70.
Gille-na-Maev, 216.
gossiprage, 22.
Gratian, Emperor, 58.
Gregory I, Pope, 73,79.
Gregory XIII, Pope, 297.
Gregory of Tours, 5.
Gundestrup Cauldron,33.

Hadrian, Emperor, 42.
Hallstatt, 11,15, 39.
Hannibal, 25,39.
Hengeist, 68.
Henry II, 93-94,98-99, 140.
Henry VIII, 114.
Henry of London, 102.
Herodotus, 14,18.
Hilary of Poiters, 67.
Hisperic Latin, 32.
Hogan Denis, 190-95.
Hogan, Michael, 150,185-89,
188,191.
Honorius, Emperor, 44.
Horsa, 69.
Humbert, Gen., 163, 197.
Hundred Years War, 125.

Iceni, 33.
Indo-Europeans, 12-13, 23.

256